QUICK ESCAPES® FROM
Philadelphia

Help Us Keep This Guide Up-to-Date

We would love to hear from you concerning your experiences with this guide and how you feel it could be improved and kept up to date. Please send your comments and suggestions to:

editorial@GlobePequot.com

Thanks for your input, and happy travels!

Quick Escapes® From series

QUICK ESCAPES® FROM
Philadelphia

The Best Weekend Getaways

FOURTH EDITION

Marilyn Odesser-Torpey

gpp®
travel

Guilford, Connecticut

All the information in this guidebook is subject to change.
We recommend that you call ahead to obtain current
information before traveling.

Editor: Kevin Sirois
Project Editor: Lynn Zelem
Layout: Joanna Beyer
Text Design: Sheryl Kober
Maps: Updated by James Fountain © Morris Book Publishing, LLC

ISSN 1537-3533
ISBN 978-0-7627-5403-8

Printed in the United States of America
10 9 8 7 6 5 4 3 2 1

To my loves, Daniel, Dana, and Kristen.

ABOUT THE AUTHOR

Marilyn Odesser-Torpey is a Philadelphia-born writer who is the travel editor for *Main Line Today* magazine and author of the first three editions of *Quick Escapes from Philadelphia* as well as the *Insiders' Guide to Pennsylvania Dutch Country* and *The Hershey, Pennsylvania Cookbook: Fun and Trivia from the Chocolate Capital of the World*.

ACKNOWLEDGMENTS

I am lucky enough to have the best family in the world: my husband, traveling companion, mapmaker, and love of my life, Dan; my daughters (and best friends), Dana and Kristen; my mother, Connie Odesser, and my sister (my other best friend) and brother-in-law, Ilene and Gary Visco. This book is dedicated to them as well as to my late father, Benjamin Odesser.

I would also like to express my heartfelt thanks to the many wonderful professionals, locals, and new friends I met along the way and who so generously shared their favorite places, experiences, and local lore with me.

Finally my deepest appreciation to my wonderful editor, Amy Lyons, and to the late Laura Strom, an editor and friend I will always remember with great respect and fondness.

CONTENTS

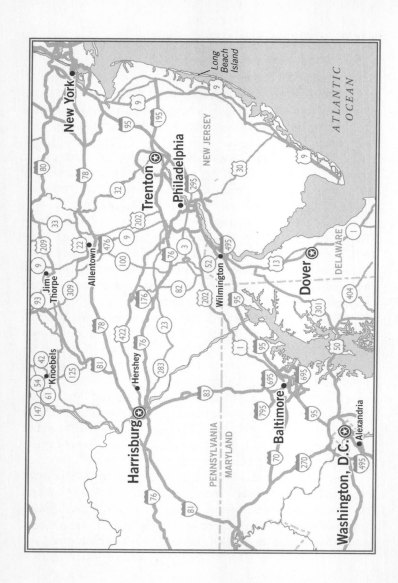

INTRODUCTION

Having been born and raised in Philadelphia, I always thought of my City of Brotherly Love as the center of the universe. After all, everybody knows that Philly is a renowned center of history and culture. And, with its close proximity to all kinds of outdoor recreational activities, we could take an easy drive "up the mountains" or "down the shore." Well, maybe the drive "down the shore" wasn't so easy if you picked the wrong time to hit the road (along with everyone else) on a sultry summer weekend.

Back then, "up the mountains" could only mean the Poconos, where the Delaware and Lehigh Rivers, along with more than a hundred lakes, streams, creeks, and ponds offered us summers filled with cool summer adventures. Winters meant whooshing down snow-covered slopes and evenings sipping hot chocolate in front of a blazing fire. "Down the shore" meant basking on the beaches and playing on the boardwalks of South Jersey.

With age and experience came a broadening of my horizons. Other shores, other mountains, and all kinds of other in-between vacation destinations in other parts of Pennsylvania and even other nearby states were waiting to be explored. And traveling to many of them has been nothing less than eye-opening. I was also surprised to realize that even places I had previously dismissed with a "been there, done that" attitude have much more to offer than I had ever imagined. During my visits to all of the places I describe, I combed each area and quizzed the locals for insider information and tips to make your travels easier and more enjoyable.

No matter what your interests or budget, whether you're in the mood to be in the middle of everything or in the middle of nowhere or if you would prefer to sleep in the lap of luxury or under the stars, there are made-just-for-you "quick escapes" only a one-and-one-half to four-hour drive away. Of course, this doesn't mean that I was wrong in believing that Philadelphia was the center of the universe. It just means that there are many new places not-so-far from home waiting to be discovered.

Before you begin your journeys, here is some general information to all of the included destinations:

HOURS OF OPERATION, PRICES, CREDIT CARDS

In the interest of accuracy and because they are subject to change, hours of operation and attraction prices are given in general terms. Always remember to call ahead. You can assume all establishments listed accept major credit cards unless otherwise noted. If you have questions, contact the establishments for specifics.

ACCOMMODATIONS PRICING

This price key reflects the average cost of a double-occupancy room during peak price period. Taxes and extras are not included. Always ask if special discounts are available.

$ less than $99
$$ $99 to $175
$$$ $176 and up

RESTAURANT PRICING

This price key reflects the average price per dinner entree (excluding cocktails, wine, appetizers, desserts, tax, and tip). You can usually expect to pay less for lunch and/or breakfast, when applicable.

$ less than $16 for entrees
$$ $16 to $30
$$$ $31 and up

UP THE MOUNTAINS
ESCAPES

UP THE MOUNTAINS ESCAPE *One*

Pocono Mountain Winter

BLUE MOUNTAIN AND JIM THORPE, PENNSYLVANIA /
2 NIGHTS

Pennsylvania's Super Slope
America's Little Switzerland
Mountain Majesty
Fairy-tale Town
Sporty Days
Romantic Nights

While Big Boulder in Lake Harmony and Jack Frost in Blakeslee are certainly great go-to ski getaway spots, they're not the only ones. Blue Mountain in Danielsville near Palmerton not only has the highest vertical drop (1,082 feet) in the state, but it's also the closest peak to Philly, only an hour-and-a-half drive away.

DAY 1/MORNING

To get to **Blue Mountain Ski Area** (1660 Blue Mountain Dr.; Danielsville; 610-826-7700; www.skibluemt.com), take I-476 north to Lehigh Valley exit 56. After the tollbooth, bear right and take US 22 east about 5 miles to PA 145 north (MacArthur Road), then continue 9 miles to the traffic light at the far end of the long bridge. Turn right onto Blue Mountain Drive and go approximately 3 miles to the traffic light in Cherryville. Drive straight through Cherryville about 3 miles to **Danielsville,** then keep going until you see the entrance sign just past the top of the mountain.

With thirty-four trails from slow to steep, mogul fields, and three terrain parks with jumps, rails, and pipes galore, Blue Mountain is perfect for rookie to racer skiers and boarders from bunny hill rookie to double black diamond daredevil. Operating hours are

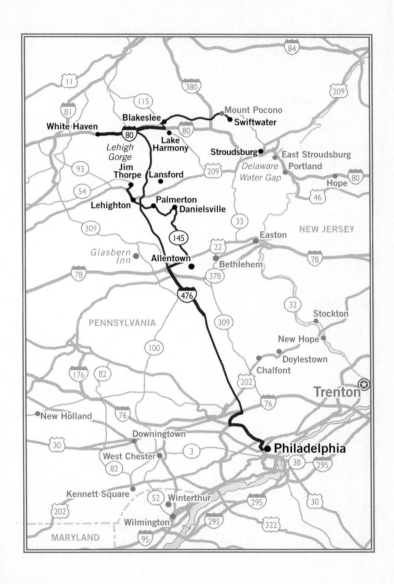

Mon through Fri from 8:30 a.m. to 10 p.m., Sat and Sun 8 a.m. to 10 p.m. Babysitting for children age 6 weeks to 5 years is available for $5 to $8 per hour until 9 p.m. every day. Ski and boarding lessons are available for every age and skill level. Equipment rentals are available. To check the day's ski conditions at Blue Mountain before you head for the slopes, call (877) SKI-BLUE.

Lift ticket prices are $39 half day/$45 full day for adults weekdays, $47/$54 weekends; $35 half or full day for kids, $38 weekends. Check for senior and weekday adult discounts. Add $10 to the lift price to add tubing to your activities. For the itinerary I am suggesting, you'll want to do that.

AFTERNOON

LUNCH   Blue Mountain has plenty of indoor casual dining options from tavern food to family-style meals where you can sit down and warm up. But if you can't bear to be separated from your skis, you can grab a burger or other quick and easy edibles at Blue Mountain's **Slopeside Pub and Grill** with its fire pit and bar located in the outside courtyard of the Summit Lodge. $. Or try **Ray's Grill on Skis** right on the slopes. $.

Now it's time to get your $10's worth as you let your posterior propel you down the mountain. Blue has nineteen slides of varying thrill levels for you to take on alone or with friends in single- or multiple-rider tubes. Hours are Mon through Thurs from 4 p.m. to 10 p.m., Fri 10 a.m. to 10 p.m., Sat and Sun 8 a.m. to 10 p.m. Tubing ticket prices for tubing alone are $23 weekdays to $30 weekends.

This evening you will be dining and lodging in the Victorian town of **Jim Thorpe.** To get there, head south on Blue Mountain Drive, then turn right onto PA 946 (West Mountain View Drive).

After 3 miles, turn right onto PA 248 (Lehigh Drive) and, after a little under 2 miles, right again onto PA 248 west. Continue for 7 miles, then turn left onto US 209. After just under 5 miles, turn right onto PA 903 (River Street), which will lead you into downtown Jim Thorpe.

EVENING

At first glance, Jim Thorpe (www.jimthorpe.com) looks like a movie set come to life with its rows of ornately trimmed Victorian homes, hilltop mansions, old-fashioned train station, and quaint little shops. In reality, the town formerly known as **Mauch Chunk** (Native American for "Bear Mountain") has had a two-centurylong tumultuous history from coal mining transport center to "America's Switzerland" tourist destination to downtrodden Depression disaster. In the hope of once again attracting tourists' attention, the town adopted the name Jim Thorpe in 1954 in honor of the renowned early-20th-century, double Olympic gold medal–winning, Native American athlete whose own roller coaster career seemed to reflect that of the town. Today, its preserved and repurposed late-19th-century buildings, small-town charm, and wealth of outdoor recreational opportunities make Jim Thorpe a unique combination of past and present.

DINNER   **Flow,** 268 W. Broadway; Jim Thorpe; (570) 325-8200; www.thecccp.org. Part art gallery, part farm-to-fork restaurant, Flow is a member of the Carbon County Cultural Project (CCCP) complex situated in a stone, mid-18th-century former wireworks factory. It focuses on local, seasonal, and organic foods. (The breads and much of the produce comes from the restaurant's own farm down the road.) There's a three-course vegetarian tasting and appropriately priced "Starving Artist" special. $$. Be sure to take a stroll through the Arisman Visitor's Gallery showcasing up-and-coming as well as established artists, and the Stabin Morykin Gallery focusing on the ethereal paintings and limited edition prints of renowned artist and CCCP co-founder Victor Stabin. The complex and restaurant are open Sun, Wed, and Thurs from 11 a.m. to 9 p.m., Fri and Sat until 10 p.m.

LODGING **Harry Packer Mansion,** 1 Packer Hill Rd., Jim Thorpe; (570) 325-8566; www.murdermansion.com. If this inn, perched high on a hill overlooking the town, reminds you of the Haunted Mansion in Walt Disney World, that's because this late-18th-century gorgeous Gothic with its cut-glass windows, hand-painted ceilings, carved mantles, and English Minton tile-accented fireplace was the model for it. $$–$$$. Two-night minimum stay is required on weekends. Ask about the mansion's murder mystery weekends and ski and stay package.

DAY 2/MORNING

BREAKFAST A full elegant breakfast is included with your room rate at the **Harry Packer Mansion.**

It's about a half-hour drive from Jim Thorpe to **Arctic Paws Dog Sled Tours** in Pocono Manor (P.O. Box 411, Swiftwater, PA 18370; 570-839-0123; www.arcticpawsdogsledtours.com) but, believe me, it's well worth the trip to have the opportunity to mush a team of beautiful Siberian huskies and take the sled ride of your life. Head north on PA 903 and go 17 miles to PA 115 north. Follow this for about 2 miles, then merge onto I-80 east; continue for a little over 9 miles until you can merge onto I-380 north via exit 293 on the left toward Scranton. After 2½ miles, take PA 940, exit 3, toward Pocono Pines/Mt. Pocono, then right onto PA 940 east/ Pocono Summit Road. Take the PA 314 ramp toward Pocono Summit/Pocono Manor. Merge onto PA 314/Manor Drive toward Pocono Manor/Swiftwater. After 1½ miles, turn right onto Swiftwater Road.

Swiftwater Road becomes Manor Drive. Arctic Paws is located at the Inn at Pocono Manor at PA 314 and Manor Drive.

The entire experience, from meeting the dogs to mushing, lasts roughly an hour, and the ride covers about 2 miles round-trip. Tours are available weekdays from 10 a.m. to 3 p.m. and weekends from 8 a.m. to 4 p.m. Cost is $50 per musher, $25 per rider. This activity is not recommended for children under 5. Reservations are required with a credit card deposit; final payment is cash-only. Warm up with some coffee, tea, cocoa, or soup at **Cafe Paws** (open weekends only).

While you're in the neighborhood, you can also take a scenic spin at the wheel of a snowmobile. **Pocono Snowmobile Rentals at Pocono Manor Golf Club** in Pocono Summit (570-839-6061; www.poconosnowmobilerentals.com), only a four-minute drive west of Arctic Paws on PA 314, offers half-hour rides for $35 for single, $50 for double daytime; $45 single, $65 double nighttime (includes bonfire with hot dogs and marshmallows). Open, weather permitting, weekdays from 10 a.m. to 5 p.m., weekends from 9 a.m. to 5 p.m. Call for reservations.

AFTERNOON

LUNCH **The New Pepperjacks,** 41 Broadway, Jim Thorpe; (570) 325-5500; www.thenewpepperjacks.com. If you're a Tex-Mex fan, you'll find your favorite fare from tacos to tostadas and fajitas to flautas on New Pepperjacks' extensive menu of Tex-Mex favorites. Open seven days for lunch and dinner, call for hours. $.

As a major coal transport center, the town had a long history that revolved around the railroad. Train enthusiasts young and old will still find plenty of locomotive-focused attractions to love, including the architecturally distinctive **Mauch Chunk Train Station,** the former **Central Railroad of New Jersey** (Packer Park, Jim Thorpe;

570-325-5810), built in 1888. In addition to serving as the town's tourist welcome center (570-325-8200; www.jimthorpepa.com) and artifacts from the town's railroading heyday, the station also functions as the home base for the **Lehigh Gorge Scenic Railway** (570-325-8485; www.lgsry.com), which offers one-hour, 16-mile roundtrip excursions in 1920s, diesel-powered passenger trains weekends May through the third weekend in Dec. Prices range from $12 to $17 for adults, $9 to $10 for children age 3 and up. "Well-behaved" dogs ride for free.

Right across the street, the **Old Mauch Chunk Model Train Display** (41 Susquehanna St., second floor of the Hooven Mercantile Building, Jim Thorpe; 570-325-4371; www.omctraindisplay.com) where you'll find a 47 X 22-foot HO scale train display consisting of more than 1,000 feet of track; engines pulling as many as 50 cars; and more than 200 houses, churches, stores, skyscrapers, and even a burning building with smoke and flames. Admission is $4 for adults, $3 for seniors, $2 for children ages 3 and under. Call for seasonal hours.

Broadway and Race Street, which runs parallel to it, comprises a particularly charming part of town that includes the more than a dozen late-19th-century mansions dubbed "Millionaire's Row" and "Stone Row," a collection of sixteen town houses said to have been inspired by Elfreth's Alley in Philadelphia. Although the three-story row houses are basically identical in design, each is individualized by some distinctive decorative window, trim, or other feature. Once the homes of railroad engineers and foremen, some of these buildings remain private residences while others provide studio and shop space for local artisans and merchants. But before you start shopping, take a tour of the magnificent late-19th-century landmark that is **Saints Mark and John Episcopal Church** (21 Race St., Jim Thorpe; 570-325-2241; www.stmarkandjohn.org), with its Tiffany stained glass windows, marble baptismal font, ca. 1860 pipe organ, and sculpted stone "rerodas" (screen behind the altar) which is modeled after the one in St. George's chapel in Windsor, England. Tours are offered Tues through Sat, from noon to 3 p.m. The cost is $5 for adults and free for children.

If browsing through antiques and collectibles boutiques is one of your favorite sports, don't miss **Rosemary Remembrances II** (10 Hill Rd., Opera House Square, Jim Thorpe; 570-325-4452; www .rosemaryremembrances.com), where Marj Reppert sells objects "found" at flea markets, yard sales, church sales, private estates, and auctions and artfully transforms them into decorative shadow boxes, storage containers, and one-of-a-kind home decor. Call for hours. At the **Carbon County Art League** at the **Second Saturdays Gallery at the Marion Hose Company,** (16 West Broadway, Opera House Square, Jim Thorpe; 610-377-1890) exhibits the works of cutting edge local artists who work in a wide range of media. Call for hours. For wearable art, check out the one-of-a-kind and limited edition fashions at **Marianne Monteleone Design** (97 Broadway, Jim Thorpe; 570-325-3450; www.shopmmdesign.com); open Thurs through Mon from 11 a.m. to 5 p.m., Tues and Wed by appointment; call for winter weekend hours. **Chatelaine** (81 Broadway, Jim Thorpe; 570-325-2224; www.chatelainepa.com) features hand-crafted jewelry from more than one hundred artists from around the country; call for hours. And don't forget the edible art at **The Country Cottage** (37 Race St., Jim Thorpe; 570-325-3836) to pick up some made-on-site pickles, jams, salsas, and other goodies; open seven days, call for hours.

EVENING

DINNER   **Moya,** 24 Race St., Jim Thorpe; (570) 325-8530; www.jim thorpemoya.com. This is a cool and classy dining spot where Ecuadorian-born owner

chef Heriberto Yunda allows local, seasonal ingredients to star in thoughtfully sim-
ple dishes such as seafood stew and braised lamb shank with apricot and sweet
sherry reduction. Open Mon, Tues, and Thurs from 5 p.m. to 9 p.m., Fri and Sat until
10 p.m., Sun until 8 p.m. $$.

LODGING Harry Packer Mansion.

DAY 3/MORNING

BREAKFAST Harry Packer Mansion.

If you think the town is pretty, wait until you take in the breathtak-
ing views as you hike, bike, or snowshoe along the many mountain
trails on exciting half- to full-day excursions ranging from easy to
extreme with **The Jim Thorpe eXperience Guided Historic Adven-
ture Tours** (37 West Broadway, Jim Thorpe; 484-225-1209; www
.thejtx.com). Along with the awe-inspiring visual perspective, you'll
also get a historical one as your guide offers background informa-
tion on the town, the ca. 1827 Switchback Railroad, Lehigh Gorge,
and the eerie Boulder Field. Full Moon Snowshoe Trips are also
available and, in season, you can also kayak and explore a coal
mine. Prices range from $45 to $75.

LUNCH Albright Mansion, 66 Broadway, Jim Thorpe; (570) 325-
4440; www.albrightmansion.com. Serves quiche, salads, and warm and cold sand-
wiches, including a tea sandwich sampler with homemade soup in a ca. 1861 Civil
War setting. $. Also moderately priced breakfasts and upscale Fri and Sat prix fixe
BYOB dinners.

Head back to Philadelphia. Begin right onto North St./PA 903 and
continue for a little more than 1 mile, turn left onto US 209 south.

Stay on 209 south for 7 miles, then take I-476 ramp to PA Turnpike toward Allentown. Drive 60 miles, then take the I-76 exit 16 toward Philadelphia/Valley Forge, merging onto I-76 via exit 16A toward Philadelphia. The trip should take about one-and-one-half hours.

There's More . . . .

Boating. **Mauch Chunk Lake Boat Rentals,** The Camp Store at Mauch Chunk Lake Park, Lentz Trail, Jim Thorpe; (570) 325-4408; www.carboncounty.com. Rent rowboats with and without motors ($20 to $30 first hour), canoes ($20 first hour), and kayaks ($15 to $20 first hour). Open from Memorial Day through Labor Day; call for seasonal hours.

Camping. **Jim Thorpe Camping Resort,** Lentz Trail, Jim Thorpe; (570) 325-2644; www.jimthorpecamping.com. Wooded tent sites, camping cabins, swimming pool and wading pools, playground, free hot showers, laundry facilities, grocery and camping supply store, games and planned activities. Fees are $28 per site for two, $55 per day for camping cabins double occupancy, two-night minimum. Recreational vehicle hook-ups are $32 (with water and electric), $38 (with water, electrical, and sewer). Air-conditioning or electric heaters and cable TV hookups are available at additional cost. Leashed pets are permitted.

Disc Golf. **Blue Mountain Ski Area,** 1660 Blue Mountain Dr., Danielsville; (610) 826-7700; www.skibluemt.com. Take the lift to play eighteen holes, $10, disc rentals extra. Open Sat from mid-Sept through end of Oct from 10 a.m. to 3 p.m.

Live Music. **The Bach and Handel Chorale,** 810 Carbon Ave., Jim Thorpe; (570) 325-4794; http://bachandhandelchorale.homestead

.com. If you're visiting during the months of Dec, Mar, or May, be sure to catch one of the four seasonal performances by this exquisite collection of local voices. The concerts are held at various locations throughout the town. Tickets range from $15 to $30 for adults, $12 to $20 for seniors and students.

Mauch Chunk Opera House, Opera House Square, Jim Thorpe; (570) 325-4439; www.mauchchunkoperahouse.com. Throughout the year this rustic 1882 entertainment center hosts concerts, children's theater, workshops, art and fashion shows, and sidewalk festivals.

Penn's Peak, 325 Maury Rd., Jim Thorpe; (610) 826-9000; www.pennspeak.com. Headliner musicians and tribute bands play this lively venue year-round. Ticket prices vary. The Peak also has a big dance floor, twin bars, a restaurant, and open-air deck with views of Beltzville Lake and the northeastern Appalachians.

Mountain Biking. **Gravity Mountain Biking.** Blue Mountain Ski Area, 1660 Blue Mountain Dr., Danielsville; (610) 826-7700; www.skibluemt.com. $20 for lift access. Open Sat from mid-Sept through end of Oct from 10 a.m. to 5 p.m.

Museums & Tours. **The Anita Shapolsky Foundation,** 20 West Broadway, Jim Thorpe; www.asartfoundation.org. One of the largest collections of American Abstract Expressionism is housed in a late-19th-century former Presbyterian Church. The church itself is a work of art with its second floor stained glass windows by Tiffany and LaFarge. Galleries are open from noon to 5 p.m. on weekends between Memorial Day and Labor Day.

Asa Packer Mansion, 128 West Broadway, Jim Thorpe; (570) 325-5259; www.asapackermansion.com. Tour the 19th-century home of one of the town's only true millionaires and the man responsible for the building of the Lehigh Valley Railroad and

Lehigh University in Bethlehem. Look for the crystal chandelier that was copied for the movie *Gone with the Wind*. The mansion is open weekends in Apr and May, Nov, and the first two weekends in Dec; seven days a week from Memorial Day to Nov 1 for one-hour docent-led tours from 11 a.m. to 4:15 p.m. Adult tickets are $8, seniors $7, students $5. Cash only.

Bear Mountain Butterfly Sanctuary, 18 Church Rd., Jim Thorpe; (570) 325-4848; www.bearmountainbutterflies.com. There's nothing as beautiful as colorful butterflies in graceful flight and you will be surrounded by numerous species in the "flutterarium." You'll also have a chance to get close (but not too close) to the environmentally endangered Central and South American poison arrow frogs. $8 for adults, $6.50 for seniors, and $6 for children. Call for seasonal hours.

Mauch Chunk Museum & Cultural Center, 41 West Broadway, Jim Thorpe; (570) 325-9190; www.mauchchunkmuseum .com. The architecture and high ornate ceilings of the museum are reminders of its origins as a church in 1843. Today it is home to a comprehensive collection of artifacts and photos that trace the history of the area. You'll be amazed by the working model of the once-world-renowned engineering innovation, the Switchback Gravity Railway. The museum is open Tues through Sun, 10 a.m. to 4 p.m. Admission is $5 for adults, $2 for children under 8.

No. 9 Mine "Wash Shanty" Anthracite Coal Mine and Museum, Dock Street, Lansford (10 miles south of Jim Thorpe on US 209); (570) 645-7074; http://no9mine.tripod.com. Ride a railcar 1,600 feet into the mountainside to see the world's oldest operating deep anthracite mine, which opened in 1855 and closed in 1972. Tours are available May through Oct; call for seasonal hours. Admission for mine tour and museum is $7.

Old Jail Museum, 128 W. Broadway, Jim Thorpe; (570) 325-5259; www.theoldjailmuseum.com. Formerly the Carbon County

Jail, this was where, in the late 1800s, seven members of the Molly Maguires were hanged. Still there are the gallows, the scary dungeon, and Cell 17, where you'll see a hand print that, according to legend, one of the prisoners left there as evidence of his innocence. Tours are offered Memorial Day through Oct, every day except Wed, from noon to 4:30 p.m., weekends only in Sept and Oct. Admission is $5 for adults, $4 for students and seniors, and $3 for children.

Pocono Jeep Tours, (484) 515-8432; www.poconojeeptours .com. Customized easy-does-it on-road or adventurous off-road rides through the mountains. A two-hour ride costs $45 per person.

State Parks. **Beltzville State Park,** 2950 Pohopoco Dr., Lehighton; (610) 377-0045; www.stateparks.com/beltzville.html. This more than 3,000-acre park offers a multitude of all-season recreational activities, many centered around the 950-acre Beltzville Lake, which is stocked with warm- and cold-water trout, bass, and other game fish and has a 500-foot beach where swimming is permitted from late May to Labor Day from 8 a.m. to sunset. Kayak, paddleboat, rowboat, pontoon, and small motorboat rentals are available. In winter, you can cross-country ski and snowshoe on 9 miles of trails and acres of open and hilly terrain. Ice fishing is also permitted.

Hickory Run State Park, RR 1 Box 81, White Haven; (570) 443-0400; www.stateparks.com/hickory_run.html. Within this 15,500-acre park are 40 miles of trails for hiking and cross-country skiing. Sandy Spring Lake is also a popular ice skating spot. Check out the dramatic landscape of Boulder Field where rock formations up to 26 feet long in a flat 1,800-foot field create an eerily dramatic landscape. In summer, the mountain laurel and rhododendron are gorgeous. Ditto for the fall foliage. Swim at the sandy beach from late May to mid-Sept, 8 a.m. to sunset.

Lehigh Gorge State Park, Jim Thorpe; www.stateparks.com/ lehigh_gorge.html. A 25-mile, gentle downhill, rails-to-trails bike trail between 800- to 1,000-foot-high mountains. The hiking is steep and requires negotiation of fast-moving waters. One of the highlights is a stop at Glen Onoko Falls with its drop of 75 feet. Pocono Whitewater Adventure Center (570-325-8430) offers bike rentals; guided mountain, wetland, and waterfall hikes; and whitewater rafting trips through the Gorge year-round, weather permitting.

Whitewater Rafting. **Jim Thorpe River Adventures,** One Adventure Lane, Jim Thorpe; (570) 325-2570; www.jtraft.com. Lehigh Gorge State Park offers some wild whitewater rafting, and this company has designed numerous trips for all ages from easy-going to hold-on-to-your-paddles that are available from Apr through Oct. Call for trip descriptions and prices.

Special Events . . . .

JANUARY
Blue Winter Festival, 1660 Blue Mountain Dr., Danielsville; (610) 826-7700; www.skibluemt.com. Dog sledding, ice carving, food, live music, and snow sports demos.

FEBRUARY
Winterfest, downtown Jim Thorpe; (570) 325-5810; www.jimthorpe .org. Ice carving and live music on Presidents' Day Weekend.

SEPTEMBER
Annual Bluegrass & Anthracite Heritage Festival, Mauch Chunk Lake Park, Lentz Trail, Jim Thorpe; (570) 325-4408; www.car boncounty.com/park. Live music from headliners and open mic

opportunities; coal mining history, exhibits, and memorabilia; food, crafters, free hayrides, environmental programs, evening bonfire.

DECEMBER

Old Time Christmas, downtown Jim Thorpe; (570) 325-5810; www .jimthorpe.org. Celebrate a Victorian Christmas beginning with a tree-lighting ceremony in the downtown park, a live nativity, Santa's arrival, live music, ghost walk, free refreshments, a traditional "mug walk" (carry a mug from business to business in the town and have it filled with various treats and treasures), and horse-drawn trolley rides.

Other Recommended Lodgings and Restaurants. . . .

PALMERTON

One Ten Tavern, 110 Delaware Ave.; (610) 826-3333; www.one tentavern.com. Mostly upscale sandwiches, pizzas and salads with some meat (or fish) and potatoes (or pasta) entrees. Open Sun noon to 6 p.m., Tues through Thurs 11 a.m. to 9 p.m., Fri and Sat until 10 p.m. $.

JIM THORPE

Café Origins, 107 Broadway; (570) 325-8776; www.cafeorigins .com. New York-chic veggie-oriented eatery serves up specialties that even carnivores will crave. Open Fri and Sat from noon to 9 p.m., Sun until 7 p.m. $–$$.

DeFeo's Manor at Opera House Square, 54 West Broadway; (570) 325-8777; www.manorbedandbreakfast.com. Ask for "The Suite" where you can even breakfast (your fridge and pantry will be fully supplied) in your own cozy turret overlooking the town and mountains. $$.

Hill Home Forge, 10 Flagstaff Rd.; (570) 325-0216; www.hill homeforge.com. Located about 1½ miles from the downtown area, this three-guest room getaway is filled with original art created by Nic East, who owns and operates this bed-and-breakfast with his wife, Eileen. $$. The couple also offers stained glass and jewelry classes.

Inn at Jim Thorpe, 24 Broadway; (800) 329-2599; www.innjt.com. This historic hotel has been charming guests including Ulysses S. Grant, Buffalo Bill, Thomas Edison, and John D. Rockefeller for over a century. Continental breakfast buffet is included. Accommodations range from standard and deluxe rooms to mini-suites. $–$$$.

J. T.'s Steak & Ale House, 5 Hazard Sq. at the Hotel Switzerland; (570) 325-4563; www.jimthorpedining.com. The J. T. stands for—who else?—Jim Thorpe. And the hearty fare is, indeed, suited to the most athletic of appetites. A specialty of the house is the twenty-four-ounce sirloin rib steak. $$. Open Sun to Thurs 11 a.m. to 10 p.m., Sat until 10:30 p.m.

Mary's Guest House, 39 West Broadway; (570) 325-5354; www .marysjimthorpe.com. Basic, comfortable, a home-away-from-home that has accommodations for up to twelve guests, whether in a private room for two or the entire 1860s town house for one, big, happy family. All guests may use the fully equipped kitchen. Bring your own towels, toiletries, and food. $—cash is preferred. *NOTE:* There is no off-street parking.

Roadies Restaurant & Bar at Penn's Peak, 325 Maury Rd.; (610) 826-9000; www.pennspeak.com. Everything from bar food to burgers, St. Louis ribs to New York Strip. Breakfast and lunch, too.

$–$$. Open Tues to Thurs 11 a.m. to 9 p.m., Sat 9 a.m. to 9 p.m., Sun to 8 p.m.

VictoriAnn Bed and Breakfast, 68 Broadway; (570) 325-8107; www.thevictoriann.com. Located on "Millionaire's Row," this lovely example of the town's impeccably restored Victorian architecture is decorated with period furnishings with a colorful garden to match. Full breakfast is included. $–$$.

For More Information . . . .

Pocono Mountains Visitors Bureau, 1004 Main St., Stroudsburg, PA 18360; (800) POCONOS (800-762-6667) or (570) 421-5791; www.800poconos.com.

Pocono Snow and Fall Foliage Hotline, in season; (570) 421-5565.

Jim Thorpe Chamber of Commerce, (570) 325-5810, www.jim thorpe.org.

UP THE MOUNTAINS ESCAPE *Two*

Pocono Mountain Summer

DELAWARE WATER GAP AREA—PLY ME A RIVER/
2 NIGHTS

> River and Mountain Sports
> Breathtaking Overlooks
> Fun Restaurants
> All That Jazz

When people talk about **Delaware Water Gap,** they are usually referring to the 70,000-acre national recreation area in Pennsylvania and New Jersey. And it truly is an idyllic spot for nature lovers of all kinds with its more than sixty hiking trails; 40 miles of Delaware River; wide variety of birds, fish, and other wildlife; and virtually unlimited opportunities to enjoy the great outdoors in whatever way you choose. Although each of the seasons has its own distinctive charm, beauty, and activities in the **Poconos,** spring and summer are really the best times to fully enjoy this area of the mountains. August is peak tourist time here and the area can get pretty crowded; you may want to plan your escape for earlier in the season or even the first few weeks of Sept when the foliage is fabulously aflame. These are also the best times to explore the town of Delaware Water Gap, along with neighboring Scotrun, Stroudsburg, East Stroudsburg, Bushkill, and Portland at your leisure. Their histories and personalities are as varied as the river that flows through the mountains. This area is about a two-hour drive from Philadelphia.

DAY 1/MORNING

From Philadelphia, take the Schuylkill Expressway (I-76) to the Northeast Extension of the Pennsylvania Turnpike (I-476); go north to I-78 east. Take I-78 east to PA 33 north then to I-80 east. Get

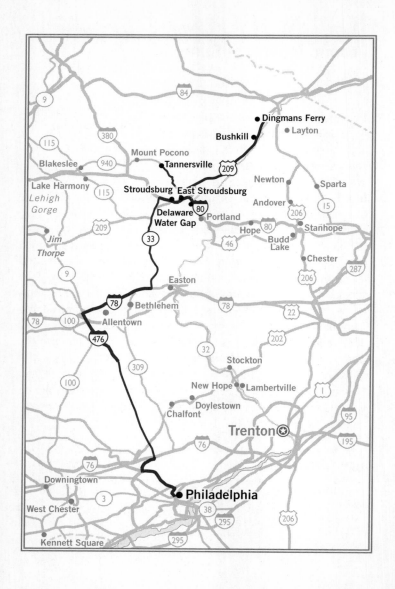

off at exit 310 for Delaware Water Gap and travel PA 611 south, which will take you into the center of the town of Delaware Water Gap.

As you enter town on PA 611, you'll see the **Water Gap Trolley Depot** (exit 310 off of I-80 at the Trolley Depot on PA 611; Delaware Water Gap; 800-275-1242; www.watergaptrolley.com) on your right. Make that your first stop and take the one-hour scenic tour. Of course, you could easily drive the route along 611 yourself, but the history and local lore offered up by your trolley driver/guide make the excursion much more interesting. Tickets are $8.50 for adults, $4 for children. Look on the Web site for a discount coupon. Call for seasonal hours.

Right across Main Street from the Trolley Depot is the **Antoine Dutot Museum and Gallery** (Main Street, PA 611; Delaware Water Gap; 570-476-4240; www.dutotmuseum.com). Inside this ca. 1850 former schoolhouse is the town's main cultural center with changing displays of local artists and Native American and other historic artifacts. Open Sat and Sun, 1 to 5 pm, Memorial Day weekend to Columbus Day weekend. Admission is a donation of $2 for adults and children aged 12 and older.

AFTERNOON

LUNCH **Everybody's Café**, 905 Main St., Stroudsburg; (570) 424-0896. Coming from Delaware Water Gap, head north on PA 611 for about 3 miles until you come to Main Street (Business 209, Stroudsburg). Situated in a Victorian home complete with ornate leaded glass doorways, graceful arches, and back-to-back fireplaces, this popular neighborhood spot is renowned for its ambitious multi-page menu and wide array of innovative vegetarian and vegan selections as well as infinite pasta combinations. Nonveggies will find plenty to keep them happy as well. $–$$. Call for seasonal hours.

For your afternoon in the sun, head north on PA 611 until it intersects PA 402. Follow 402 north about 18 miles to **Pecks Pond Backwater Outfitters** (Peck's Pond; 570-775-7237; www.peckspond.com). Instead of paddling a boat on the local waters, you can glide along propelled by your own legs and a small paddle on a seatlike "float" that will allow you to access backwater streams and ponds without disturbing the wildlife. A six-hour outback nature trip with guide and equipment costs $129 per person and can be tailored specifically for individuals who want to fish, bird-watch, or take photographs. Peck's Pond Backwater Outfitters also offers guided fishing outings and canoe, kayak, and electric motor boat rentals. Call for seasonal hours.

EVENING

DINNER   **Antelao Restaurant,** 84 Main St.; Delaware Water Gap; (570) 426-7226; www.antelaorestaurant.com. Be sure to make reservations for dinner. This intimate gem of a BYOB has only six tables. Culinary Institute of America graduate chef Michael DeLotto and his wife, baker and herb-grower Elvi, create beautiful food such as chicken breast or salmon roulade and artichoke and ricotta crepe from kalamata olive and sun-dried tomato tapenade from locally-sourced, seasonal ingredients. $$. Dinner is served Thurs through Sun 5 p.m. to 9 p.m. If you want to consider bringing along a bottle of a local wine, go to **Sorrenti's Cherry Valley Vineyards** (570-992-2255; www.cherryvalleyvineyards.com) in Saylorsville for a taste of Chardonnay, dry Proprietor's White, or semidry Proprietor's red. To get there, take US 209 south for about 6½ miles; it will become PA 33 south. Drive another 3 miles and exit toward Saylorsburg. Turn left on Old Route 115, then another left onto Lower Cherry Valley Road. The winery is open weekdays from 10 a.m. to 6 p.m., Sat and Sun 1 to 5 p.m.

LODGING   **Stroudsmoor Country Inn,** Stroudsmoor Road, Stroudsburg; (570) 421-6431; www.stroudsmoor.com. From Delaware Water Gap, take I-80 west to PA 191 south; turn right and follow 191 to the top of the mountain, where you'll make the first right onto Stroudsmoor Road (the entire trip, including the mountain-climbing expedition, should take five minutes or less). Situated on 200 acres overlooking the city, this family-owned and -operated inn has antique-furnished guest rooms, suites, and cottages; some have whirlpool baths, fireplaces, Italian marble bathrooms, and/or private balconies. Enjoy a bountiful breakfast each morning. Among the many on-site amenities are indoor and outdoor pools, whirlpool, and full-service spa. $$–$$$.

DAY 2/MORNING

BREAKFAST Stroudsmoor Country Inn. Whatever you have, from egg dishes to pancakes, make sure you sample the inn's signature iced raisin bread. Yum! The restaurant is also open to the public for breakfast, lunch, a la carte and buffet dinners, and Sunday brunch. Dress comfortably and pack plenty of suntan lotion for exploring the trails, waterfalls, and other natural attractions of the Delaware Water Gap National Recreation Area. Before you head there, however, pick up a single- or triple-decker sandwich-to-go at the **Water Gap Diner,** a block off Main Street, PA 611, at 55 Broad St., Delaware Water Gap; (570) 476-0132. $. To make your sweet tooth happy, make a quick stop at the **Village Farmer and Bakery,** Main Street, PA 611, across from the Water Gap Trolley Depot; (570) 476-9440, an old-fashioned family-run farm stand that sells oven-fresh cookies, brownies, thirty varieties of pies, and other home-baked goods.

Whether you're an experienced hiker at the top of your form or someone who simply appreciates fabulous scenery, the **Delaware Water Gap National Recreation Area** (570-828-2253; www.nps .gov/dewa) has a trail for you. At **Dingmans Falls Trail** (1 mile west of US 209 at Dingmans Ferry) a ½-mile walk along the forest floor through a hemlock-canopied grove will bring you face to face with Silver Thread Falls, with its graceful 80-foot drop, and Dingmans Falls, with its two-tiered, 130-foot drop. The 1⁸⁄₁₀-mile forested loop at nearby George W. Child Recreation Site takes you to three additional waterfalls along Dingmans Creek. Wooden stairs and boardwalks make it easy for you to safely get a close look. About 12 miles north is Raymondskill Falls, a seven-tiered 175-foot beauty that drops in seven stages.

AFTERNOON

LUNCH **George W. Child Recreation Site.** A wonderful spot to enjoy your picnic lunch is in the hemlock-shaded glen along Dingmans Creek.

Before you leave the park area, get in your car and take the Dingmans Ferry access road to US 209; then follow 209 north to the toll bridge to New Jersey. A few hundred yards after you cross the bridge, take the right-hand turn and follow the signs for about 2½ miles to **Peters Valley Crafts Center** (19 Kuhn Rd., Layton, NJ; 973-948-5200; www .petersvalley.org). Located in a green, peaceful valley, this center is actually a community of working/teaching studios for resident artists ranging from blacksmiths to photographers to woodworkers. You can visit the store and gallery anytime of year (call for seasonal hours) to see and purchase works by artists-in-residence and more than 300 artisans from around the country. From May through Sept, the artists open their studios to the public for two- to five-day classes and self-guided tours. In fall, the center hosts a juried craft show with deSuntrations and hands-on kids projects.

EVENING

DINNER **Deer Head Inn,** 5 Main St., PA 611, Delaware Water Gap; (570) 424-2000; www.deerheadinn.com. During the town's annual Celebration of the Arts weekend in Sept, this modest little gathering spot is known as "jazz central" because it's such a popular hangout for the performers and their fans. Actually, that nickname applies all year long—and has for more than forty years. The dinner menu serves up basic, but well-made, fare with some interesting touches such as broccoli rabe pesto on penne, and crab and avocado salad on the pan-seared salmon. A perennial favorite is the unadorned New York strip steak. For an extra $5 to $12 you can stay for the music. Usually the Deer Head Inn is very easy-going and relaxed—except during Celebration of the Arts when it's insane, so make reservations and don't be late! $–$$. Call for seasonal hours.

LODGING   Stroudsmoor Country Inn.

DAY 3/MORNING

BREAKFAST   Stroudsmoor Country Inn.

From Stroudsburg take I-80 west; get off at exit 304 onto US 209. Turn right at Shafer's School House Road, then left on Business Route 209. Follow the signs to **Quiet Valley Living Historical Farm** (1000 Turkey Hill Rd., Stroudsburg; 570-992-6161; www.quiet village.org), about 1½ miles down the road. On this 60-acre farm, you can visit the original house, barn, smokehouse, and tool sheds owned by an 18th-century German immigrant family. Open mid-June to Labor Day, Tues through Sat 10 a.m. to 5 p.m., Sun noon to 5 p.m. as well as selected days in spring and fall. Watch a period-clad farm family go about their daily chores. Admission for adults $10, $5 for children age 3 to 12.

LUNCH   **Barley Creek Brewing Company,** Sullivan Trail and Camel-back Road, Tannersville; (570) 629-9399; www.barleycreek.com. Take I-80 west for about 7 miles to exit 299/Tannersville, then make a right onto PA 715 north. Take your first left onto Sullivan Trail and follow it about 1 mile to Camelback Road. If you get there by 12:30 p.m., you can have a free tour and tasting. But even if you miss the tour, be sure to order your favorite style from refreshing, golden ale to rich, dark stout to go with your burger, shepherd's pie, ribs, or other pub selection. Even the nonalcoholic Birch Beer is homemade. $–$$. Open midweek and Sun from 11 a.m. until at least 9:30 p.m. and Fri and Sat nights until 10:30 p.m.

AFTERNOON

Glen Brook Golf Club (Hickory Valley Road, Stroudsburg; 570-421-3680; www.glenbrookgolfclub.com). Guests at Stroudsburg Country Inn are entitled to special rates and tee times at this local landmark course with its challenging rolling hills, water play, and mountain backdrop. Greens fees range from $45 weekday, $54 weekends riding; $27 to $54 walking. Non-golfers might prefer an essential oil wrap, energy balance facial, garden Swedish massage, outdoors if weather permits at **The Spa at Stroudsmoor Country Inn by Shear Design** (570-424-9061). Hours are Wed through Sun from 9 a.m. to 5 p.m. Other hours are available at the spa's Stroudsburg location.

To head home, take US 209 south toward PA 33 south/Snydersville; after 6½ miles, 209 becomes 33. Keep driving for 18½ miles, then merge onto US 22 west toward Bethlehem/Allentown. After another 16½ miles, merge onto I-476 south toward I-276 Philadelphia exits 44–20. After 42 miles, take I-76 exit east via 16A on the left toward Philadelphia.

There's More . . . .

Camping. **Mountain Vista Campground,** 50 Taylor Dr., East Stroudsburg; (570) 223-0111; www.mtnvistacampground.com. Wooded tent sites; water, sewer, and electric hook-ups; camping store; laundry; stocked fishing pond; tennis, volleyball, game room; planned activities and entertainment. Open Apr through Oct; call for seasonal rates.

Museums & Tours. **Olde Engine Works Marketplace,** 62 North Third St., Stroudsburg; (570) 421-4340; www.oldeengineworks.com. This hundred-year-old former machine shop now houses 125 antiques and collectibles dealers. Call for seasonal hours.

Stroud Mansion, 900 Main St., Stroudsburg; (570) 421-7703; www.monroehistorical.org. On the former site of a French and Indian War fort, Revolutionary War Colonel Jacob Stroud, founder of the town that bears his name, built this twelve-room Georgian home for his son, John in 1795. Today it displays four floors of historic artifacts, antique toy and textile collections, a Victorian parlor, and a recreated colonial-era cellar kitchen. Open year-round Tues through Fri 9 a.m. to 4 p.m., first and third Sun 1 to 4 p.m. (Come at either 10 a.m. or 2 p.m. for a one-hour guided tour.) Admission is $8 for adults, $6 for seniors and students.

Shopping. **Stockade Miniatures** at 4 North Sixth St., Stroudsburg; (570) 424-8507; www.stockade-miniatures.com. The store is dedicated to selling new and old toy soldiers from every era and every part of the world. Open Mon through Fri 10 a.m. to 5 p.m., Sat 11 a.m. to 4 p.m.

Resorts. **Camelback Mountain Resort,** 1 Camelback Rd., Tannersville; (570) 629-1661; www.skicamelback.com. Skiing hours in season are Mon through Thurs 9 a.m. to 9 p.m., Fri until 10 p.m., Sat 8:30 a.m. to 10 p.m., Sun until 9 p.m. Tubing hours are Mon through Thurs 2 p.m. to 8 p.m., Fri until 9 p.m., Sat 9 a.m. to 9 p.m., Sun until 8 p.m. Lift tickets are $45 weekdays,

$55 weekends for adults; children and seniors $33 weekdays, $40 weekends. If you purchase tickets online, you'll save $2. Tubing tickets for all times and all ages are $25.

Camelbeach, 1 Camelback Rd., Tannersville; (570) 629-1661; www.skicamelback.com. This flip-season attraction of Camelback Ski area features water slides ranging from "kids only" to speed slides. At Kahuna Lagoon, you can brave the biggest waves in the Northeastern U.S. or you can tube a lazy river. Call for seasonal hours. Ticket prices are $35 for adults, $24 for children and seniors. Online adult ticket discounts are available.

Tubing. **Pack Shack Adventures,** 88 Broad St., Delaware Water Gap; (570) 424-8533; www.packshack.com. Rent tubes for a giddy glide down the river from mid-Apr through Oct. Hours are midweek 9 a.m. to 6 p.m., weekends 8 a.m. to 6 p.m. Rentals cost $27, save $2 with advance reservation.

Special Events . . . .

JUNE
Annual Celtic Festival, Shawnee Mountain Ski Area, exit 309 off I-80, Hollow Road, Shawnee-on-Delaware; (570) 421-7231; www.shawneemt.com. A weekend of nonstop Irish and Scottish music and dancing, including bagpipe bands and parade, working sheepdogs, and traditional foods and crafts.

AUGUST
Annual Pocono State Craft Festival, Quiet Valley Living Historical Farm, 1000 Turkey Hill Rd., Stroudsburg; (570) 476-4460; www.poconocrafts.com. Demos and displays showcase the multi-media talents of about 70 artisans from around the country and Canada. Activities for kids include creating their own crafts.

SEPTEMBER

Delaware Water Gap Celebration of the Arts, Delaware Water Gap; (570) 424-2210; www.cotajazz.org. Held annually the weekend after Labor Day, this three-day outdoor event attracts thousands of jazz fans from all over for music, arts and crafts, and all kinds of food.

OCTOBER

Pocono Garlic Festival, Shawnee Mountain Ski Area, exit 309 off I-80, Hollow Road, Shawnee-on-Delaware; (570) 421-7231; www .shawneemt.com. This Labor Day event is all about the beloved bulb, locally grown and featured in every kind of recipe from roasted pig to ice cream and funnel cakes and is the inspiration of multi-media craft. There's also live music—don't know how the performers will incorporate garlic, but surely if they can they will.

Timber & Balloon Festival, Shawnee Mountain Ski Area, exit 309 off I-80, Hollow Road, Shawnee-on-Delaware; (570) 421-7231; www.shawneemt.com. A weekend of balloon launches and rides; lumberjack shows with log rolling, pole climbing, axe and chainsaw contests; pig races; chairlift rides; skydiving exhibitions; music; food and crafts.

Other Recommended Lodgings and Restaurants . . . .

SCOTRUN

Great Wolf Lodge, 1 Great Wolf Dr.; (866) 958-9653; www.great wolf.com. There are no rainy day blues at this Disney-esque accommodation with its own almost 80,000-square-foot indoor waterpark. Other activities such as the Harry Potter–like interactive MagiQuest and spa are a la carte. $$$ for basic Family Suites that sleep four, some with gas fireplaces, whirlpools, and/or private balconies or patios. Themed suites for kids feature bunk beds tucked away in their own in-suite " wolf cave," "Northwoods tent," or "log cabin."

SHAWNEE-ON-DELAWARE
Buttermilk Falls Bed and Breakfast, 5231 Buttermilk Falls Rd.; (570) 426-7440. Four tidy attractive rooms situated on three-and-a-half acres with waterfall and stream for fishing. $$.

Stony Brook Inn Bed & Breakfast, River Road; (570) 424-1100; www.stonybrookinn.com. Three pretty rooms and one suite with adjoining sitting room. $–$$.

For More Information . . . .

Pocono Mountains Visitors Bureau, 1004 Main St., Stroudsburg, PA 18360; (800) POCONOS (800-762-6667) or (570) 421-5791; www.800poconos.com.

UP THE MOUNTAINS ESCAPE *Three*
The Skylands, New Jersey
THE GREAT OUTDOORS IN THE GREAT NORTHWEST/
2 NIGHTS

Rainbow Caverns
Sparkling Waters
Cowboys and Outlaws
Caviar and Pearls

About an hour northeast of Phil-adelphia begins New Jersey's "Great Northwest," a nearly 100-mile, five-county span known as the **Skylands.** Stretching all the way up to the dividing line that separates the Garden State from New York, the Skylands region encompasses two national parks, 60,000 acres of state parkland, and mile upon mile of scenic lakes, rivers, hills, and farmlands. Low-key small towns along the way invite visitors to slow down and stick around.

One of my favorite Skylands destinations is **Sussex County** at the region's northernmost tip, which begins about an hour from the Pennsylvania border. One state forest and six state parks account for one-third of Sussex County's total land mass, while the Kittatinny Mountains form its northwestern boundary.

With all of the fishing, swimming, fishing, golfing, biking, hiking, and other warm weather activities Sussex County has to offer, summer is generally regarded as peak season, when many of the accommodations are at their highest. However, when you consider the fabulous foliage of fall and great Alpine and cross-country skiing in winter, the Skylands is truly a four-season destination.

DAY 1/MORNING

On the way to your overnight accommodations in the town of Hamburg in Sussex County, I would recommend a stop in the historic,

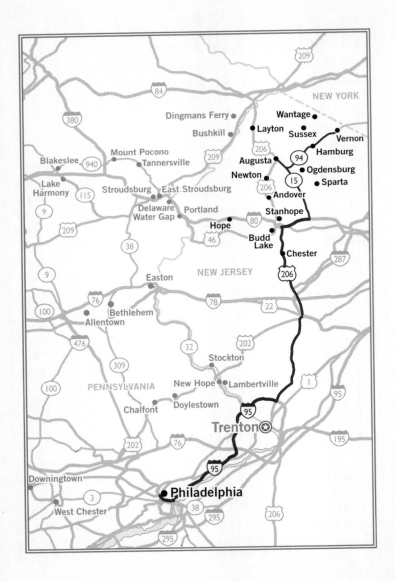

artsy and boutique shop–filled town of **Chester,** located in Morris County just southwest of Sussex. To get there, Take I-95 north toward Trenton for close to 40 miles; take exit 7B, then merge onto Lawrenceville Rd./US-206 north toward Lawrenceville/Princeton. Continue to follow the US-206 north signs for a little over 39 miles, then take a slight right at Main St. which runs through the heart of Chester (http://chesternj.org). The trip to Chester should take a total of about 1¾ hours.

Once known as "Black River," Chester's history as a farming area dates back to the early 1700s, but its real boom period was during the area's iron mining days in the latter half of the 1800s. That's when most of the buildings now housing more than 100 antique, art, and boutique shops were built. Chester is an easy walking town, so park anywhere on Main Street (aka NJ 24 or CR 513) and browse your way along its tree-lined streets and lanes and hidden courtyards.

AFTERNOON

LUNCH   The Publick House Tavern & Inn, 111 Main St., Chester, NJ; (908) 879-6878; www.chesterpublickhouse.com. In the early 1800s, this place was a well-known stagecoach stop. So make this historic spot your first stop in Chester for a lunch of lush, brandy-laced lobster bisque followed by a big Angus burger, Maryland-style crab cake, or Italian frittata. $.

On Chester's Main Street you'll find a combination of some things old and some things new. **The Chester Antique Mall** (427 Route 24; 908-879-7836; www.cantiquemall.com) features a collection of more than 25 dealers specializing in 18th- and 19th-century furniture, glass, china, pottery, and art. Open Tues through Sat 10:30 a.m. to 5 p.m., Sun 11:30 a.m. to 5 p.m. For creations of the more current kinds, **Chester Crafts & Collectibles** (26 Main St.; 908-879-2900) showcases the works of more than 50 regional artisans. Open daily from 10:30 a.m. to 5:30 p.m. And check out the cool kaleidoscopes at **Stained Glass Boutique** (76 E. Main St.; 908-879-7351). Open Mon 11 a.m. to 4:30 p.m., Tues 11 a.m. to 5 p.m., Wed through Fri 10:30 a.m. to 5 p.m., Sat 10 a.m. to 5:30 p.m. and Sun 11 a.m. to 5:30 p.m. Along the way, snack on a scoop or two of the house-made fanciful flavors (Smurf?) from **Taylor's Ice Cream Parlor** (18 E. Main St.; 908-879-5363). Open Mon through Thurs 10:30 a.m. to 9:30 p.m., Fri through Sun 10:30 a.m. to 10 p.m. If you're craving cookies or favor fruit, you'll have to make your way across big and busy US 206 to **Alstede Farms** (84 CR 513/Old Route 24; 908-879-7189; www.alstedefarms.com), a 365-acre family-owned operation where you can also pick your own fruits, veggies, and flowers. Open every day of the year; call for seasonal hours. Close by is **Cooper Gristmill** (66 Route 24; 908-879-5463; www.morrisparks.net), an operational early 19th century reproduction of one of the water-powered, stone mills that fueled the economy in the mid- to late-18th century. Tours led by costumed guides are available daily from Apr through Oct, weekends only the rest of the year; call for seasonal hours and special events.

EVENING

It's about a 50-minute drive to your dining and lodging destination in Hamburg. To get there from Cooper Gristmill, head northwest on West Main Street/NJ 24 toward Mill Ridge lane, then take the second left onto US 206 north. In less than 8 miles, take the ramp onto I-80 east and drive less than 7 miles to exit 34 toward NJ 15/Wharton/Dover/Sparta. Turn right onto North Main Street, then take a slight right toward NJ 15 north. When you get to NJ 15 north, take a slight left, in a little less than 10 miles, look for Country Road 517 exit toward Sparta/Franklin. Turn right at CR 517/New Sparta Avenue, then, in 5 miles, turn left at NJ 23 north. In a little less than 4 miles, turn right at NJ 94 north/Vernon Avenue, then turn right at Wild Turkey Way. **Crystal Springs Resort** (www.crystal golfresort.com) will be on your right-hand side. Crystal Springs is an expansive resort with two luxury hotels, two spas, and twelve restaurants, cafes, and bistros.

DINNER **Restaurant Latour,** Crystal Springs Country Club, One Wild Turkey Way, Hardyston, NJ; (973) 827-1587. With elegant, white tablecloths this restaurant is Crystal Springs' top-of-the-line dining spot featuring an imaginative classic French-meets-contemporary-American seasonal menu. Couple the high-caliber food with a more than 64,000-bottle wine cellar and you have an outstanding dining experience, whether you order a la carte or the seven-course chefs dégustation. $$$. Open Thurs through Thurs 5 p.m. to 9 p.m., Fri and Sat 5 p.m. to 10 p.m., Sun 4 p.m. to 8 p.m. Reservations are required.

LODGING **Minerals Resort & Spa at Crystal Springs,** NJ 94 and Chamonix Drive, Vernon NJ; (973) 827-5996. If you're traveling with the family, this Aspen-style resort offers a full-service nursery and all kinds of day and evening kid-friendly activities including arts and crafts, nature walks, sports and swimming, tennis and golf lessons. Accommodations range from deluxe guest rooms to presidential suites, some with stone living room and bedroom fireplaces, Jacuzzi, and balcony. Hotel amenities include seven indoor/ outdoor heated nature pools, Jacuzzis, steam room, and sauna. $$–$$$. **Grand Cascades Lodge,** NJ 94, Vernon, NJ; (973) 827-5996. If you're looking for a romantic getaway, this lodge combines wooden beam and natural stonework mountain design with Old World European ambience. Accommodations range from basic guest rooms to two-bedroom suites, some with one or two fireplaces, Jacuzzis, balconies, and gourmet kitchens. The $7 million Biosphere Pool Complex is a tropical oasis with a heated indoor freeform pool, underground aquarium, 140-foot water side, Jacuzzi, steam room, and sauna. $$$.

DAY 2/MORNING

···

BREAKFAST Minerals and Grand Cascades each has its own distinctive restaurant with a substantial and delightful morning menu. At Mineral Springs, **Kites Restaurant** serves such specialties as eggs Benedict or Florentine and crème brûlée French toast. $. Breakfast is available Mon through Fri (a la carte) 8 to 11 a.m. and Sat and Sun (buffet) 7 to 11 a.m. On the menu at Grand Cascades' **Crystal Tavern** are huevos rancheros and breakfast club sandwich. $. Sun through Fri a la carte breakfast and Sat continental buffet are served 7 to 11 a.m.

After breakfast, go outside and play. Seven public and semiprivate courses within a 5-mile radius of the resort offer experiences ranging from the Minerals Family Golf Center to the 27-hole Great Gorge Country Club to the super-challenging Crystal Springs. Call the resort for greens fees. Non-golfers can find fun at **Mountain Peak Ski Resort's Waterpark** (200 Route 94, Vernon, NJ; 866-787-1924, www.mountaincreek.com) about two minutes west on NJ 94. The park has more than two dozen rides including cliff jumps, wave pool, high slides, and tube rides. Call for seasonal hours and prices. In winter, Mountain Peak has a wide range of terrains for skiing, snowboarding, and tubing for all ages and skill levels. Adult lift tickets are $45 weekdays to $62 weekends; tubing is $16 to $20 per hour.

AFTERNOON

···

LUNCH **Chatterbox Drive-In,** 1 State Hwy. 15, Augusta, NJ; (973) 300-2300; www.chatterboxdrivein.com. About a half-hour southwest of Crystal Springs is this *Happy Days*–style restaurant. Take NJ 94/McAfee Road a little less than 14 miles, then turn right on NJ 15/NJ 94. After 3 miles, NJ 15 becomes US 206/ Hampton House Road. Continue about 1 mile until you reach the restaurant. From

Memorial Day through Labor Day, car-hops will bring your half-pound burgers, "Big Wazoo" (kielbasa), or pierogies right to your car. Fifties- and sixties-themed inside seating area is also open year-round. The Chatterbox is open Sun 11:30 a.m. to 8 p.m., Mon through Thurs until 9 p.m. and Fri and Sat until 9:30 p.m. $.

For more than fifty years, **Wild West City** (50 Lackawanna Dr., Stanhope, NJ; 973-347-8900; www.wildwestcity.com) has been bringing that rootin,' tootin,' shootin' American era to life with a well-researched antique accented recreation of Dodge City, Kansas, in the late 19th century. It offers a full day's schedule of twenty-two live street theater shows featuring cowboys, outlaws, roping, riding, even the capture of Jesse James—with the help of audience members. Admission is $13.50 for adults, $12.50 for children. The park is open weekends only from May to mid-June and from Labor Day to Columbus Day, seven days from mid-June to Labor Day. Hours are 10:30 a.m. to 6 p.m.

EVENING

DINNER **Black Forest Inn,** 249 US 206, Stanhope; (973) 347-3344; www.blackforestinn.com. It's only a two-minute drive, heading southwest on Lackawanna Drive/CR 207 towards CR 206, then turn left. Don't expect kitschy decor or food; this is serious European-style fare served in a lovely, low-key setting. The schnitzels (pork or veal cutlets) are tender and elegantly sauced, the sauerbraten a delicate balance of sweet and sour. You also can't go wrong with a side of homemade spätzle, potato dumpling, or red cabbage. If you get there between 4:30 p.m. and 6 p.m., you'll get a great deal on the three-course prix-fixe dinner. $$. Fri evening buffets are pricier, but worth the opportunity to sample so many of the restaurant specialties. Dinner is served Mon, Wed, Thurs, and Fri 4:30 to 6 p.m.; Sat 5 to 10 p.m., Sun 1 to 8 p.m. The restaurant is also open for lunch.

Take in an evening performance at **Pax Amicus Castle Theatre** (23 Lake Shore Dr., Budd Lake, NJ; 973-691-2100; www.paxamicus .com, located right across the Morris County border, 10 minutes southwest of the restaurant. Go south on US 206 north for half a mile, then take the ramp toward International Trade Center straight onto International Drive north. Make a slight right onto US 46, turn right onto Manor House Road, right onto St. James Road, and finally left onto Lake Shore Drive. The theater, a grand reproduction of a 15th-century chateau, will be on your left. For more than 30 years, Pax Amicus has been presenting a year-round schedule of Broadway and off-Broadway productions, Shakespearean, and other classic plays as well as children's theater, comedians, and other performing artists. Tickets for matinees and evening performances generally range from $12 to $25. Call for productions and times.

LODGING   **Crystal Springs Resort.** It's just under an hour drive back. Go back to St. James Road, turn left onto Manor House Road, then left again onto US 46 east. Stay on 46 east for 3 miles, then merge onto I-80 east toward Somerville/ New York. About 7½ miles down the road take exit 34 toward NJ 15/Jefferson/Dover/ Sparta. Take a slight right onto North Main Street/CR 634, then another slight right onto NJ 15 north. Drive 10 miles on NJ 15 until you reach the CR 517 ramp toward Sparta/Franklin. Turn right onto CR 517, then left onto NJ 23/CR 517. Follow NJ 23 for a little less than 4 miles to NJ 94/Vernon Avenue. Follow NJ 94 for about 6½ miles.

DAY 3/MORNING

You definitely don't want to leave Crystal Springs Resort without a treatment or two at Elements or Reflections Spas. **Elements at Minerals Resort** (973-864-5850) offers a variety of innovative services and products including a signature copper flake-infused moisturizer for the face and body, triple-layer exfoliating salt formula, and multiple-mud wrap. **Reflections at Grand Cascades Lodge** (973-823-6550) features ultra-posh treatments made with powdered pearls, crushed Champagne grape seeds, white truffles, and caviar. Call the spas for hours, prices, and reservations.

And before you depart from Vernon, another must-do is a visit to **Bobolink Dairy and Bakeyard** (42 Meadow Burn Rd., Vernon, NJ; 973-764-4888; http://shop.cowsoutside.com), just eight minutes northeast of the resort. Go northeast on CR 515/Stockholm Road toward NJ 94/McAfee Vernon Road and continue to follow 515 for about 3 miles. Take a slight left onto Princes Switch Road, then right onto Meadow Burn Road. At Bobolink, Nina and Jonathan White craft artisanal cheese from milk from their own cows. Nearly every other Sun from May through Oct, they invite the public to participate in four-hour cheese-making classes ($75, check the Web site for schedules). The farm is open for sampling and selling Wed to Fri from noon until 6 p.m., Sat and Sun from 9 a.m. to 5 p.m.

BRUNCH   **Perona Farms,** 350 Andover–Sparta Rd., Andover, NJ; (973) 729-6161; www.peronafarms.com. Even though it isn't likely that you resisted snacking on some cheese and crusty bread at Bobolink, you're probably ready for a bigger meal. And you'll find the area's best-loved brunch spot about 40 miles southwest at Perona Farms. Turn left from Meadow Burn Road onto Prices Switch Road/CR 515 and follow to where 515 merges with NJ 94. In about 8 miles, turn left onto NJ 23, then, after almost 4 miles, right onto CR 517/Munsonhurst Road. Follow CR 517 about 9 miles to Andover Sparta Road. "Sunday Bruncheon" at the glamorous, almost-century-old, family-owned and -operated Perona Farms has long been a tradition for locals. The lavish buffet includes a fresh seafood bar, nine hot dishes, made-to-order waffles and doughnuts, chef's carving stations, and other juice-to-dessert items. $$. Perona Farms offers Sunday Bruncheon seatings from 10:30 a.m. to 1:30 p.m.

AFTERNOON

....

To learn more about Sussex County's history as an important mining center and, at the same time, view some truly dazzling natural phenomena, take a twelve-minute ride northeast to **Sterling Hill Mining Museum** (30 Plant St., Ogdensburg, NJ; 973-209-7212; www .sterlinghillminingmuseum.org). Go northeast on CR 517/Andover Sparta Road toward Current Drive, turn right onto Sparta Avenue/ CR 517 after 2 miles, then follow CR 517 for a little under 5 miles. Turn left onto Brooks Flat Road, then right onto Plant Street. Opened sometime before 1739, Sterling Hill was one of the oldest mines in the country and the last operating underground mine in New Jersey when it closed in 1986. Between this zinc ore mine and one in nearby Franklin, a world-record-breaking 350 different mineral species have been uncovered, more than two dozen of which have not been found anywhere else on the planet. The area also holds the world record for the number of fluorescent minerals uncovered here, earning it the title "Fluorescent Mineral Capital of the World." As part of the two-hour underground tour, you'll see a spectacular array of glowing red and green zinc ore exposed in the mine walls under ultraviolet light. (You can take a piece home.) Six hundred more fluorescent minerals and more than 20,000 artifacts from the mine's boom days are on display in museums on the grounds. Admission for adults is $10. Call for seasonal tour days and times.

To get back to Philadelphia, head south on CR 517/Main Street toward Edison Avenue, follow CR 517 for almost 4 miles, then turn left to merge onto NJ 15 south toward I-80. After 10 miles, merge onto I-80 east toward New York. In another 9½ miles, take exit 43 toward Morristown/Mahwah. Keep right at the fork to merge onto I-287 south, then continue for close to 24 miles. Take exit 17 to merge onto US 202 south/US 206 south toward US

22 west/Somerville/Flemington. Stay on 206 south for close to 25 miles, then merge onto I-95 via the ramp to Pennsylvania. Stay on I-95 for 36 miles. The trip home should take you a little over two-and-one-half hours.

There's More . . . .

Amusement Parks. **Land of Make Believe & Pirate's Cove,** 354 Great Meadows Rd., Route 611; Hope, NJ; (908) 459-9000; www.lomb .com. More than two dozen amusements, water rides, and other attractions for all ages at this more than fifty-year-old park. Call for summer schedule. Admission for adults is $21, $23 for children.

Camping. Sussex County offers a wide variety of public and private park camping options from primitive tent sites to yurts to fully equipped cabins. For more information, go to www.newjerseyvisitorsnetwork.com, www.sussex.nj.us, and www.state.nj.us/dep/parks and forests.

Fishing. **Sussex County's Lake Wawayanda,** Wawayanda Creek and Kittatinny Valley State Park's Lake Aeroflex are stocked with salmon. Skylands waters also teem with trout, perch, bass, and all types of other fish. For more information, go to www.njfishandwild life.com.

Hiking and Mountain Biking. With so many miles of state park and forest land, some of which run along the Appalachian trail, the opportunities are endless for hikers and bikers of every age and skill level. You can hike beside rivers and watch for barred owls, great blue herons, wood ducks, and more than forty species of butterflies in wildlife sanctuaries. For more information, go to www.sussex.nj.us, www.njskylands.com, www.state.nj.us, and www.njwildlifetrails.org.

Diablo Freeride Park, 200 Route 94, Vernon, NJ; (888) 767-1914; www.diablofreeridepark.com. More than 40 freeride and downhill trails for all skill levels. $38 for lift ticket. May to end of Oct.

Spectator Sports. **Sussex Skyhawks,** Skylands Park, 94 Championship Place, Augusta, NJ; (973) 300-1000; www.sussexskyhawks .com. Professional Canadian–American League baseball at family-friendly prices: $10 for reserved seats, $8 general. Call for May to Sept home-game times.

State Parks. **High Point State Park,** 1480 Route 23, Sussex, NJ; (973) 875-4800; www.stateparks.com/high_point.html. At 1,803 feet above sea level, the view of mountain, river, farmland, and forest in three states from the High Point Monument is worth the more than 200-stair climb to the top. Lake Marsha has a lifeguard protected beach and spring-fed waters. Hikers and mountain bikers will find more than 50 miles of well-marked trails, including portions of the Appalachian Trail. In winter, 15 km of groomed trails, half of which are covered by artificial snow, are open for cross-country skiing; rental equipment is available. Entrance fees are $5 weekdays, $10 weekends from Memorial Day weekend to Labor Day.

Tours. **Spring Valley Equestrian Center,** 56 Paulinskill Lake Rd., Newton, NJ; (973) 383-3766; www.springvalleyequestriancenter .com. Hourlong trail rides along the Paulinskill Valley Trail are $30, half-hour rides for kids 8 and under are $25.

Special Events . . . .

(Events take place at Sussex County Fair Grounds, 37 Plains Rd., Augusta, NJ, unless otherwise indicated.)

MARCH

Springfest in Sussex County; (973) 948-9448; www.springfestgar denshow.com. Thirteen gardens are designs using creative uses of natural stone, ponds, water falls, garden plants, and flowers; expert speakers and consultations; marketplace and kids' activities.

AUGUST

New Jersey State Fair–Sussex County Farm & Horse Show; (973) 948-5500; www.newjerseystatefair.org. Ten-day agricultural fair features farm animals, horse shows, carnival rides and games, art and model train exhibits, chainsaw artist, monster trucks, dog show, and other activities and entertainment.

Other Recommended Restaurants and Lodgings

ANDOVER

Andover Diner, 193 Main St.; (973) 786-6641; www.andoverdiner .com. Breakfast all day, lunch and homemade pies. $.

GLENWOOD

Glenwood Mill Bed and Breakfast, 1860 Route 565; (973) 764-8660; www.glenwoodmill.com. Renovated 200-year-old grist mill has two guest rooms and two suites with bubble jet tubs and gas fireplaces. Full breakfast. Close to hiking trails. $$.

LAFAYETTE

Lafayette House Restaurant, Old Lafayette Village, between NJ 94 and NJ 15; (973) 579-3100; www.thelafayettehouse.com. Located in Old Lafayette Village shopping area. Serving seafood, steaks, and specialty Chesapeake chicken stuffed with crabmeat. Open for dinner Mon to Thurs 4:30 to 10 p.m., Fri and Sat 5 to 11 p.m.,

Sun 4:30 to 9 p.m. $$. Lunch, tavern menu, and Sun brunch are available.

NEWTON

Andre's Restaurant & Wine Boutique, 188 Spring St.; (973) 300-4192; www.andresrestaurant.com. Sophisticated American menu changes twice monthly. Wine suggestions with each dish. Open for dinner Wed and Thurs 5 to 9 p.m., Fri and Sat 5 to 10 p.m., Sun until 8 p.m. $$–$$$. More moderately priced tavern menu, too.

Wooden Duck Bed and Breakfast, 140 Goodale Rd.; (973) 300-0395; www.woodenduckinn.com. Main and carriage house rooms and suites on 1,600 acres with swimming pool and adjacent to Kittatinny State Park and two stocked lakes within walking distance. Full breakfast included. $$–$$$.

SPARTA

The Homestead Restaurant, 294 N Church Rd.; (973) 383-4914; www.homesteadrest.com. Rustic dining spot specializing in almost a dozen burger variations named after Western movies. Take the two-pound Legend burger challenge and earn a place in the Homestead Hall of Fame. Steaks and ribs, too. Mon through Wed and Sun from 11:30 a.m. to 9 p.m., Thurs to 10 p.m., Fri and Sat to 11 p.m. $–$$.

STANHOPE

The Whistling Swan Inn Bed and Breakfast, 110 Main St.; (973) 347-6369; www.whistlingswaninn.com. Charming Victorian home features ten guest rooms and two suites with two-person Jacuzzis, fireplaces, and mini-fridge. Full buffet breakfast. $$–$$$.

VERNON

Alpine Haus Bed and Breakfast Inn, 217 Route 94; (973) 209-7080; www.alpinehausbb.com. Eight antique-furnished guest rooms and two suites with gas fireplaces and Jacuzzis in an 1887 Federal Style Inn and Carriage House. Full hot breakfast. $$.

Mountain Creek, 200 Route 94; (866) 787-1924; www.mountain creek.com. One- to three-bedroom condos, some slopeside, with fireplaces and kitchens, private balconies, ski-in/ski-out. Pool, gym, and on-premise massage studio. A la carte breakfast on week-days. $$–$$$.

WANTAGE

High Point Country Inn, 1328 Route 23 North; (973) 702-1860; www.highpointcountryinn.com. Pet-friendly motel on seven acres with pool minutes from High Point State Park and the Appalachian Trail. "Snack-pack" breakfast. $.

For More Information . . . .

New Jersey Skylands Guide; www.njskylands.com.

Skylands of NJ Tourism Council; (800) 4SKYLAND; www.skylands tourism.org.

Sussex Skylands Chamber of Commerce; (973) 579-1811; www .sussexcountychamber.org.

UP THE MOUNTAINS ESCAPE *Four*

Berkeley Springs, West Virginia
ETERNAL SPRINGS/2 NIGHTS

Rejuvenating Waters
Heaven-sent Hands
Abundant Art
George's Bathtub

Long before the first Europeans set foot in the New World, Native Americans from Canada to the Carolinas were making regular pilgrimages to this lovely Appalachian mountain valley in West Virginia's eastern panhandle to bathe in warm mineral spring waters legendary for their curative powers. Early colonists also believed that "taking the waters" at Medicine Springs or Warm Springs, as it was called back then, could cure their aches and ailments.

In fact, George Washington was so taken with "ye fam'd warm springs" that in 1776 he and a group of his family and friends became landowners in the area and dubbed it "The Town of Bath" after England's premier spa. Bath quickly became a favorite watering hole for the socially prominent—and the site of gambling and parties so wild they prompted a member of the clergy to warn of the "overflowing tide of immorality" that threatened to engulf any who dared to go there.

Today, the only sign of wildlife is the furred and feathered kind you can glimpse from the scenic mountain trails. But the crystal-clear 74.3-degree waters from its springs continue to work their magic on those who come seeking comfort for body and soul.

Five year-round spas offer distinctly different menus of therapeutic and beauty treatments in settings ranging from state-park basic to state-of-the-art luxurious. **Berkeley Springs** is also a mecca for artists and craftsmen, who provide a feast for the eyes in galleries and shops and on public buildings.

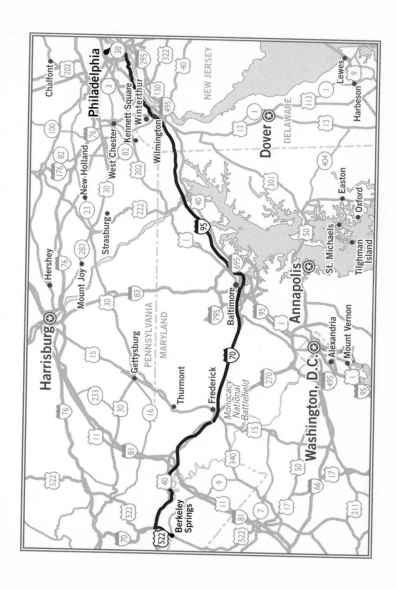

DAY 1/MORNING/AFTERNOON

It's a four-hour (165-mile) drive from Philadelphia to Berkeley Springs, so start early to take full advantage of the smorgasbord of pampering the town has to offer. Take I-95 south to the I-695 west exit (49B), toward I-70/Towson, Maryland. Merge onto I-695 north. Take the I-70 west/I-70 exit (16), toward Frederick. Keep left at the fork in the ramp, then merge onto I-70 west. Stay on I-70 west until you reach the US 522 south exit (18) on the left toward Hancock/Winchester. Merge onto US 522 south and follow it for 6 miles; it will become Washington Street and take you straight into the heart of Berkeley Springs. *IMPORTANT NOTE:* Don't depend on your GPS to guide you in this area or you'll just get angry and throw it out the window.

LUNCH **Earth Dog Café,** 398 S. Washington St., Berkeley Springs, WV; (304) 258-0500. There's probably no better place to acclimate yourself to the laid-back attitude in this town than Earth Dog Café, where peace signs and tie-dye shirts remind diners of the heyday of the hippie movement. If you're a barbecue buff, try one of the hickory smoked specialties such as pork ribs or shoulder, brisket, or chicken—the sauce is really something special. Or go for a smothered hot dog. Breakfast is available all day, and the cafe is also open for dinner. $. Open Mon through Thurs 7 a.m. to 8 p.m., Fri until 9 p.m., Sat 8 a.m. to 9 p.m., Sun until 8 p.m.

Berkeley Springs State Park may seem like a pretty grandiose name for the five-acre patch of green at the corner of Washington and Fairfax Streets. But considering that the town's lifeblood runs through it, the designation seems much more appropriate.

In the park, be sure to pay homage to **George Washington's Bathtub,** a tongue-in-cheek tribute to—but authentic reproduction of—the hollowed-out crude sand- and rock-lined pools from G. W.'s spa days. In addition to soaking in the waters, our health-seeking ancestors liked to swig it, too. And that hasn't changed. Every day streams of people from all over the county come to fill up their bottles, jugs, and other vessels from the free public tap.

For a truly down-to-earth (and budget-friendly) spa experience, you can't get any more authentic (or inexpensive) than the **Old Roman Bath House** (2 S. Washington St., Berkeley Springs, WV; 304-258-2711; www.berkeleyspringssp.com). No fancy whirlpools, just totally serene immersion in your own private 750-gallon walk-in tub of mineral spring water heated to 100 to 102 degrees ($10 for a twenty-minute bath; $40 to $45 weekdays, $70 to $80 weekends with Swedish massage). Infrared treatments are also available. Open daily 10 a.m. to 6 p.m., Fri until 9 p.m. Apr 1 through Oct 31.

Cross the street to **The Bath House Massage & Health Center** (21 Fairfax St., Berkeley Springs, WV; 304-431-4698; www.bath house.com). In addition to your basic and hot stone massages, the menu features many globally-inspired treatments such as a Moroccan Body Ritual, Tuscan Wine Peel, Balinese Body Polish, and Russian Massage. Prices range from $75 to $120. Aromatherapy spa and infrared saunas are also available. Call for hours.

Just a five-minute drive up the mountain is the renowned Robert Trent Jones-designed, eighteen-hole, par 72, championship public course at **Cacapon State Park Resort** (Cacapon State Park, Berkeley Springs, WV; 304-258-1022; www.cacaponresort.com/golf.htm). From downtown, turn right at the corner of Fairfax and Washington Streets. Washington Street turns into US 522. Take US 522 south about 10 miles to the park entrance. Driving range, pro shop, and private lessons ($30) are available. Greens fees vary by season and day of week—for eighteen holes, it ranges from $27 to $32, $18 for off-season.

EVENING

....

DINNER   **Tari's Cafe,** 123 North Washington St., Berkeley Springs, WV; (304) 258-1196. Probably the liveliest dining spot in downtown Berkeley Springs. Crab soup and crab cakes, in sandwiches, salads, and even on top of fettuccini, are the big draws at this country-style, local art-filled popular spot. $–$$.

If you long for the days when movie theaters had personality (and reasonable prices), take in the 8 p.m. show at the **Star Theatre** (Congress and North Washington Streets, Berkeley Springs, WV; 304-258-1404; www.starwv.com/star) any Fri through Sun evening (also Thurs in summer). A true mom-and-pop operation, this vintage Depression-era movie house is as famous as for its popcorn (made in a 1947 popper) as it is for its flicks. Movies are $3.75 for adults, $3.25 for children. Take note of the theater's stained-glass windows with the dancing star designs. They were created by a self-taught local artist who calls himself Ragtime.

LODGING   **Highlawn Inn,** 304 Market St., Berkeley Springs, WV; (304) 258-5700; www.highlawninn.com. To find your bed for the night (and your breakfast tomorrow morning), take Washington Street to Market Street, just south of the park and springs. Turn left onto Market and follow it 2 blocks to the top of the hill. Originally built for a Victorian bride, this elaborate abode was meticulously restored by innkeeper Sandra Kauffman and her husband, Tim, to regain its aura of romance. Sink-in sofas flank the working fireplace in the antiques-filled parlor area. A wrap-around porch takes full advantage of the inn's hilltop perch. Highlawn also includes three adjacent buildings, each distinctive in character. $$–$$$.

DAY 2/MORNING

BREAKFAST **Highlawn Inn.** Sandra is known far and wide for her sumptuous breakfast buffets featuring freshly squeezed juices; homemade breads, pastries, and egg and vegetarian dishes spiked with fresh herbs from her garden; fruited oatmeal; and custom-blended coffee.

Head back up to Cacapon State Park for a leisurely stroll or ambitious hike on 20 miles of blazed trails. Park maps and trail guides are available at the front desk of the **Cacapon State Park Resort.** Throughout much of the year, naturalist-guided walks are also available. At the park's stables you can arrange for a one-hour ($24) or longer trail ride through the forested mountainside from Easter through Thanksgiving. For a different experience, try "wobble trap" (clay pigeon) shooting. Open seven days Sept through May from 10 a.m. to 4:30 p.m., Memorial Day through Labor Day until 5:30 p.m. Cost is $21 with shotgun and shells, $7 if you bring your own.

Need to cool off? There's also an open-to-the-public lake, complete with diving boards, lifeguard, and lovely white, sandy beach. Rowboats and paddleboats are available for rental. Open Memorial Day weekend through Labor Day weekend.

When you're ready to leave the park, take US 522 north about 9 miles until it intersects with WV 9. Make a left onto WV 9 and go about 4 miles until you come to **Panorama Overlook** (aka Prospect Peak Scenic Overlook). The breathtaking view from this rugged, rocky peak encompasses the Potomac and Cacapon Rivers nearly 1,000 feet below and three states—Maryland, Pennsylvania, and West Virginia. Although the road is open to hikers year-round, it is accessible by car only from May through Oct.

AFTERNOON

> **LUNCH** **Panorama at the Peak,** 1 Prospect Peak Lane, Panorama Overlook, Berkeley Springs, WV; (304) 258-9847; www.panoramaatthepeak.com. You won't be able to tear yourself away from the view, so head on WV 9 west across from Panorama Peak to this restaurant. Locally-sourced trout, chicken, lamb, and other meats and produce are gently handled without fuss or frills. The menu includes some creative vegetarian selections, too. $–$$. Call for seasonal hours.

To showcase the talents of the many amateur and professional artists and crafters who call Berkeley Springs home, the local **Morgan Arts Council (MAC)** has opened a gallery (open Sat and Sun 11 a.m. to 5 p.m., call for additional hours) on the first floor of a 40,000-square-foot former cold storage building called the **Ice House** (corner of Independence and Mercer Streets, Berkeley Springs, WV; 304-258-2300; www.icehouseartistsco-op.com). On display (and for sale) are works representing more than thirty local artists and a wide range of disciplines, including sculpture, forged iron, abstract mosaics, wearable art, and handcrafted furniture. On selected evenings, the Ice House also hosts lectures, literary discussions, plays and musical performances, and classes on an eclectic variety of topics. On Sat evenings in July and Aug, MAC sponsors free concerts at Berkeley Springs State Park. Blues, jazz, country, string band, Caribbean, or international music sounds extra good with a magnificent mountain view in the background.

For more local art, stop in at **Mountain Laurel Gallery** (1 North Washington St., Berkeley Springs, WV; 304-258-1919; www.mtn-laurel.com), where you'll find six rooms and two floors filled with arts and crafts from more than 150 artists from around the country and Canada. The focus in on local talent who produce some pretty cool items including hardwood kitchenware, "stream of consciousness" photography, and whimsical pottery with personality. Hours are Mon through Sat 10 a.m. to 6 p.m., Sun until 5 p.m. **Old Factory Antique Mall** (282 Williams St., Berkeley Springs, WV; 304-258-1788; www.oldfactoryantiquemall.com), has 20,000 square feet of antiques and crafts plus its signature Almost Heaven Fudge. Hours are 10 a.m. to 5 p.m. Then there's the **Glass Coven** (145 Wisteria Lane, Berkeley Springs, WV; 304-258-2629; www.glass coven.com), which focuses on decorative, functional, and wearable fused-, stained-, and mosaic-glass items.

EVENING

DINNER   **Lot 12 Public House,** 117 Warren St., just 1 block south of Highlawn Inn, Berkeley Springs, WV; (304) 258-6264; www.lot12.com. Chef/owner Damian Heath creates sophisticated seasonal food in an intimate setting. Menu musts include crisp goat-cheese medallions on baby spinach and crisp roasted duck with rosemary potato cake and pear chutney. The vegetarian "shepherdless pie" is a meatless marvel. $$. Open Apr through Nov, Thurs through Sun beginning at 5 p.m.; Dec through Mar, Fri, Sat, and Sun from 5 p.m. Be sure to make reservations.

LODGING   Highlawn Inn.

DAY 3/MORNING

BREAKFAST   Highlawn Inn.

Just across the Maryland border and a nine-minute drive north of Berkeley Springs along US-522/WV-9 is the town of Hancock.

Rent a bike at **C & O Bicycle** and take a ride along the twenty-two-and-a-half-mile Western Maryland C & O Canal Rail Trail.

Prices range from $9.50 for two hours to $30 for 24 hours. Open late Mar/early Apr through end of Oct; seven days in summer when school is out; six other times (closed Tuesday). Hours are 8 a.m. to 6 p.m. 9 S. Pennsylvania Ave.; Hancock, MD; (301) 678-6665; www.candobicycle.com.

LUNCH   **Troubadour Lounge** (25 Troubadour Lane; Berkeley Springs, WV; (304) 258-9381; www.troubadourlounge.com. This place is tricky to find, but you won't find an eatery or owners with more destination-worthy personalities. Not only do you get to chow down on some burger, country ham sandwich, or even a T-bone steak for extremely modest prices, but you get to dine in the middle of the **West Virginia Country Music Hall of Fame and Museum** as owner 70-something-year-old "Joltin'" Jim McCoy (yes, he's one of THOSE McCoys) tells you about his long-time career as a performer and producer. Open Tues, Wed, and Sun 1 to 10 p.m., Thurs until 11 p.m., Fri and Sat until to 1 a.m. $. To get there from downtown Berkeley Springs, take US 522 south past four stoplights; pass the Dairy Queen on the right, then make a left onto Route 13, Winchester Grade Road. Continue on Route 13/Winchester Grade Road for about 3 miles. Make a left just before the sharp blind curve onto Spriggs Road, then continue past the road sign for Daveda Court (it will be on your left). Stay on Spriggs Road all the way to the end, then make a left at the intersection onto Highland Ridge Road. Go to the bottom of the hill and the Troubadour Lounge will be on your left. My advice is to take this trip during daylight hours because the tricks and signage can be confusing. But do go there; if I, who am seriously directionally impaired, found it, so can you!

AFTERNOON

Surely you have time to treat yourself to one more spa treatment before you head for home. At **Atasia Spa** (206 Congress St., Berkeley Springs, WV; 304-258-7888; www.atasiaspa.com), located just a block from the springs, Thai massage is a specialty. Owner

Frankie Tan's soothing foot massage followed by a steaming hot towel and heated oil neck and shoulder massage is the signature treatment. Services range from $45 to $135. The spa is open daily 9 a.m. to 6 p.m.

There's More . . . .

Camping. **Cacapon Hideaway;** (304) 258-4141; www.cacaponhide away.com. One hundred acres of campground located near the Cacapon and Potomac Rivers and a nature conservancy with hiking trails. The property has a large pond for fishing, paddle boats, a playground, and canoe and fishing pole rentals. Wooded sites, some with electric, all with fire rings and fire rings. Camping cabins are also available. $.

Fishing. **Sleepy Creek Lake,** West Virginia Department of Natural Resources; (304) 558-2758; www.wvdnr.gov. This man-made lake, located in the Sleepy Creek Wildlife Management Area, is a great place to catch trophy bass, crappie, and northern pike. Night fishing is permitted. Call for directions.

Nature and Recreation Programs. **Cacapon Resort State Park,** www .cacaponresort.com. Year-round naturalist-guided bird walks and night hikes with campfires. Programs are offered daily from Memorial Day through Labor Day and Tues through Sat from Sept through May.

Shopping. **1000 Points of Peace,** 20 Daveda Ct., Berkeley Springs, WV; (304) 258-5885; www.1000pointsofpeace.com. Local stained glass artist, Ragtime, and friends create one-of-a-kind peace signs and symbols of hope, peace, and family. Call for an appointment.

Berkeley Springs Farmers' Market, US 522 & Fairfax St., Berkeley Springs, WV; www.berkeleyspringsfarmersmarket.com. Seasonal fruit, vegetables, and plants; meats and dairy; bakery and prepared food items from local farms and producers. Open Thurs and Sun in spring, summer, and early fall. Call for specific hours.

Jules Enchanting Gifts and Collectibles, 13 Fairfax St., Berkeley Springs, WV; (304) 258-9509; www.julesenchantinggifts.com. Whimsical figurines and other fun stuff from spinning steel eye-catchers to frameable, shaped puzzles. Call for hours.

Sage Moon Herb Shop, 15 Fairfax St., Berkeley Springs, WV; (304) 258-9228; www.sagemoonherbshop.com. A wide variety of bulk herbs, teas, and herbal blends plus home-made natural, organic body care products and mood-mellowing flower essences. Call for hours.

Spas. **Five Senses Spa,** The Country Inn at Berkeley Springs, 110 S. Washington St., Berkeley Springs, WV; (304) 258-2210; www.thecountryinnatberkeleysprings.com. European facials for women and men, total body, exclusive essential oils massage, and cleansing and toning Yon-Ka Aromarine Mud Wrap. Services range from $65 to $140. Ask about mid-week specials.

Spectator Sports. **Hagerstown Speedway,** 15112 National Pike, Hagerstown, MD; (301) 582-0640; www.hagerstownspeedway.com. Year-round racing fast-track racing. Admission is $10 for adults, free for children under 12.

Special Events . . . .

Call (800) 447-8797 for more information about the following events:

JANUARY THROUGH MARCH

Winter Festival of the Waters. A celebration of the healing and economic powers of the town's warm springs. At January's Spa Feast, you can sample more than fifty-five different body treatments at the spas as well as workshops and special dinners. During the last full weekend in February Berkeley Springs hosts its world-renowned annual International Water Tasting which brings still, sparkling, and municipal tap waters from around the world for a professional wine-tastinglike competition. To commemorate the first visit by America's first president to the Berkeley Springs in March 1748, the town throws a George Washington's Bathtub Celebration, featuring a weekend of $1 specials throughout the town.

APRIL

Uniquely West Virginia Wine & Food Festival. Two days of eating and drinking locally-grown and -made products.

MAY

Berkeley Artists' Springs Studio Tour; www.berkeleyspringsstudio tour.org. Held twice a year, on Memorial Day Weekend and the second weekend after Columbus Day. Visit twenty-six working artists in seventeen locations

OCTOBER

Apple Butter Festival. Celebrate the harvest with daylong apple butter making, apple butter and cake competitions, a parade, live music, turtle races, beard and mustache contest, and more than 200 food, crafts, and antiques booths.

Other Recommended Restaurants and Lodgings . . . .

BERKELEY SPRINGS

Ambraehouse at Berkeley Springs featuring Wine with Me, 98 North Washington St.; (304) 248-2333; www.ambraehouse.com. Three suites named after wines with jetted soaking tubs in a completely refurbished 1907 former home. Complete breakfast is included. $$. Wine with Me—Innkeeper Lisa Bowman offers food and wine tastings and appreciation classes.

Angus & Ale, 146 Southridge; (304) 258-7575; www.angusandale .com. Fried gator tail is a popular add-on to the steaks. $–$$. Open Mon 4 to 8 p.m.; Tues, Fri, and Sat 11:30 a.m. to 9 p.m.; Wed and Thurs to 8 p.m.; Sun 8 a.m. to 8 p.m. Lunch and Sunday brunch, too.

Berkeley Springs Cottage Rentals; (304) 258-5300, www.berkeley springscottagerentals.com. Numerous one- to five-bedroom chalets, cottages, and cabins in the downtown, riverside, and countryside areas. Some may have fishing and swimming ponds, hiking trails, and other amenities. Rates start at $.

Cacapon Resort State Park, 818 Cacapon Lodge Dr.; (304) 258-1022; www.cacaponresort.com. Lodge rooms: Forty-eight basic rooms offer year-round mountain and golf course views. The lounge has a fireplace. Children under 12 stay free. No pets. $. Cabins: Three types of cabins offer year-round rentals. Modern and standard cabins, which sleep four to eight, feature stone fireplaces and fully equipped kitchens; some accommodate pets. $–$$. Bungalows: Open Apr through Oct, these accommodations sleep up to four and come with living/dining/bedroom with built-in double bunks and shower. Two-night minimum is required on weekends. $.

The Country Inn at Berkeley Springs, 110 S. Washington St.; (304) 258-2210; www.thecountryinnatberkeleysprings.com. Distinctively decorated rooms and suites situated in a historic inn and contemporary addition. For the ultimate in privacy, book The Treehouse guest cottage. Onsite are the Five Senses Spa and four restaurants. $$–$$$.

The Manor Inn Bed and Breakfast, 234 Fairfax St.; (304) 258-1552; www.bathmanorinn.com. Five guest-room Victorian with featherbeds, clawfoot tubs, and Jacuzzis serves breakfast in an antique-decorated dining room or, weather permitting, on the large front porch. $. Ask about mid-week discounts.

Mi Ranchito Mexican Restaurant, 141 Independence St.; (304) 258-4800; www.miranchitomx.blogspot.com. Mexican classic appetizers, entrees, and combos. Prices are mostly $, some $$. Open Mon through Sat 11 a.m. to 8 p.m., Sun lunch is served, too.

Rose Cafe, one-half block from US 522 (51 Independence and Washington Streets); (304) 258-6023; www.maryrosecafe.com. Sushi for two for $30; Thai green, Indian vegetable, shrimp, and chicken curries. $$. Open daily 9:30 a.m. to 5:30 p.m.

Sleepy Creek Tree Farm Bed and Breakfast, 37 Shades Lane; (304) 258-4324; www.maggiedot.com. Situated on an eight-acre Christmas tree farm on Sleepy Creek, 4 miles east of Berkley Springs, this two guest room sits on the creek, features a pond stocked with hybrid striped bass, gardens, and wooded trails. Breakfast is included. Well behaved pets welcome. $$–$$$.

Tony's Butcher Block, 2880 Valley Rd.; (304) 258-4770; www.tonysbutcherblock.com. Open Tues through Sat 8 a.m. to 5 p.m. A great place to pick up your picnic fare as well as signature Maryland Blue Crabs steamed and cakes. Try the West Virginia pepperoni rolls. $.

For More Information . . . .

Travel Berkeley Springs Visitor Center, 304 Fairfax St., Berkeley Springs, WV 25411; (304) 258-9147; www.berkeleysprings.com. Open Mon through Fri 9 a.m. to 5 p.m., Sat until 3 p.m.

DOWN THE SHORE
ESCAPES

DOWN THE SHORE ESCAPE *One*
Long Beach Island, New Jersey
SMALL ISLAND, BIG FUN/2 NIGHTS

Soft Sugar Sand
Hanging Ten
Chowder Champions
Sailing the Sky

When summer turns sultry, the lure of the shore is irresistible. And, with so many different seaside experiences such a short drive away from Philly (that is, if you hit the road early enough to beat everyone else who has a wave craving), you can pack a lot of sun and fun into a couple of days.

If you're looking for glitz, stick with Atlantic City. For boardwalks, you'll have to go to Ocean City, the Wildwoods or Cape May. **Long Beach Island**'s only boardwalk was washed away by a storm in 1944. No one seems to miss it.

Many of the long-time locals wistfully talk about how much their southern Ocean County, NJ, barrier island has changed over the years. In some ways, it definitely has. For example, some landmark structures have given way to new multimillion-dollar homes. At the same time, others have been painstakingly restored to their Victorian graciousness as private residences and B&Bs. And while some generations-old businesses have changed hands and sometimes even identities, new ones are bringing a renewed vitality to communities steeped in tradition.

Connected to the New Jersey mainland by the Manahawkin Bay bridge, Long Beach Island is located about 1¾ hours from Philadelphia. The entire island is only 18 miles long from south (where you cross over the bridge) to north and 6 blocks wide, bounded by the Atlantic Ocean and Barnegat Bay.

To get to Long Beach Island from Philadelphia, take I-95 north about 4 miles, then turn left onto Kaighn Avenue/NJ 70E. Continue

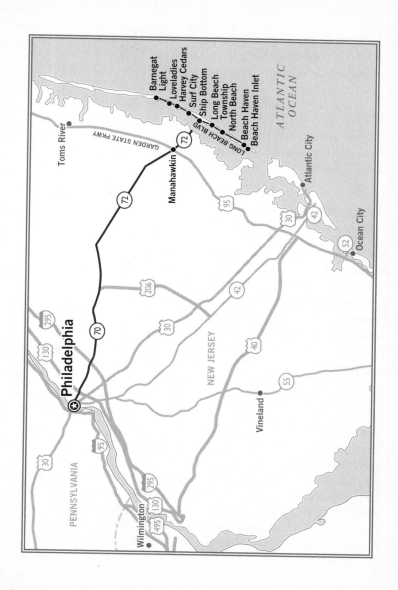

for 26 miles, then turn onto NJ 72 east. Stay on 72 for about 30 miles, then turn right onto S. Long Beach Boulevard/CR 607; continue for about half a mile. You will enter Long Beach Island at Ship Bottom, NJ.

Long Beach Boulevard is the main drag. Turn right on it and you will head toward Long Beach Township, North Beach, Beach Haven, and Beach Haven Inlet (aka Holgate) at the island's south end. Turn left and you will head toward Surf City, Harvey Cedars, Loveladies, and Barnegat Light at the north end.

DAY 1/MORNING

If it's a family vacation you're after, make the right turn after the bridge and head south to **Beach Haven.** As you approach the town (or borough, as they call it), the road becomes Bay Avenue. But even if you don't catch the name change, you'll know you've arrived when the kids catch site of the amusement park in the middle of the downtown area. For adults, Beach Haven also offers sophisticated accommodations and dining, theater, a renowned nautical museum, and all kinds of shopping, all within easy walking distance.

Just because there isn't a boardwalk doesn't mean you won't find the rides and games that are so much of the family seashore experience. Whether you're a kid or just remember being one, **Fantasy Island** (320 W. Seventh St.; 609-492-4000; www.fantasy islandpark.com), offers good old-fashioned fun without all the bells and whistles of big theme parks. The little ones will find plenty of age-appropriate rides, but if it's thrills you're after, skip the bumper cars and choose the 65-foot-high Ferris wheel with its breathtaking view of the bay and ocean. Rides are pay-as-you-go for 75 cents per token; expect to shell out an average of four to five tokens per ride.

On Fri nights, a POP (pay one price) wristband gets you all the rides you want from 2 to 7 p.m. for only $15. Check out the schedule for magic and exotic animal shows on selected summer evenings. The park is open from Memorial Day to Labor Day; call for seasonal hours. Right next door, **Thundering Surf Waterpark and Adventure Golf** (Eighth Street and Bay Avenue; 609-492-0869; www.thunder ingsurfwaterpark.com) has six giant single- and double-tube water slides, smaller slides and Dancing Fountains for the younger set, and a lazy river for floating. (Two hours: $23 for adults and children, $8 for toddlers and senior citizens. Eighteen holes of minigolf costs $10 for adults, $7.50 for kids). Call for seasonal hours.

AFTERNOON

LUNCH **Country Kettle Chowda,** Bay Village, Ninth & Bay Avenue, Beach Haven, NJ; (609) 492-2800; www.bayvillagelbi.com. Or **Stefano's California Grill & Pizza,** Thirty-fourth Street & the Boulevard, Beach Haven Terrace, NJ; (609) 492-1200; www.stefanoslbi.com. With more than 100 restaurants and delis on the island, you can't possibly go hungry, but, for a real taste of the local cuisine, don't miss the area's signature and highly controversial white and red clam chowders. The words "award-winning chowder" are not taken lightly on Long Beach Island. Every fall for the past two decades, local eateries battle to bowl over thousands of voracious voters with their robust reds and velvety whites during the colossal cook-off called **Chowderfest.** Although everyone has his or her own favorite, many agree that, for a knock-out New England white, multiple Grand Prize Award winner Country Kettle Chowda is always a good bet. Order it in a crusty bread bowl for a real stick-to-your-ribs lunch. (The lobster bisque is to die for, too.) $. Call for seasonal hours. If it's Manhattan red that makes your mouth water, head for this category's Grand Prize grabber, Stefano's California Grill & Pizza. $. Call for seasonal hours.

About three minutes south of Beach Haven, you can rent a one- or two-person sit-on-top kayak; four-person, 16-foot skiff boat (perfect for crabbing or fishing as well as for just cruising) or 22- to 24-foot pontoon boat for ten at **Holgate H2O Sports** (Holgate Marina, 83 Tebco Terrace, Long Beach, NJ; 609-492-1342; www.holgateh2o sports.com). Rentals are available from Memorial Day through Oct 1; call for seasonal days, hours, and prices. Check the company's Web site for discount coupons.

Four cameras mounted atop the ca. 1859 **Barnegat Lighthouse,** at the island's northernmost extremity, capture a real-time 170-feet-above-sea-level panoramic perspective and relay the images to the landmark's **Interpretive Center** (Barnegat Light, NJ; 609-494-2016). But if you can handle the climb up Old Barney's 217 steps (and don't mind paying $1 to do it), the breathtaking view is worth the effort. Inside the interpretive center, the history of the lighthouse and the need to protect the Barnegat Bay, Atlantic Ocean, and maritime forest surrounding it are explained in images and text. At night, the beacon shines as it did more than 150 years ago. The lighthouse is open Apr 1 through Oct 31 9 a.m. to 4:30 p.m. daily, and the rest of the year 9 a.m. to 3:30 p.m.

In the adjacent **Barnegat Lighthouse State Park,** free interpretive programs explore the environment, including the flora and fauna that inhabit one of the last remnants of maritime forest on the island. For bird watchers, this is a worth-the-trip spot during spring and fall migration. Picnics along the inlet are available or you're welcome to spread your blanket on the sand along the jetty. From the base of the lighthouse, a concrete walkway with handrails stretches a quarter mile out into the Atlantic so visitors can fish for striped and black sea bass, bluefish, flounder, and other species; watch the boats; and maybe catch a glimpse of the playful harbor seals and harlequin ducks that hang out here.

EVENING

....

DINNER   **Cinnamon Bay Caribbean Grill** (affectionately known as CBCGs), 7601 Long Beach Blvd., Harvey Cedars, NJ; (609) 361-CBCG; www.cinna monbaycaribbeangrill.com. So what if you can't make it to the Bahamas, Jamaica, or Trinidad? CBCGs brings the flavors of those tropical islands to Long Beach Island, courtesy of Culinary Institute of America owner/chefs Mary and Rob Garton. You probably won't be able to decide which of the exotic coconut shrimp, curry crab cake, empanadas, conch fritters, or jerk chicken wing appetizers to try, so go for the sampler and taste them all! For your entree, try the jerk pork, baby back ribs, or Trinidadian chicken curry. $$. Ask about the Early Bird Special. Call for seasonal hours. In July and Aug, live musical performances ranging from reggae to folk are scheduled.

Take in a show at the **Surflight Theatre** (Engleside and Beach Avenues, Beach Haven, NJ; 609-492-9477; www.surflight.org), the island's only live professional theater for more than sixty years. Presentations include classic and current Broadway dramas and musicals, as well as live musicians and comedians (tickets are $20 for adults, $10 for children). Children's favorite stories are also brought to the stage on Wed through Sat for 6 p.m. performances ($10 for all tickets). Call for seasonal performance schedule.

After the theater curtain falls, the entertainment at **The Show Place Ice Cream Parlor** (204 Centre St. and Beach Avenue, Beach Haven, NJ; 609-492-0018, www.theshowplace.org) where the singing and dancing "waitri" serve up kid-size "Little Me" sundaes and all kinds of fancy ice-cream concoctions with Broadway show names. Open Memorial Day through Labor Day. $.

LODGING   **Julia's of Savannah,** 209 Centre St., Beach Haven, NJ; (609) 492-5004; www.juliasoflbi.com. Accommodations on the island run the gamut from beach-block bed-and-breakfasts to a retro-on-the-outside, contemporary-on-the-inside boutique hotel. Keep in mind that many require a two-night minimum stay on summer weekends and all nights in July and Aug, so check before you book. Julia's of Savannah's convenient location in Beach Haven's historic district only a block-and-a-half from the beach isn't the most compelling reason for choosing it as your home away from home; owners Tom and Angela Williams' hospitality is. While all nine rooms in their restored Victorian bed-and-breakfasts are cheerful and cozy, some have extra luxuries such as private porches, whirlpool tubs, fireplaces, and an old-fashioned claw-foot soaking tub. Off-street parking, beach badges, chairs, towels, and bicycles are included. Open Feb through the first week in Dec. $$$.

Most of the accommodations provide badges with your stay. You'll probably want to pick somewhere that provides off-street parking as well, because available on-street spaces, while free, are often scarce.

DAY 2/MORNING

BREAKFAST **Julia's of Savannah.** Angela's full, bountiful breakfasts are creative and plentiful, showcasing New Jersey fresh fruits.

Now it's time to break out the bathing suits. Miles of soft sand beach await. From mid-June through Labor Day, beach badges are required for everyone between the ages of 12 and 64. They can be purchased on each beach by "Beach Badge Checkers." Daily rates vary by beach and range from $5 to $8 per day; look on www.njlbi.com for exact rates for each of the island's six municipalities.

To ensure that everyone is able to share the seaside experience, there are at least seventy wheelchair ramps leading to the beaches. In Long Beach Township (which encompasses two-thirds of the

Long Beach Island coastline and 17 communities including Beach Haven, Branch Beach, Holgate and Loveladies), sandy-terrain-capable adult- and child-size wheelchairs called "Beachwheels" are also available. Numbers are limited so be sure to reserve in advance (www.longbeachisland.com).

With 18 miles of ocean-side beach, it's easy to find your own place in the sun. All of the beaches are family-friendly, but, for really little ones, the calmer waters of the numerous bay beaches, many in Long Beach Township, might be preferable. If you're looking for a more sedate spot on the sand, Branch Beach, Loveladies, North Beach, Holgate, and Harvey Cedar are less commercialized and, therefore, usually quieter.

You could spend the morning jumping waves or soar 300 to 500 feet above them as you fly solo or in tandem with **LBI Parasailing** (Sixth Street and the Bay at Lighthouse Marina, Barnegat Light, NJ; 609-361-6100; www.lbiparasail.com). Cost for an eight- to ten-minute solo or ten- to twelve-minute tandem ride is $65 per person; Check the Web site for flight discount coupons. Open every day beginning at 8 a.m.

AFTERNOON

LUNCH Engleside Inn, 30 Engleside Ave., Beach Haven, NJ; (609) 492-1251; www.englesideinn.com. This is the place to go for beachside dining. Have a fresh tomato and mozzarella with honey vinaigrette topped with grilled chicken or fish, burger, or Cajun fish or chicken sandwich by the pool, on the patio or at the bar at the Sand Bar (they serve margaritas, daiquiris, and other cool tropical drinks, too) or in the sushi bar. $. Call for seasonal hours.

For a couple of different ways to enjoy the water, you can rent a one- to three-passenger wave runner by the hour or half-hour at

Route 72 Wave Runner (2390 East Bay Ave., Manahawkin, NJ; 609-361-7147; www.route72waverunner.com). Rental hours are 9 a.m. to 7 p.m. from Memorial Day Weekend through Labor Day Weekend, then weekends only through Sept 30.

Long Beach Island has long been a mecca for surfers. That's because board bearers are welcome on at least twenty-five beaches on the island, seven of which are dedicated to the sport. Holyoke Avenue in Beach Haven, between North First and North Third Streets in Surf City are among the most popular surfing spots. Others are located on North Beach Haven; Brant, Brighton, and Haven Beaches; and The Dunes (www.njlbi.com). If you need some surfing supplies, **"The Original" Ron Jon Surf Shop** (901 Central Ave., Ship Bottom, NJ; 609-494-8844; www.ronjonsurfshop.com), a Long Beach Island fixture since 1959.

If you haven't been on a board, but have always wanted to, take a lesson with the **Matador Surfing Academy** (http://matadorsurf boards.com) at the **Brighton Beach Surf Shop** (8511 Long Beach Blvd., Long Beach Township, NJ; 609-492-0342; http://brighton beachsurfshop.com) or **Wave Hog Surf Shop** (620 Long Beach Blvd., Ship Bottom, NJ; 609-494-1040; http://wavehogsurfshop .com.) Available from Apr until Nov, Matador offers 1½-hour semi-private instruction for beginners and up for $45 and private for $64. Instruction for special needs surfers are $100. And an hour with one of the school's surf coaches ($40) can help even the most experienced competitive surfers hone their skills. Board and wetsuit rentals are included in the lesson prices.

EVENING

| DINNER | **Raimondo's Restaurant,** 1101 Long Beach Blvd., Ship Bottom, NJ; (609) 494-5391. This is an upscale Italian dining spot that doesn't |

rely on red sauce. You have to try the Spiedini alla Romana appetizer, Parmesan-battered layers of bread, mozzarella, eggplant, and prosciutto with anchovy sauce, and the Cape Sante Carbonara entree with blackened Barnegat Light sea scallops over spaghetti tossed with bacon, pancetta, and caramelized shallots in a cracked black pepper and Parmesan sauce. Yes, it's a lot of verbiage, but every ingredient deserves to be named in these two outstanding dishes. Call for seasonal hours. $$–$$$.

Catch the magnificent Long Beach Island sunset or next morning's sunrise on the beach. Times are listed on www.njlbi.com.

Stop by **Café Bacio** (1511 Long Beach Blvd., North Beach Haven, NJ; 609-492-7702; www.cafebacio.com) for an espresso or cappuccino and some signature New York cheesecake, gelato, or ice cream. $. On Tues and Thurs nights, the specialty is chocolate fondue, on Mon and Wed it's s'mores.

LODGING	Julia's of Savannah.

DAY 3/MORNING

BREAKFAST	Julia's of Savannah.

In summer, when the blues are biting, rent a rod (or bring your own) and head out 15 miles offshore with John Larson on his twin-engine catamaran *Miss Barnegat Light* (Eighteenth Street and Bayview Avenue, Barnegat Light, NJ; 609-494-2094, www.missbarnegat light.com). Larson takes out fishing parties ($50 for adults, $45 for seniors, $40 for kids, includes bait) from 8 a.m. to 2 p.m. daily from late May through late Sept, Fri only in Oct.

AFTERNOON

....

LATE LUNCH/EARLY DINNER   **daddy O,** 4401 Long Beach Blvd., Brant Beach, NJ; (609) 494 1300; www.daddyohotel.com. Outside it's old-fashioned seashore, but inside is contemporary cool with a menu to match. $ if you stick with the innovative flatbreads (try the white clam or the shrimp and spicy chorizo), fish and shrimps, sandwiches, panini and shared plates. daddy O serves lunch and dinner throughout the year. Call for seasonal hours.

Before you head home, don't forget to pick up a little "thank you" gift for the people next door who walked your dog, watered your plants, or took in your mail while you were sunning yourself on the sand. Make it easy on yourself and stop in at **Historic Viking Village** (Nineteenth Street and Bayview Avenue, Barnegat Light, NJ; www .vikingvillageshows.com), a collection of rustic converted fishing shacks that now house cute little boutiques that sell everything from nautical antiques and vintage country home accessories to contemporary clothing for all ages. Since Viking Village is located at the docks, you just might get to see some of the local fishermen bringing in their catch of the day. It is also home to the fishing vessel *Lindsay L* owned by Kirk and Pam Larson. The scalloper portrayed the *Hanna Bodan* in the movie *The Perfect Storm.*

As for the "thank you" gift, you can never go wrong with any combination of the more than twenty-six flavors of hand-whipped heaven from John Maschal's **Country Kettle Fudge** (Bay Village, Ninth & Bay Avenue, Beach Haven, NJ; 609-492-2800; and Twentieth & Long Beach Boulevard, Surf City, NJ; 609-494-2822; www .countrykettlefudge.com). Yum, triple chocolate! Oh yes, they have prettily packaged salt water taffy, too.

To get home, turn left at West Eighth Street off of Long Beach Boulevard, then take a slight left at East Bay Avenue/NJ 72 west. Follow 72 west for about 7 miles until you reach the ramp of the

Garden State south/NJ 444 south. Take the Parkway about 14 miles, continue on US 9 south for a little over 2 miles, then continue onto NJ 444 south for almost 11 miles until you come to exit 38A for the Atlantic City Expressway toward Camden/Philadelphia. Merge onto the Expressway and stay on for 37 miles. Continue onto NJ 42 north for about 7 miles, then merge on I-76 west. Take a slight right at I-676 north (sign will also say Camden/Ben Franklin Bridge) and stay on for close to 6 miles, then take the US 30 West/I-676 West ramp.

There's More . . . .

Bike Rentals. **Surf Buggy LBI,** 1414 Long Beach Blvd., Surf City, NJ; (609) 361-3611; www.surfbuggylbi.com. Bicycle and surrey rentals. Call for beach cruiser, hybrid, road bike, adult tricycle, tandem, kid's bike, and other prices. Surrey rentals cost $22 per hour for a single, $30 for a double.

Golfing. **Ocean Acres Country Club,** 925 Buccaneer Lane, Mana-hawkin, NJ; (609) 597-9393; http://allforeclub.com. Challenging eighteen-hole public golf course with practice putting green and lessons. Call for seasonal hours, greens fees.

Museums & Tours. **Evening Ghost Tours of Historic Beach Haven;** (609) 709-1425. A one-and-one-half-hour family-oriented spooky stroll. $15 for adults, $8 for children under age 12; 20 percent of ticket price goes to the Long Beach Island Historical Association. Tues and Wed evening from mid-June through early Sept; call for seasonal hours. Reservations only.

    Long Beach Island Foundation of the Arts & Sciences, 120 Long Beach Blvd., Loveladies, NJ; (609) 494-1241; www.lbifsci ence.org. Exhibits works by local and national artists. Open Thurs through Sun 9 a.m. to 4 p.m. On Wed from early June through mid-Aug, there's a conservation-focused "Hands-On the Bay" wetlands nature walk. $5 per person. On Fri from 10 a.m. to noon from late June through late Aug, free Bayshore Walks & Seining allows you to net and study some aquatic critters.

Museum of New Jersey Maritime History, Dock Road and West Avenue, Beach Haven, NJ; (609) 492-0202; www.museumofnjmh .com. Artifacts from prehistoric times and from various shipwrecks; scrimshaw; and antique nautical and diving equipment. Donations appreciated. Open daily 10 a.m. to 4 p.m. in June; until 6 p.m. in July and Aug; Fri, Sat, and Sun until 4 p.m.

Shopping. **Unshredded Nostalgia,** 323 S. Main St. (US 9), Barnegat, NJ; (800) 872-9990; www.unshreddednostalgia.com. Show biz and other memorabilia ranging from $5 celebrity glamour shots up to several thousand dollar cels from classic animated movies. Call for seasonal hours.

Special Events . . . .

(Unless otherwise specified, contact the Southern Ocean County Chamber of Commerce, 265 West Ninth St., Ship Bottom, NJ 08008; 609-494-7211; www.visitlbiregion.com.)

JULY
Annual Long Beach Island Art Festival, Long Beach Island Foundation of the Arts and Sciences, 120 Long Beach Blvd., Loveladies, NJ; (609) 494-1241; www.lbifoundation.org. More than 170 artists present original works and demos.

Annual "Memories by the Bay" Classic Car Show, Tenth Street and Waterfront Park, Ship Bottom, NJ; (609) 494-2171; www.shipbot tom.org.

JULY AND AUGUST
Barnegat Light Amateur Sand Sculpting Contest, Street Beach Ocean; Barnegat Light, NJ 08006; (609) 494-9296; www.barn light.com. A more than two-decade tradition, this twice-monthly competition attracts some pretty talented beach builders to vie for prize ribbons.

SEPTEMBER
Annual Irish Festival, Ship Bottom Boat Ramp Parking Lot, Tenth and Shore Avenue, Ship Bottom, NJ; www.lbiaoh.com. Irish music, dancing, games, and food sponsored by The Ancient Order of Hibernians.

OCTOBER
Annual Long Beach Island Chowder Cook Off, Taylor Avenue ball field, Ninth Street and Taylor Avenue in Beach Haven. Culinary giants of the island demonstrate their mollusk mettle for major bragging rights. Taste and vote for your favorite red and white.

MID-OCTOBER TO EARLY DECEMBER
Annual Long Beach Island Surf Fishing Classic. More than half-a-century old, this eight-weeklong tournament, one of the longest-running fishing contests on the east coast, attracts close to a thousand contestants who vie for thousands of dollars in cash prizes for striped bass and bluefish.

Other Recommended Restaurants and Lodgings . . . .

Go to www.visitlbiregion.com for a list of beach rentals. Thirty-eight Long Beach Island real estate offices can help you find rental properties from rustic cabins to modern duplexes to fit your needs and budget.

BARNEGAT LIGHT

The Sand Castle Bayfront Bed and Breakfast, 710 Bayview Ave.; (609) 494-6555, www.sandcastlelbi.com. Five guest rooms and two suites 2 blocks from the ocean beach. Heated indoor swimming pool and Jacuzzi; full breakfast; bicycles; and beach badges, chairs, and umbrellas. $$$.

BEACH HAVEN

Buckalew's Restaurant, Tavern and Cafe, 101 N. Bay Ave.; (609) 492-1065; www.buckalews.com. This historic eatery has long been famous for its tomato pies—large and personal size. The white with ricotta, fresh mozzarella, basil, tomato, and garlic is a winner, too. $–$$.

Chicken or the Egg, 207 North Bay Ave.; (609) 492-3695; www .492fowl.com. Breakfast is served any time—how much better can life be! $. Open every day (except Tues) from 7 a.m. to 9 p.m. for lunch and dinner, too.

Gables, 212 Centre St.; (888) LBI-GABLES; www.gableslbi.com. Newly restored landmark bed-and-breakfast has five period-antique-decorated guest rooms, four with whirlpool spa tubs, one with claw-foot bubble jet tub and all with either fireplaces or iron stoves. $$$. **Gables Restaurant.** upscale menu featuring local, organic, and sustainable ingredients changes daily. $$–$$$. Breakfast, lunch, and brunch tea are also available. Call for seasonal hours.

BEACH HAVEN CREST

Bisque, Seventy-ninth Street and Long Beach Boulevard; (609) 361-2270; www.bisquelbi.com. The ambience is casual, the continental menu is super-classy—think pistachio-crusted salmon with Dijon cream sauce. Ask about the four-course prix-fixe "Twilight

Dinner Special." $$–$$$. Open seven days year-round, serving dinner from 5 p.m., BYOB.

HARVEY CEDARS
Plantation Restaurant, 7908 Long Beach Blvd.; (609) 494-8191; www.plantationrestaurant.com. Tropical, beachy vibe with ceiling fans, rattan furnishings, and seafood-leading menu. Nice selection for vegetarians as well. $$$. Open year-round for dinner from 4 p.m. Lunch and light fare/bar menu is available from 11:30 a.m. to 4 p.m.

SHIP BOTTOM
Greenhouse Café, corner of Sixth Street & Long Beach Boulevard, Ship Bottom, NJ; (609) 494-7333; www.greenhousecafelbi.com. Open year-round Mon through Thurs 8 a.m. to 9 p.m. and Sat and Sun until 10 p.m. Its New England white and Manhattan-style red have been named chowder champs more than a dozen times. The rest of the seafood offerings (and there are plenty of them), pastas, meat entrees, and pizzas range from classic to creative. $$. Open for breakfast and lunch, too.

For More Information . . . .

Long Beach Island Business Alliance; www.njlbi.com.

Long Beach Island Guide; www.longbeachisland.com.

Southern Ocean County Chamber of Commerce; (609) 494-7211, www.visitlbiregion.com.

DOWN THE SHORE ESCAPE *Two*

The Beaches of Southern Delaware

LEWES AND REHOBOTH BEACH—SANDS OF TIME/
2 NIGHTS

Reel Fun
Parrots in the Trees
Crazy Coasters
Kids and Kites

Although to many Philly residents "down the shore" traditionally refers to the beaches of South Jersey, the Garden State certainly does not have a monopoly on fun by the sea. Only a two-and-a-half-hour drive from Philadelphia in **Sussex County,** Delaware, **Lewes** has had a tumultuous history: as an ill-fated Dutch whaling settlement in 1631, as a target for late-17th-century pirate raids and cannon bombardment during the War of 1812, and as a crucial Atlantic coastline defense post during World War II. You can still see the remnants of the town's early years in its carefully restored homes (one with a cannonball still lodged in its wall), museums, and lookout towers—even on the rolling sand dunes of nearby Cape Henlopen. Fortunately peace now reigns over this lovely Lewes as well as over the adjacent miles of virtually unspoiled ocean and bay beaches and the protected shoreline ranging from dunes to freshwater wetlands to pine forests. By the way, if you want to endear yourself to the natives, keep in mind that Lewes is pronounced "loo-iss," not "looz" as in "youse."

By day **Rehoboth Beach,** located only eighteen minutes from Lewes, is an old-fashioned shore town, complete with boardwalk and lots of town-sponsored activities for the whole family. By night it takes on a more sophisticated personality, its streets sparkling with the lights of myriad eclectic shops, restaurants, and nightspots.

Like most East Coast shore points, peak season at the beaches of southern Delaware is from Memorial Day to Labor Day. So if you

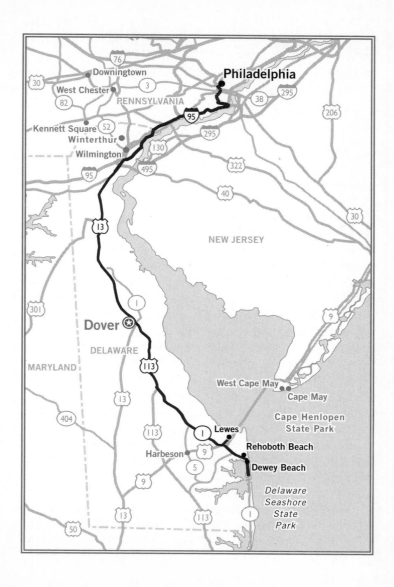

want to miss the crowds, consider going in the late spring or early fall. The beaches are just as beautiful then, and most of the shops are open.

DAY 1/MORNING

To get to Lewes, take the Schuylkill Expressway (I-76) east to I-95. Take I-95 south for 28 miles to I-295. Travel north on 295 for 1 mile until you reach Route 13/Route 40; then follow Route 13 south for 66 miles to Route 1. Follow Route 1 south 18 miles to WV 9, then WV 9 for 2 miles into Lewes.

Start at the **Zwaanendael Museum** (102 Kings Hwy. at Savannah Road, Lewes, DE; 302-645-1148; www.history.delaware.gov). Although its elaborate architecture and stonework facade are decidedly 17th-century European, this eye-catching building was actually built in 1931 to commemorate the 300th anniversary of the arrival of the area's—and the state's—first settlers. The original whaling colony quickly came to a tragic end, but this replica of the city hall that stood in their native city of Hoorn, Holland, in 1631 preserves and shares its history and artifacts. Other exhibits and displays tell the stories of the British bombardment of Lewes during the War of 1812, the town's long career as a major port of trade, and the *DeBraak,* a captured Dutch-built ship sailing under the English flag that was sunk by a storm off Cape Henlopen in 1798. Open Wed through Sat 10 a.m. to 4:30 p.m. Admission is free.

For a single $5 admission price, you can tour a number of other significant sites, beginning with the **Lewes Historical Society Complex** (Shipcarpenter and West Third Streets, Lewes, DE; 302-645-7670; www.historiclewes.org). For this ambitious project, the society transported nine 18th- and 19th-century buildings, including an early Swedish log house, doctor's office, one-room schoolhouse, country store, and residences, from all over Lewes and its neighboring towns to this beautifully landscaped site. It then restored and accurately furnished them to give us a glimpse of the personal and working lives of their former occupants. Tours are available mid-June through mid-Sept, Mon through Sat 11 a.m. to 4 p.m. For an additional $2, you can also visit the Historical Society's three other sites: the **Cannonball House Marine Museum** (118 Front St., corner of Front and Bank) with its patched-over hole in the wall where a British cannonball from the War of 1812 remains lodged; the **Ryves Holt House** (Second and Mulberry Streets), built in 1665, the oldest known house in the state, and the **Lightship Overfalls** (on Pilottown Road on the Lewes & Rehoboth Canal), commemorating the ship that protected the entrance to Delaware Bay from 1892 to 1961. These museums are open during the summer Mon through Sat from 11 a.m. until 4 p.m.

Be sure to include a visit to the **1812 Memorial Park,** located right across Front Street where you'll find, then the site of an important defense battery, now a commemorative park marked by guns from that encounter as well as one from an abandoned pirate vessel and another used during World War I.

AFTERNOON

LUNCH **Second Street Grille,** 115 West Second St., Lewes, DE; (302) 644-4121. CIA graduate Ray Richardson's lovely storefront restaurant offers lunch, light fare, dinner, and Sunday brunch in a relaxed atmosphere filled with art and soft music. Try house specialties spicy Maryland crab soup and crispy calamari with chili mayo or the fresh catch of the day in a sandwich or on a Caesar salad. $–$$. Open Wed, Thurs, and Fri from 11:30 a.m. to 9 p.m., Sun 11 a.m. to 10 p.m., Sun until 5 p.m. (call to ask about seasonal extended Sun dinner hours).

About 1 mile east of Lewes is **Cape Henlopen State Park** (15099 Cape Henlopen Dr., Lewes, DE; 302-645-8983; www.destateparks .com), a naturalist's paradise with 4,000 acres of every type of terrain, including ocean and bay beaches, rolling dunes (such as the 80-foot-high Great Dune), pine forests, salt marshes, and freshwater wetlands. These varied environments make the park the perfect habitat for a wide variety of plants and animals, including a number of rare and endangered species. During migrating seasons, it provides a much-needed resting place and feeding area for many types of birds. And for us it offers a place to swim, sun, fish, and explore the interpreted nature trails for hours without ever getting bored. You'll also find an unparalleled view of the Delaware Bay and Atlantic coastline from the top of the World War II Observation Tower. Open to the public; admission is included with your $8 per carload park entrance fee. The park is open from 8 a.m. to sunset year-round.

Before you begin your explorations, pay a visit to the Nature Center (open 9 a.m. to 4 p.m. year-round), which has five 1,100-gallon marine aquariums, a touch tank, and interpretive exhibits. For a few extra dollars, you can participate in guided canoe trips, birdwatching expeditions, wetland explorations, and other educational and recreational programs that are available on a regular basis.

EVENING

Have an early dinner because you've got an appointment at 6 p.m. that's going to take up the rest of your evening.

DINNER **Gilligan's Restaurant & Harborside Bar,** 134 Market St., Lewes, DE; (302) 644-7230; www.gilliganswaterfront.com. No, it's not the SS *Minnow,* but it is a former Key West fishing boat now moored on the canal in Lewes. In addition to lots of atmosphere, Gilligan's offers upscale seafood selections such as macadamia-crusted grouper with mango-lime butter and chef/owner Cheryl Tilton's signature "no-filler" crab cake. If the weather permits, relax with a drink at the bar on the covered deck on top of the boat, where you can watch the sunset and the boats as they return to the harbor. $$–$$$. Open Tues through Sun 11 a.m. to 1 a.m.

Now that you've gotten your sea legs, take a half-night (6 p.m. to 10:30 p.m.) fishing expedition offered in season at **Fisherman's Wharf** (Anglers Road and the Canal; 302-645-8862; www.fish lewes.com). Price is $40 per person; call for seasonal schedule as well as rates for full-night and daytime fishing expeditions. Rod and reel rentals are $7. Sight-seeing and dolphin-watching cruises are also available.

LODGING   **The Hotel Rodney,** corner of Second and Market Streets, Lewes, DE; (302) 645-6466; www.hotelrodneydelaware.com. This downtown boutique hotel combines contemporary and antique furnishings and accents to create distinctive room and suite decor. $$–$$$.

DAY 2/MORNING

BREAKFAST   **The Buttery,** 142 Second St. (Second and Savannah Streets), Lewes, DE; (302) 645-7755; www.butteryrestaurant.com. Treat yourself to a lavish Sunday brunch here at this lovely restaurant where, for only $20 per person, you get fresh fruit and pastries; Champagne, Mimosa, or Bloody Mary; and a choice of entrees including eggs savannah with crab Florentine, crepes a la fruits de mer, and petite filet mignon and eggs. Open for lunch and dinner, too. Call for seasonal hours.

Head for **Rehoboth Beach** by driving west on US 9 for a little under 2 miles then turn left onto Coastal Highway south and follow it for 3½ miles. Turn slight left onto Rehoboth Avenue Ext/DE 1 ALT and follow that for less than a mile to the next roundabout. Take the roundabout to the second exit onto Rehoboth Avenue.

Go east on any street and you'll find yourself face to face with the white sands, natural dunes, and foaming surf of Rehoboth Beach. Don't fight the urge—kick off your shoes and dig your toes into the wet sand along the water's edge. Then take a leisurely walk and let the sounds of the waves and calls of the shorebirds melt your city stress away. Be sure to keep your eye on the horizon. If you're in the right place at the right time, you might even see dolphins frolicking right off the shoreline.

If the winds cooperate, you might even want to fly a kite. Don't have one? No problem! Just take a short walk over to **Rehoboth Toy & Kite Company** (67 Rehoboth Ave. or One Virginia Avenue on the Boardwalk, Rehoboth Beach, DE; 800-250–KITE or 302-227-6996). You'll find the basic single-line Deltas for beginners, a wide array of stunt models, and colorful, whimsical shapes. Call for seasonal hours.

AFTERNOON

LUNCH **Nicola Pizza,** 8 North First St. (right off the boardwalk), Rehoboth Beach, DE; (302) 227-6211; www.nicolapizza.com. This is the home of the Nic-o-boli, a locally beloved creation of ground beef, cheese, and sauce rolled in dough, its cousins the Nic-spin-oli with spinach, and the "Nico e Bolito" with chicken and jalapeño peppers. Ask about the "healthy heart" Nic-o-boli. $. Call for seasonal hours.

You can rent a 16-foot runabout (half-day $199) or skiff (half-day $102) at **Rehoboth Bay Marina** (Collins Street, Dewey Beach, DE; 302-226-2012; www.rehobothbaymarina.com). To get there, drive just over a mile on DE 1 north for less than a mile, then turn left at

DE 24W/John J. Williams Highway; you will see the marina on your right. The marina is open Memorial Day through Labor Day, seven days a week. Half-day rentals are from 8 a.m. to noon and from 1 p.m. to 5 p.m. Call for Apr, Sept, and Oct hours.

Head back to Rehoboth Beach via DE 1 north for about 3 miles until it becomes King Charles Street. Follow King Charles Street until you come to Silver Lake. When you get to the lake, keep your eye on the sky, or at least on the higher tree branches, near the electrical transformer, and you might be lucky enough to spot one of the wild Monk Parakeets (a type of South American parrot with shocking green plumage) that nest there year-round. How they originally got there is anybody's guess (many locals believe they are the descendants of a pair of runaway pets), but watching these beautiful birds make themselves at home so far from their tropical native habitat is a thrilling experience.

EVENING

DINNER   **Back Porch Cafe,** 59 Rehoboth Ave., Rehoboth Beach, DE; (302) 227-3674; www.backporchcafe.com. A real treasure that offers a savvy, sassy menu that belies its quaint, understated exterior. Locally grown ingredients give an extra intensity to such creations as lager-brined prime rib of pork, crispy brown rice and black bean rissole, and grilled loin of rabbit. As for dessert, I have only one thing to say—get one along with cup of coffee en flambé. If the weather is amenable, ask to sit outside on the upper or lower deck. Enjoy live music every Thurs and Fri evening during the summer. $$–$$$. Open for dinner daily at 6 p.m., for lunch and Sunday brunch from 11 a.m. to 3 p.m. and "Après Surf" daily from 3 to 5:30 p.m.

After dinner check out the sights and sounds on the boardwalk, a milelong fun but not frantic promenade with miniature golf, arcades, and a small amusement park. If you're here at 8 p.m. on any summer weekend, you can gather round the **Rehoboth Beach Memorial Bandstand** (302-664-2288; www.rehobothbandstand .com), right off the boardwalk at Rehoboth Avenue, for a free old-fashioned band concert at 8 p.m.

LODGING   **The Bellmoor,** 6 Christian St., Rehoboth Beach, DE; (302) 227-5800; www.thebellmoor.com. A romantic getaway spot, this inn is tucked away on a quiet side street, yet only a couple of blocks from the heart of the action. Some of the pretty rooms and suites offer private balconies with garden views, marble baths, fireplaces, hydrotherapy tubs, and/or wet bars. Breakfast and afternoon tea and cookies are included. There are also two outdoor swimming pools (one for adults only along with an indoor-outdoor hot tub). $$$. Extra pampering can be arranged at the on-site spa.

DAY 3/MORNING

Wake up early so that you can enjoy an early bike ride on the board-walk (permitted 5 a.m. to 10 a.m. May 15 through Sept 15). If you need a rental, **Wheels Bicycle Shop,** (4100 Highway One; Rehoboth Beach, DE; 302-227-6807; www.rehoboth.com) has all kinds at prices beginning at $6 per hour.

BREAKFAST   **The Bellmoor.** Linger over your complimentary country breakfast in the garden.

What boardwalk would be complete without an amusement park? Rehoboth has **Fun Land** (6 Delaware Ave., Rehoboth Beach, DE; 302-227-1921) a traditional family-owned affair with eighteen rides, including a haunted mansion, bumper cars, "Gravitron" and sea dragon coaster, midway games, and an arcade. There's no admission price; rides are pay-as-you-go. Open Mother's Day Week-end through Labor Day. Call for hours.

AFTERNOON

LUNCH **Jakes Seafood House,** two locations: Downtown Rehoboth at 29 Baltimore Ave., Rehoboth Beach, DE; (302) 227-6237; and Highway One at 19178 Coastal Hwy., Rehoboth Beach, DE; (302) 644-7711; www.jakesseafoodhouse .com. The seafood bisque is chock full of lobster, shrimp, scallops, and lump crab meat. The seafood specialties range from the expected to the surprising—think Jamaican jerk shrimp salad and "twisted mahi mahi sandwich." There's a raw bar at the Highway One location. $–$$. The downtown location is open only from Apr to Oct; the Highway One location is open year-round. Open seven days; lunch is served from 11:30 a.m.; call for seasonal hours.

Check out what's going on at the **Rehoboth Art League** (12 Dodds Lane, Lewes, DE; 302-227-8408; www.rehobothartleague.org). This cluster of four rustic buildings and lovely gardens is the setting for a wide variety of exhibits, programs, and special events all year long. It is also the site of the 1743 **Homestead** house, now a museum featuring restored rooms of period furnishings. Admission is free. Open Mon through Sat 10 a.m. to 4 p.m., Sun noon to 4 p.m.

Rehoboth Beach's shopping district, concentrated along Rehoboth Avenue and Wilmington Street, is lively and has an international flavor. At the Tideline Gallery (146 Rehoboth Ave., Rehoboth Beach, DE; 302-227-4444; www.tidelinegallery.com) the colorful two-legged Eve lamps and silly stoneware egg separators will make you giggle, while the seriously artistic and functional glass and pottery selections will appeal to your decorating diva. It's hard to believe that the intricately detailed, ultradelicate hanging sculptures at **Scandinavian Occasions** (125 Rehoboth Ave., Rehoboth Beach, DE; 302-227-3945) are actually paper cuts, a traditional Scandinavian craft. **Panache** (129-B Rehoboth Ave., Rehoboth Beach, DE; 302-227-9229; www.panachegalleryde

.com)—and P2 upstairs—features handmade contemporary crafts made by artisans all over the country.

EVENING

DINNER   **Cultured Pearl,** 19 Wilmington Ave., Rehoboth Beach, DE; (302) 227-8493; www.culturedpearl.us. For the timid, a section of the menu devoted to "East Meets West" compromises pairings of shrimp and vegetable tempura with filet mignon and mashed potatoes. But for an authentic experience, stick to the a la carte sushi bar or, even better, a chef's combination "sushi sara." $$–$$$. Dinner is served nightly year-round from 4:30 p.m.

To return to Philadelphia, take DE 1 north for 71 miles; keep north at the fork to stay on for an additional 6½ miles. Stay straight to go onto DuPont Hwy/US 13 north for 8½ miles. Take I-495 north about 10 miles. Stay straight to go to I-95 north and continue for 22 miles. It should take you about two-and-half hours to get home.

There's More . . . .

Antiquing. For antique jewelry, go to **Chatelaine's,** 119 Second St., Lewes, DE; (302) 645-1511. If you're in browsing mode, try **Lewes Mercantile Antiques,** 109 Second St., Lewes, DE; (302) 645-7900; www.lewes-antiques.com. Or visit **Heritage Antique Market,** 130 Highway One, Lewes, DE; (302) 645-2309, which has over 50 dealers.

Ferries. Cape May–Lewes Ferry, Cape Henlopen Drive, Lewes, DE; (302) 645-6364; www.cmlf.com. A relaxing 17-mile (seventy minutes one-way) ride across Delaware Bay. Leave the car in the parking lot and purchase a foot-passenger fare ($10 one way, $8 return for adults in peak season). A free shuttle in Cape May will take you to the downtown hot spots. Operates daily.

Golf. **The Rookery Golf Course,** Route 1 just north of Lewes (mailing address: RR 3, Box 183, Milton, DE 19968); (302) 684-3000; www.rookerygolf.com. Eighteen-hole public course adjacent to wetlands. Open year-round; peak season fees are $69 for eighteen holes.

Shopping. Two of the most fun shops in Lewes are **The Stepping Stone,** 107 Market St., Lewes, DE; (302) 645-1254; www.steppingstonelewes.com, which features one-of-a-kind works from artists from all across the United States, and **Puzzles,** 108 Front St., Lewes, DE; (302) 645-8013, has everything from rustic handcrafted wooden designs to the latest Rubik's mind teasers.

Lavender Fields Farm, 18864 Cool Spring Rd., Milton, DE, about 15 minutes from Lewes; (302) 684-1514; www.lavenderfieldsde.com. Pick a bouquet, stroll among two dozen varieties of aromatic blooms, or purchase lavender-spiked products at the on-farm store. Open 10 a.m. to 4 p.m. every day from June 1 to Oct 1 and on Sat and Sun until Dec 31. Don't miss the Lavender Fields Labyrinth, a duplicate of the one embedded in the floor of the Cathedral of Chartres.

Preservation Forge, 114 West Third St., Lewes, DE, (302) 645-7987. Artist John Austin Ellsworth keeps the craft of blacksmithing alive while producing wonderful items for the home and garden. Hours vary other seasons, so call first.

Tanger Outlets, 1600 Ocean Outlets, Route 1, Rehoboth Beach, DE; (302) 226-9223; www.tangeroutlet.com. More than 130 name-brand outlets along a 2-mile stretch of Route 1. (Remember, shopping in Delaware is tax free!) Mon through Sat 9 a.m. to 9 p.m., Sun 11 a.m. to 7 p.m.

State Parks. **Beach Plum Island Nature Preserve,** 42 Cape Henlopen Dr., just north of Lewes, DE; (302) 645-8983; www.destate parks.com/downloads/surf-fishing/beach-plum.pdf. A satellite of Cape Henlopen State Park, most of this 129-acre barrier island is protected to preserve the habitat for native plants. But you are welcome to stroll the beach or do some surf fishing (required permit is available at the park office). Open 24 hours Mar 1 to Dec 31.

Delaware Seashore State Park, 39415 Inlet Rd., Rehoboth Beach, DE; (302) 227-2800; www.destateparks.com/park/delaware-seashore. A 2,000-acre recreational area and nature preserve offering ocean and bay bathing with modern changing areas and showers, surfing, surf fishing, and bird watching. Open daily 8 a.m. to sunset year-round; entrance fee is $8 per car. Camping sites (302-539-7202), available Mar 1 to Nov 30, accommodate tents to RVs with hookups for electricity, water, and sewer on some sites. Fees are $30 to $38 per night, Mar 1 through Nov 30.

Special Events . . . .

(Unless otherwise specified, call 877-465-3937 for more information.)

MARCH
Easter. Easter Promenade, Rehoboth Beach Convention Center, 229 Rehoboth Ave., Rehoboth Beach, DE; (302) 227-2233. Parades and other seasonal family activities. Free.

Great Delaware Kite Festival, Cape Henlopen State Park, Lewes, DE; (302) 645-3937. Held annually on Good Friday, this event features kite-flying competitions, vendors, food, and entertainment.

Rehoboth Beach Chocolate Festival, Rehoboth Beach Convention Center; (302) 227-2772, www.rehomain.com. Unlimited tastings and contests for pros and home cooks in categories from cookies to cakes to the intriguing "most unusual."

MAY
British Motorcar Show, Lewes Historical Society Complex, Lewes, DE; (302) 645-8073. Vintage and modern Austin Healeys, Jaguars, MGs, Morgans, Triumphs, and their ilk compete for prizes.

JULY
Fireworks on Rehoboth Beach; (302) 227-2772, www.rehomain .com. July 4 display attracts more than 80,000 viewers.

AUGUST
Annual Sand Castle Contest, Fisherman's Beach, north end of Rehoboth Beach boardwalk; (302) 741-8204 or (302) 741-8210. Amateur sculptors of all ages compete for cash prizes. Free.

OCTOBER
Annual Sea Witch Halloween & Fiddler's Festival, throughout Rehoboth Beach; (800) 441-1329 or (302) 227-2233. Costume contests for people and pets, giant parades, entertainment, crafts, beach games, scavenger hunt, and shop-to-shop trick or treating for the kids. At the Fiddler's Festival, musicians compete for cash prizes.

Boast the Coast Maritime Festival and Coast Day, town of Lewes, DE; (302) 645-8073; www.coastalsussex.com. Best known for its spectacular lighted boat parade, this festival also has seafood tasting, local bands, and magic show for the kids.

Coast Day, University of Delaware Hugh R. Sharp Campus in Lewes, DE; (302) 831-8083; www.ceoe.udel.edu. This fun and educational ecologically-oriented event features tours of research ships and visits with scientists, hands-on scientific activities, marine exhibits, crab races, close-ups with dogfish sharks and other marine life, seafood cooking demos, and boat races.

Rehoboth Beach Autumn Jazz Festival; (800) 29–MUSIC; www .rehobothjazz.com/ajf. Over thirty venues throughout Rehoboth and Dewey Beach areas. three days of concerts, seminars, jazz brunches, and art exhibits.

NOVEMBER
Rehoboth Beach Independent Film Festival, Midway Shopping Center, Route 1, Rehoboth Beach, DE; (302) 645-9095; www .rehobothfilm.com. Three days of critically acclaimed national and international films, workshops, and guest speakers.

Other Recommended Restaurants and Lodgings . . . .

LEWES
At Daily Market, 420 East Savannah Rd.; (302) 645-8284. You can pick up a deli sandwich and your favorite snacks for your picnic at the beach. While you're there, be sure to check your sunscreen supply. $. Open 365 days a year.

The Blue Water House Bed and Breakfast, 407 E. Market St.; (302) 645-7832. Colorful, quirky accommodation with tropical decor located between downtown Lewes and Delaware Bay Beaches. Two-night minimum in peak season. $$ per night.

Inn at Canal Square, 122 Front and Market Streets; (302) 644-3377; www.theinnatcanalsquare.com. Rooms and suites overlooking Lewes harbor. $$$.

King's Homemade Ice Cream Shops, 201 Second St.; (302) 645-9425; and Union St., Milton, DE; (302) 684-8900; www.kingsicecream.com. Family-owned and -operated, homemade ice cream since 1972. $.

La Rosa Negra, 1201 F Savannah Rd.; (302) 645-1980. Homemade pastas and other Italian specialties. $$. Call for seasonal hours.

Savannah Inn, 330 Savannah Rd.; (302) 645-0330; www.savannahinnlewes.com. Rooms and suites in newly renovated brick Victorian. Therapeutic massage and retreat weekends. $$$. Two-night minimum during peak season.

REHOBOTH BEACH

Arena's Famous Bar & Deli Restaurant, 149 Rehoboth Ave.; (302) 227-1272 and **Arena's Café,** 4113 Highway One, Rehoboth Beach, DE; (302) 226-CAFE; www.arenasdeliandbar.com. A wide variety of big sandwiches, including veggie and build-your-own selections, and fresh salads; great for picnic packing. Open daily 11 a.m. to 1 a.m. $.

Blue Moon Restaurant, 35 Baltimore Ave.; (302) 227-6515; www.bluemoonrehoboth.com. Restored Victorian beach house featuring upscale modern American cuisine. Daily veggie entree. Small plates $–$$, dinner entrees $$–$$$. Open seven days year-round; dinner from 5:30 p.m. and Sunday brunch 10:30 a.m. to 2 p.m.

Boardwalk Plaza Hotel, Olive Avenue at the Boardwalk; (302) 227-7169; www.boardwalkplaza.com. Gracious Victorian hotel with guest rooms furnished with antiques and period reproductions, indoor-outdoor spa pool, on-site fine dining restaurant.

Canalside Inn, Canal & Sixth Street; (302) 226-2006; www.canal side-inn-rehoboth.com. Contemporary, pet-friendly; pool. Breakfast, bikes, and beach chairs are included. $$–$$$.

Crystal Restaurant, 620 Rehoboth Ave.; (302) 227-1088. It doesn't look like much from the outside, but this unassuming little restaurant has endeared itself to the locals with good food at cheap prices. $. Open year-round for breakfast, lunch, and dinner.

Dogfish Head Craft Brewing & Eats, 320 Rehoboth Ave.; (302) 226-2739; www.dogfish.com. Free tours of the company's "home base," where experimental brews are featured once a month and vodka, gin, and rum are made in the upstairs distillery. Tours are offered Tues, Wed, and Thurs at 4:30 p.m. The pub menu includes a horribly named, deliciously tasty appetizer called The Dogpile—get it!—and everything from wood-grilled pizzas to steaks. $–$$. Open daily year-round noon through dinner.

Eden, 32 Baltimore Ave.; (302) 227-3330; www.edenrestaurant .com. Upscale fare—risotto du jour, Maine lobster/local crab tower, signature key lime pie, thoughtful wine list. $$–$$$.

Homestead at Rehoboth Bed & Breakfast, 35060 Warrington Rd.; (302) 226-7625; www.homesteadatrehoboth.com. Adult only, pet friendly converted farmhouse with four guest rooms. Continental breakfast included. $$–$$$.

La La Land, 22 Wilmington Ave.; (302) 227-3887. Dine on La La Land and Sea and other specialties al fresco in the private tropical garden. $$$.

Sea Witch Manor & Spa, Bewitched and **BEDazzled Bed-and-Breakfasts,** 71, 67, and 65 Lake Ave.; (302) 226-9482. Three romantic bed-and-breakfasts (BEDazzled's decor is old Hollywood glam), each with its own distinctive personality, gourmet breakfast, small on-site spa. $$–$$$.

Victoria's at Boardwalk Plaza Hotel, Olive Avenue and the Boardwalk; (302) 227-0615; www.boardwalkplaza.com. Lovely surroundings, including outdoor, boardwalk-side patio; excellent food such as signature cream of crab soup, seafood mélange, and veggie terrine. $$–$$$. Open for breakfast, lunch and dinner. The Sunday brunch is outstanding. Sun through Thurs 7 a.m. to 9 p.m., Fri and Sat 7 a.m. to 10 p.m.

For More Information . . . .

Delaware Tourism Office, 99 Kings Hwy., Dover, DE 19901; (866) 284-7483; www.visitdelaware.com.

Lewes Chamber of Commerce and Visitors Bureau, 120 Kings Hwy., Lewes, DE 19958; (302) 645-8073; www.leweschamber.com.

Rehoboth Beach/Dewey Beach Chamber of Commerce, 501 Rehoboth Ave., Rehoboth Beach, DE 19971; (302) 227-2233; www.beach-fun.com.

Southern Delaware Tourism Office, 103 West Pine St., Georgetown, DE 19947; (302) 856-1818; www.visitsoutherndelaware.com.

DOWN THE SHORE ESCAPE *Three*

Annapolis, Maryland
MARITIME MASTERPIECE/2 NIGHTS

Yacht Races
Naval Academy
Schooner Sails
Historic Digs

For more than three centuries, the Chesapeake Bay has been a primary source of commerce, culture, and cuisine for the people in **Annapolis.** Known as "America's Sailing Capital," it remains a city of sailors from the midshipmen of the U.S. Naval Academy to the after-work yacht racers.

Annapolis is also a great walking city, with streets that fan out from its centerpiece state capitol. It's a good thing, too, because there's plenty to see here, including the nation's largest collection of surviving 17th- to 19th-century buildings, ranging from humble, early wood-frame abodes to lavish English-style mansions.

DAY 1/MORNING

Annapolis is only about a 130-mile, two-and-a-half-hour drive from Philadelphia. To get there, take the Schuylkill Expressway (I-76) to I-95 and drive south on I-95 past Baltimore, about 120 miles to I-97. Travel south on I-97 for 21 miles and you will come to US 301/US 50. Take US 50 east to exit 29A (St. Margarets Road). Turn right at the light and go straight 2.3 miles. Make a left U-turn onto Brownswood Road; then take the first right onto Forest Beach Drive and continue for 1½ miles for a delicious introduction to Maryland's famous crabs (see Cantler's Riverside Inn, below).

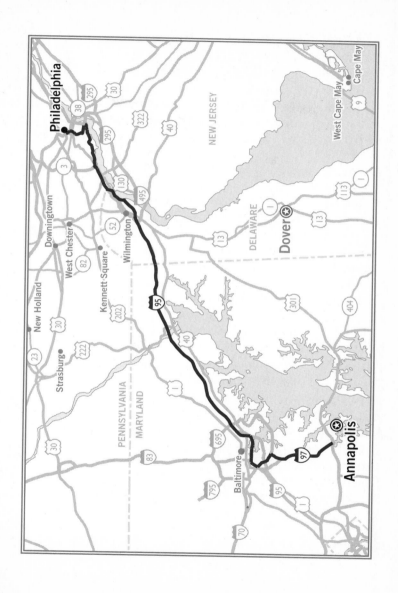

AFTERNOON

LUNCH **Cantler's Riverside Inn,** 458 Forest Beach Rd., Annapolis, MD; (410) 757-1311; www.cantlers.com. Here you can feast on award-winning seafood specialties, including just about every preparation of crab from dip to soup to steamed as well as stuffed into shrimp, rockfish and crepes. $–$$. Open for lunch and dinner Sun through Thurs 11 a.m. to 11 p.m., Fri and Sat 11 a.m. to midnight.

Reverse your tracks back to US 50 west, which will take you across the Severn River Bridge. Take exit 24A Rowe Boulevard/MD 70. Follow Rowe Boulevard to State Circle, crowned by the Maryland State House. Bear right on Rowe Boulevard to Northwest Street, then left. Turn right into Gotts Court Garage, which is located next to the **Annapolis Visitor Center** (26 West St., Annapolis, MD; 410-280-0445; www.visitannapolis.org). At the garage, your first hour is free; then it's $1.25 per hour, maximum $10.

The **Maryland State House** (100 State Circle, Annapolis, MD; 410-974-3400; www.msa.md.gov) sits on a hill at the hub of the city. This impressive structure—which for nine months in 1783–84 served as the nation's capitol—has a remarkable history and split personality—literally. A broad black line on the floor divides the original 1770s wood and plaster section from the early 1900s marble addition.

One of the many highlights of your tour is the room where, in 1783, George Washington resigned his commission as commander in chief of the Continental Army and where, less than a month later, the Treaty of Paris officially ending the Revolutionary War was ratified. Open Mon through Fri 9 a.m. to 5 p.m., Sat and Sun 10 a.m. to 4 p.m. Tours are given at 11 a.m. and 3 p.m.

In the 18th century, Maryland Avenue was the most fashionable residential street in the city. Stretching from State Circle to the gate of the U.S. Naval Academy, it is still the epitome of style with its diverse collection of exclusive galleries and shops. At **Annapolis Pottery** (40 State Circle, Annapolis, MD; 410-268-6153; www.annapolispottery.com) you'll never find anyone asleep at the wheel. You can chat with the artisans as they handcraft original stoneware vases, pots, and other decorative items. Open Mon through Sat 10 a.m. to 6 p.m., Sun until 6 p.m.

You'll find more local arts and crafts at the **Maryland Federation of Art—Circle Gallery** (18 State Circle, Annapolis, MD; 410-268-4566; www.mdfedart.org) which is open Tues through Sun 11 a.m. to 5 p.m. and the **League of Maryland Craftsmen** (216 Main St., Annapolis, MD; 410-626-1277; www.artinannapolis.com) which is open Mon through Fri 10 a.m. to 5:30 p.m., Sat 10 a.m. to 6 p.m., Sun noon to 5:30 p.m.

From Maryland Avenue, turn right onto Prince George Street. At No. 186 is the **William Paca House & Garden** (410-263-5553; www.annapolis.org), the private residence of one of the four Marylanders who signed the *Declaration of Independence*. The five-part restored structure is a splendid example of 18th-century architecture. Particularly beautiful is the two-acre terraced Eden out back, where you can admire the brilliant colors of the flowers, the clever fish-shaped pool, and the air of absolute serenity. Open Mon through Sat 10 a.m. to 5 p.m., Sun noon to 5 p.m. Call for winter hours. Admission for combined house and garden tour is $8 for adults, $7 seniors, and $5 for children.

EVENING

DINNER **Carrol's Creek,** 410 Severn Ave., Annapolis, MD; (410) 263-8102; www.carrolscreek.com. Located across Spa Creek in Eastport. If you like, you can walk from the downtown area over the Spa Creek Bridge. Or you can take the three-minute drive starting from Prince George Street, take a right onto Maryland

Avenue. Turn right onto King Georg Street, then right again onto Randall Street. Enter the next roundabout and take the second exit onto Compromise Street. Compromise becomes Sixth Street. Turn left onto Severn Avenue; the restaurant will be on your left. Whether you walk or drive, look for the bright red awning. In addition to its spectacular bayfront view, Carrol's Creek is renowned for its Maryland-accented American cuisine. There are crab cakes and raw and fried oysters, as well as a killer savory crab cheesecake with a pecan-Old Bay crust. But spring for the Chef's Dinner, which allows you to add cream of crab soup, salad, and dessert to any entree for an extra $14. $$$. Lunch hours are Mon through Sat 11:30 a.m. to 4 p.m.; dinner Mon through Thurs 5 to 9 p.m., Fri and Sat until 10 p.m., Sun at 3 p.m. Sunday brunch is served from 10 a.m. to 1:30 p.m.

After dinner in season you can sit out on the restaurant's deck/lounge and watch the yachts returning to the neighboring Annapolis Marina from the Wed evening races. Better yet, the Kaye family will take you for a two-hour sunset sail aboard their 74-foot schooner *Woodwind,* a replica of the luxury "yachts" of the early 20th century. *Woodwind* departs from Pusser's landing at the **Annapolis Marriott Waterfront Hotel** (80 Compromise St.; Annapolis, MD; 410-263-7837; www.schoonerwoodwind.com) next to City Dock seven days a week at 6:30 p.m. mid-Apr through the beginning of Nov. Sunset (and weekend) cruises are $37 per person for adults, $22 for children. Weekday daytime cruises are $34 for adults, $22 for children weekdays. From May to the end of Sept, the Kayes also offer Fri and Sat overnight boat-and-breakfast packages for two ($289) that include a double stateroom, two-hour sail, and breakfast. For overnight reservations call (410) 263-1981.

LODGING   **Historic Inns of Annapolis,** 58 State Circle, Annapolis, MD; (410) 263-2641; www.historicinnsofannapolis.com. This is really three 18th-century inns—Governor Calvert House, Robert Johnson House, and Maryland Inn—all centrally located across from State Circle and adjacent to Church Circle. Each of the three is distinctive in personality, and all are delightfully furnished with period antiques and reproductions. If you have a favorite among the inns, you can make a request to stay there when you make your reservation. $–$$ (reserve online to get the lowest rates).

DAY 2/MORNING

BREAKFAST **Treaty of Paris Restaurant,** 16 Church Circle at the Maryland Inn, Annapolis, MD; (410) 263-6340; www.historicinnsofannapolis.com. Here you can enjoy a real Maryland-style breakfast in an authentic 18th-century setting. You'll find your favorite traditional morning fare, but, for some genuine local flavor, try the "Sea and Eggs," featuring soft shell crabs, shrimp and crab cream sauce, and grilled sausage. $–$$ for breakfast. The restaurant serves lunch and dinner, too. $$–$$$. Breakfast hours are Sat and Sun 8 a.m. to 2 p.m., lunch Sat and Sun 11:30 a.m. to 2 p.m.; dinner hours are Thurs through Sat 5:30 to 9:30 p.m.

Head east on Maryland Avenue until it dead-ends at King George Street; turn right on King George, keep going straight, and you will find yourself at Gate 1, the main visitors entrance of the **United States Naval Academy.** One of Annapolis's best-known landmarks for the past 150 years, this 338-acre campus—officially known as the "Yard"—is home to a brigade of 4,000 and a faculty of 580. Right inside the gate is the **Armel-Leftwich Visitor Center** (52 King George St.; Annapolis, MD; 410-293-8687; www.usna.edu), where you can arrange for a guided tour of the Yard's many attractions. Guided tours are offered year-round, seven days a week. Fees are $9 for adults, $8 for seniors, $7 for students. Note that you will need a photo ID to enter the Yard.

At precisely 12:05 p.m. weekdays, the entire brigade assembles for noon meal formation, an impressive event complete with ceremonial swords and drums and bugles that takes place in front of Bancroft Hall, the largest dormitory in the western hemisphere and home to the entire brigade. Close by is a statue of the famous Indian warrior Tecumseh, to whom the midshipmen send their pleas for benevolence prior to important football games and tests.

One of the most prominent features of the Yard—and of the Annapolis skyline—is the Chapel, with its magnificent Tiffany Studios-designed stained-glass windows. Beneath the Chapel is the elaborate and eerily beautiful "undersea" Crypt of John Paul Jones with its black-and-white marble sarcophagus supported by carved porpoises, covered with sculpted seaweed, and surrounded by models, photos, and mementos tracing the career of this famed Revolutionary War hero. Call for seasonal hours.

Preble Hall houses the **U.S. Naval Academy Museum** (410-267-2108), with four galleries showcasing a collection of more than 35,000 artifacts and artworks spanning centuries of naval history. Among the exhibitions are 1,210 medals from thirty countries dating from 254 B.C. to A.D. 1936, and 600 historic American and captured flags, including some that have been to the moon. One of the most riveting exhibits is the Class of 1951 Gallery of Ships with its awe-inspiring selection of precision-carved ship models crafted from wood, gold, and bone by artisans from the 16th to the 19th centuries. By the way, the last mentioned were carved from leftover beef bones by French prisoners of war being held in England during the Napoleonic conflicts. The museum is open Mon through Sat 9 a.m. to 5 p.m., Sun 11 a.m. to 5 p.m. Admission is free.

AFTERNOON

LUNCH **Harry Browne's,** 66 State Circle, Annapolis, MD; (410) 263-4332; www.harrybrownes.com. This longtime lunch and dinner tradition for Annapolitans and visitors has a moderately priced menu full of delicious surprises. It offers homemade soups, pastas, and quiche that regularly change with the availability of fresh ingredients and the imagination of the chef. Always available are the excellent cream of crab soup, chili served in a sourdough *boule,* and, of course, signature crab cakes. Lunch hours are Mon to Sat 11 a.m. to 3 p.m., dinner Mon to Sat 5:30 to 10 p.m., Sun 4:30 to 9 p.m. Champagne brunch is served Sun 10 a.m. to 3 p.m.

During the warm weather, one Sat a month is public dig day at **Historic London Town House and Gardens** (839 Londontown Rd., Edgewater, MD; 410-222-1919; www.historiclondontown.org), Maryland's largest archaeological dig. Take US 50 west to MD 665/ Aris T. Allen Boulevard. Get off at the second exit and make a right-hand turn onto MD 2. You'll go over the South River Bridge. The third traffic light is Mayo Road; turn left onto Mayo, then left again onto Londontown Road and continue to the end of the road. On those special Saturdays, you can work alongside the pros who are searching for the lost forty dwellings, shops, and taverns that once comprised the bustling 17th-century tobacco port called London. On other days this site is still worth visiting for a tour of the one building that remains, an 18th-century mansion where you can learn about life in old-time London, and eight acres of gorgeous gardens. Open Wed through Sat 10 a.m. to 4 p.m., Sun noon to 4 p.m. Mar through Dec, Wed to Fri only Jan and Feb. Guided house tours are $10 adults, $9 seniors, $5 children.

DINNER Rams Head Tavern, 33 West St., Annapolis, MD; (410) 268-4545; www.ramsheadtavern.com. Adjacent to State Circle is the second major focal point of the city, Church Circle. Go halfway around Church Circle to West Street to reach your destination for dinner. Steak is a specialty. $$–$$$. Open Mon to Sat 11 a.m. to 2 a.m., Sun 10 a.m. to 2 a.m.; Sunday brunch 10 a.m. to 2 p.m.

Follow up your dinner with an evening of music in an intimate venue that has hosted the likes of Greg Allman, Leon Russell,

Kathy Mattea, and Arlo Guthrie at the **Rams Head on Stage** (410-268-1131; www.ramsheadonstage.com). Ticket prices vary widely per performer, but they tend to be in the mid-teens to mid-twenties range. The tavern offers a great dinner and show combo that gives you 10 percent off your entire meal check and a free beer nightcap (with ticket stub) after the show. You'll also get two hours free parking at Gotts Garage.

LODGING   Historic Inns of Annapolis.

DAY 3/MORNING

BREAKFAST   **Cafe Normandie,** 185 Main St., Annapolis, MD; (410) 263-3382. There's nothing quite as romantic as savoring cups of cappuccino at a cozy table in a rustic French country bistro. Try something exotic, perhaps eggs Basque with ratatouille and cheese. The crepes are heavenly and the warm tarte tatin divine. It's open for lunch and dinner, too. $–$$. Hours are Mon to Thurs 11 a.m. to 10 p.m., Fri to 10:30 p.m., Sat and Sun 9 a.m. to 10:30 p.m.; closed daily from 3:30 to 5 p.m.

If you want to take home a piece of Maryland history, head for the City Dock area for a stop at the **Historic Annapolis Foundation Museum Store and Welcome Center** (77 Main St., Annapolis, MD; 410-268-5576; www.annapolis.org). This extensive collection in a restored 1810 warehouse reflects the architectural, social, cultural, and maritime history of the city through 18th-century reproductions, hand blown glassware, books, and other decorative and educational items. Open Mon through Sat 10 a.m. to 5 p.m., Sun noon to 5 p.m.

HistoryQuest (99 Main St., Annapolis, MD; 410-267-6656) is tour and information central and home of **Fleming's Bake Shop.** Hours of operation are Mon to Sat 9:30 a.m. to 5 p.m., Sun 11 a.m. to 5 p.m. There's also a small gift shop at the **William Paca House,** located at 186 Prince George St. Hours are Sat 10 a.m. to 5 p.m., Sun noon to 5 p.m. Check for winter hours.

For the best selection of U.S. Naval Academy and Annapolis clothing and accessories, go to **Peppers** (133 Main St., Annapolis, MD; 410-267-8722). They even have Navy-style gear for newborns! Straight ahead is **City Dock.** On the sidewalk at the head of City Dock is the **Kunta Kinte–Alex Haley Memorial** commemorating the arrival in 1767 of the African slave who was immortalized in his descendant Haley's book *Roots,* as well as all of the others who were brought here in bondage.

AFTERNOON

LUNCH **49 West Coffeehouse,** 49 West St.; Annapolis, MD; (410) 626-9796; www.49westcoffeehouse.com. The coffeehouse serves substantial fare for breakfast, lunch, and dinner. You could make a meal of an assortment of appetizers such as chipotle shrimp skewers and smoked salmon with bagel chips, pico de gallo and dill chive cheese spread. $–$$. Call for hours. (Check out the artwork on the walls, each month a different local artist is featured.)

Take a last turn on the water with **Kayak Annapolis, LLC** (P.O. Box 3501; Annapolis, MD 21403; 443-949-0773; www.kayakannapolistours.com). They offer two-and-a-half-hour guided sit-on-top kayak tours of Spa Creek; $65 for adults, $50 for children under 12. Morning (7:30 a.m.), afternoon (11:30 a.m.), and evening (3:30 p.m.) tours are available.

To return to Philly, get on US 50 heading west and retrace your route from day one. It should take about two-and-a-half hours.

There's More . . . .

Museums & Tours. Annapolis Maritime Museum, 723 Second St., Eastport, Annapolis, MD; (410) 295-0104; www.amaritime.org. Four-hundred years of maritime history through artifacts, art, and a variety of programs. Seasonal tours of Thomas Point Shoal Lighthouse including docent-narrated boat ride. Call for seasonal museum hours and tour schedules.

Annapolis Carriage. Purchase tickets at HistoryQuest, 99 Main St., Annapolis, MD; (410) 267-6656; www.annapoliscarriage.com. Coachman-narrated rides are 20 to 25 minutes ($20 for adults, $10 for children) or 40 to 50 minutes ($35/$15). Call for seasonal hours.

Annapolis Food Tours, Capital City Colonists; (410) 295-9715; www.capitalcitycolonials.com. Three-hourlong, 1-mile tasting tour takes you to historic sites (and even a private home) for samplings of crab, ice cream, cabbage rolls, wine, and more. $42 for adults, $32 for kids.

Annapolis Segway Tours, 131 Prince George St., Annapolis, MD; (800) 979-3370; www.annapolissegwaytours.com. $45 for one hour, $65 for two. Hours are Mon through Sat 10 a.m. to 5 p.m., Sun from noon. Advance reservations are required.

Annapolis Tours, (410) 268-7601; www.annapolis-tours.com offers a number of different guided walking tours of the city (call for seasonal schedules) including the **Four Centuries Tour,** which includes Maryland State House interior, US Naval Academy, and historic downtown. $16 adults, $4 students. Bring a photo ID. **African American Heritage Tour** encompasses three centuries of history from slavery to today. Bring photo ID. **Haunted Ghost Tour,** spirit-seeking by candlelight. $16 for adults, $10 for children.

Discover Annapolis Tours, departs from visitor center, 26 West St.; Annapolis, MD; (410) 626-6000; www.discover-annapolis.com.

Forty-minute ($14 adults, $9 children) and one-hour ($14/$7) historic downtown tours on air-conditioned trolleys. Call for seasonal hours.

Hammond Harwood House, 19 Maryland Ave., Annapolis, MD; (410) 263-4683; www.hammondharwoodhouse.org. This restored pre-Revolutionary War residence provides a look at Annapolis history from the perspective of a family who lived here. Open Apr through Oct, Wed through Sun noon to 5 p.m. Admission is $6 for adults, $5.50 for students, $3 for children under 6.

Watermark Cruises of Annapolis, (410) 268-7601; www.watermarkcruises.com. Forty-minute narrated cruises of Annapolis Harbor and U.S. Naval Academy or of residential areas including history from the 17th century to present. $12 for adults, $5 for children. Call for seasonal hours.

State Parks. **Sandy Point State Park,** 1100 East College Parkway (off PA 50/301 at the Bay Bridge western terminus); (410) 974-2149; www.dnr.state.md.us. Chesapeake Bay beaches for swimming and boating (boat rentals are available), fishing; hiking and biking trails. Open daily year-round, 6 a.m. to 9 p.m. from Memorial Day to Labor Day; daytime use only rest of year. $5 per person weekdays, $6 weekends. Discounts for seniors and young children.

Theatre & the Arts. **Annapolis Summer Garden Theatre,** 143 Compromise St., Annapolis, MD; (410) 268-9212; www.summergarden .com. This outdoor community theater performs Shakespeare and Broadway under the stars from Memorial Day to Labor Day. Performances Thurs through Sat evenings at 8:30 p.m. Tickets are $18—ask about the "Eats and Seats" discounts.

Banneker-Douglass Museum, 84 Franklin St., Annapolis, MD; (410) 216-6180; www.bdmuseum.com. Open Tues through Sat 10 a.m. to 4 p.m. This museum of African-American arts and culture features changing exhibits, lectures, films, and publications. Free.

Maryland Hall for the Creative Arts, 801 Chase St., Annapolis, MD; (410) 263-5544; www.marylandhall.org. In addition to hosting indoor and outdoor art exhibits, the city's primary community arts center is home to the Annapolis Symphony Orchestra, Chorale, Opera, and Ballet Theater. Call for performance schedules and ticket prices.

Special Events . . . .

MAY

Chesapeake Bay Bridge Walk. Lots of locals and visitors gather every year to take this 4½-mile stroll. Why? Because it's there! Call (877) BAYSPAN after 6:30 a.m. on the day of the walk to see if it is cancelled due to unfavorable weather conditions.

END OF AUGUST THROUGH LATE OCTOBER

Maryland Renaissance Festival, Crownsville Road (between MD 450 and MD 178), Annapolis, MD; (800) 296-7304; www.renn fest.com. Bawdy, brawling re-creation of a 16th-century English village, jousting, and other revelry. $18 for adults, $15 for seniors, $8 for children.

SEPTEMBER

Anne Arundel County Fair, MD 178 (General's Highway), Crownsville, MD; (410) 923-3400; www.aacountyfair.org. Carnival midway rides, agricultural and craft demonstrations, outdoor skills contests, livestock sale, live bands, tractor pulls, skunk races.

Maryland Seafood Festival, Sandy Point State Park, Annapolis, MD; (410) 626-8922; www.mdseafoodfestival.com. Weekend after

Labor Day. Three-day seafood extravaganza including Maryland crab soup cook-off. $10 admission.

Other Recommended Restaurants and Lodgings. . . .

ANNAPOLIS

Annapolis Ice Cream Company, 196 Main St.; (443) 482-3895; www.annapolisicecream.com. About fifty regular plus a number of seasonal flavors made onsite.

Charles Inn Bed-and-Breakfast, 74 Charles St.; (410) 268-1451; www.charlesinn.com. Period art and furnishings in a restored Civil War-era home. Continental breakfast weekdays, full meal weekends. $$–$$$.

Galway Bay Irish Pub, 63 Maryland Ave.; (410) 263-8333; www.galwaybayannapolis.com. Corned beef and cabbage, shepherd's pie, Chesapeake oyster, and Irish bacon. $–$$. Mon to Sun 11 a.m. until "late."

Lemongrass, 167 West St.; (410) 280-0086; www.kapowgroup.com. You'll crave the crispy green beans and asparagus and other stellar selections you don't have to be able to pronounce to love. $. Lunch is Mon to Fri 11:30 a.m. to 3 p.m., Sat noon to 4 p.m.; dinner Mon to Thurs 5 to 10 p.m. Fri and Sat until 11 p.m., Sun 4 to 10 p.m.

Middleton Tavern, 2 Market Space, City Dock; (410) 263-3323; www.middletontavern.com. Oyster (and shrimp) shooters; seafood raw, steamed, smoked, and fried. $$–$$$. Also open for lunch. Hours are Mon to Fri 11:30 a.m. to 1:30 a.m., Sat and Sun from 10 a.m. (Dinner from 5 p.m. to midnight.)

The O'Callaghan Hotel Annapolis, 174 West St.; (866) 782-9624; www.ocallaghanhotels.com. Boutique Irish hotel with on-site restaurant. $$–$$$.

Reynolds Tavern, 7 Church Circle; (410) 295-9555; www.reynolds tavern.org. Three beautiful guest rooms in one of oldest taverns in the U.S. $$$. On-premises restaurants serving lunch, afternoon tea, and dinner.

Severn Inn, 1993 Baltimore Annapolis Blvd.; (410) 349-4000; www.severninn.com. Upscale waterfront dining featuring seafood and dry-aged strip steak. $$$. Lunch Mon to Sat 11:30 a.m. to 2:30 p.m.; dinner Mon to Thurs 5 to 9 p.m., Fri and Sat until 10 p.m. Pub serves until 11 p.m. weekdays and weekends. Sunday buffet brunch 10 a.m. to 2 p.m.

For More Information . . . .

Annapolis & Anne Arundel County Conference and Visitors Bureau; (410) 280-0445; www.visitannapolis.org.

Maryland Office of Tourism; (866) 639-3526; www.visitmaryland .org.

DOWN THE SHORE ESCAPE *Four*

Maryland's Eastern Shore—St. Michaels, Oxford, Tilghman Island, and Easton
FOLLOW THE DOTTED COASTLINE/2 NIGHTS

It isn't only the Chesapeake Bay Bridge that separates Maryland's Eastern Shore from the rest of the world. It is an entire way of life. Here, the last of the once extensive fleet of oyster-dredging skipjacks—

> Skipjack Sails
> Sensational Seafood
> Bay Watch
> Funky Flamingos

and their rugged crews—still ply the bay and deliver their catch of the day directly to the kitchens of waterfront restaurants. And boat builders still practice their centuries-old craft to construct and restore majestic wooden sailing ships for work, display, and pleasure.

As you travel south, then east along the coast, you'll pass through little dots of towns only about fifteen to twenty minutes apart, some with names you know (such as St. Michaels and Tilghman Island), and others, such as Grasonville, Oxford, and Easton, that may not be quite as familiar. Along the way you'll become acquainted with beautiful rivers named Choptank, Tuckahoe, Wye, Miles, and Tred Avon.

Peak visitor time along the Eastern Shore is during the summer. But the early fall brings a back-to-normal tranquility as well as awe-inspiring arrays of fall foliage for those who like to avoid the crowds.

DAY 1/MORNING

Although there are shorter, more direct routes to **St. Michaels** from Philadelphia, this one allows you to have a taste of some of

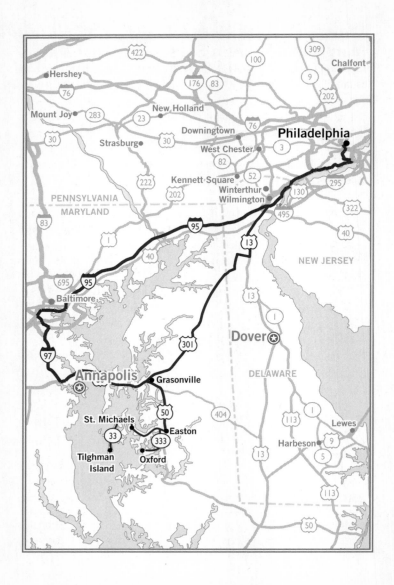

the Eastern Shore's best seafood and visit one of the area's most beautiful wetlands sanctuaries along the way. The trip will take about three hours and twenty minutes (about ½ hour longer than usual). Take I-76 (Schuylkill Expressway) to I-95 south past Baltimore. Just beyond the city, follow signs for I-695 east toward Glen Burnie. This is a left-hand exit. Follow I-695 until it merges with I-97 south (also a left-hand exit). Take I-97 south until it merges with US 50 east. Follow US 50 past Annapolis and across the Bay Bridge to exit 42, Kent Narrows. Follow the blue directional signs to Harris Crab House in Grasonville.

AFTERNOON

LUNCH   **Harris Crab House** at the Kent Narrows, 433 North Kent Narrows Way, Grasonville, MD; (410) 827-9500; www.harriscrabhouse.com. You know the seafood is fresh because while you eat you can watch the local watermen deliver their day's catch of clams, crabs, and oysters right to the dock of the Harris family's processing plant next door. The red and white crab soups are to die for. And go ahead and order the crabs by the bucket and claims by the pail. In my opinion, their "secret seasoning" is better than the ubiquitous Old Bay. $–$$. Open for lunch and dinner 11 a.m. to 10 p.m. 365 days.

Go back toward US 50, but instead of getting back onto the highway, turn left onto MD 18 and follow it for about 2 miles. Turn right at Perry Corner Road and go ½ mile to the entrance of the wetlands center, which is on the right.

Chesapeake Bay Environmental Center, aka Horsehead Wetlands Center, (Grasonville, MD 410-827-6694; www.bayrestoration .org), is 500 acres of protected land where you can see Mother Nature at her wildest. Stop at the Visitor Center for a brief acquaintance with some of the types of butterflies, insects, and other forms of life that call this environment home. Outside the picture window is one of six ponds where you can watch the resident and visiting waterfowl in their natural habitat. Take the Boardwalk ⅔ mile across the salt meadow and climb to the top of the 15-foot tower. Explore the beautiful trails that wind past the butterfly-and-hummingbird garden, wildflowers, and habitat ponds. Borrow a net from the visitor center to let the kids go seining in the tidal pool. More than 200 species of birds have been spotted here. Canoes and kayaks are also available for self-guided water tours of the center from May through Oct. Open 9 a.m. to 5 p.m. daily year-round. Admission is $5 for adults, $4 for seniors, and $2 for youths (5 to 18).

Retrace your steps from the environmental center to get back onto US 50 east. When the road divides into US 301 and US 50, keep following US 50 east toward Ocean City. As you approach Easton, watch for signs for St. Michaels. Turn off US 50 onto MD 322. At the light near the shopping centers, turn right onto MD 33 toward St. Michaels. MD 33 will turn into Talbot Street, the town's main thoroughfare, lined with shops, restaurants, and other enticing places.

Make a right-hand turn from Talbot onto Mill Street at Navy Point and you'll come to the **Chesapeake Bay Maritime Museum** (213 N. Talbot St., St. Michaels, MD; 410-745-2916, www.cbmm .org). Highlights include a floating fleet of restored workboats and the three-story 1879 Hooper Strait Lighthouse. Pull up a crab or eel pot or tong for oysters at Waterman's Wharf or become an apprentice for the day and learn traditional boatbuilding from a real shipwright ($45 per session). The museum is open seven days a week year-round. Hours are 10 a.m. to 6 p.m. in summer; call for other seasonal hours. Admission is $13 for adults, $10 for seniors, $6 for youths 6 to 17, and free for children under 6.

EVENING

DINNER **208 Talbot,** 208 N. Talbot St., St. Michaels, MD; (410) 745-3838; www.208talbot.com. Co-owner and executive chef, Brandan Keegan creates a globally-inspired surf and turf menu (lamb tagine, Alsatian choucroute, signature fish and chips). $$. Three- and four-course prix-fixe dinners ($$$) are available nightly. There's also a fun food "Eatery" (burgers, carnitas). $. Both restaurants are open Wed through Sat from 5:30 p.m.

LODGING **The Parsonage Inn,** 210 N. Talbot St., St. Michaels, MD; (410) 745-8383; www.parsonage-inn.com. You can't miss this restored brick Victorian with its own steeple; it's a truly dramatic sight. If you're a history buff, ask for one of the bedrooms in the original part of the building. The inn provides bikes to borrow. And get ready for a beautiful breakfast cooked by Culinary Institute of America graduate "Chef Bill." Afternoon tea is also included. $$–$$$.

DAY 2/MORNING

BREAKFAST The Parsonage Inn.

Borrow a set of wheels from the inn and explore the town in the early morning before the shops open or take a back roads trail such as the **Tred Avon Circle Bike Trail** (ask the innkeepers or contact the Talbot County Visitor Center). If you're feeling particularly ambitious, you can ride 7 miles to the **Oxford–Bellevue Ferry** (27456 Oxford Rd., Oxford, MD; 410-745-9023; www.oxfordbellevueferry .com), the oldest privately-owned ferry service in the country, dating back to 1683. For $6 round-trip, you and the bike can take the ¾ mile (seven-to-ten minutes) across the Tred Avon river to the quiet little town of **Oxford.**

AFTERNOON

....

LUNCH   **Oxford Market,** 203 South Morris St., Oxford, MD; (410) 226-0015; www.theoxfordmarket.com. Pick up a cup of soup, chili, or a sandwich, and definitely some homemade cookies. Open every day from 7 a.m. to 8 p.m. Enjoy it across the street at a picnic table overlooking the river.

Take the ferry back across and ride to St. Michaels. From the downtown area, follow MD 33 (Talbot Street) for 14 miles until you reach the Knapp's Narrows Draw Bridge. Cross the bridge and you're on **Tilghman Island.**

Had you visited the Eastern Shore in the late 19th century, you would have seen hundreds of sailing boats called skipjacks dredging for oysters out in the Chesapeake Bay. Today you can still see—and sail on—the real thing with fifth-generation waterman Captain Wade Murphy Jr. on a two-hour sail on his 1886 skipjack, the *Rebecca T. Ruark* (410-829-3976 or 410-886-2176; www.skipjack.org), North America's last working sailboat. Captain Wade still offers demonstrations as part of his journey into maritime history. Daytime and sunset sails are available seven days a week; call for times. $30 per person, $15 for children under 12. If you want to do some crabbing or fishing yourself, Captain Wade also offers a "Waterman for a Day" sail aboard *Miss Kim,* an authentic Chesapeake crab boat. $75 per person.

EVENING

....

DINNER   **Bay Hundred Restaurant,** 6176 Tilghman Island Rd., Tilghman, MD; (410) 886-2126; www.bayhundredrestaurant.net. You'll want to linger over your lunch as you watch watermen at work and sailboat sailors at play. Chef/owner Mark Chew's menu covers all of the bay and sea basics. Try the lobster &

shrimp a la Bowen smothered in a creamy cheese and white wine sauce. $–$$. Top off your meal with a tropical cocktail at the restaurant's outdoor Markaritaville Tiki Bar. Open year-round Sun to Thurs 11 a.m. to 10 p.m., Fri to Sun until 11 p.m. (Bar is open until 1 a.m.)

| LODGING | The Parsonage Inn. |

DAY 3/MORNING

| BREAKFAST | The Parsonage Inn. |

You can't leave St. Michaels before checking out some of the cool, one-of-a-kind shops along and around Talbot Street. Belly up to the tasting bar and sample some of the more than 4,000 salsas, hot sauces, and mustards, some house-made at **Flamingo Flats** (100 South Talbot St., St. Michaels, MD; 410-745-2402; http://flamingo.onwebshowcase.com). They also have those wonderfully tacky pink flamingos and windup crabs you've been looking for. Open Apr through Dec 10 a.m. to 5 p.m.; Jan to Mar Thurs to Mon. For crustaceans of the chocolate variety, head to **St. Michaels Candy & Gifts** (216 South Talbot St., St. Michaels; 410-745-6060; www.candyisdandy.com). Call for seasonal hours. It's a five-minute drive away from downtown Talbot Street, but if you're into truly unique art, a visit to the old barn that houses **Turtle Cove Mosaic Gallery** (23944 Porters Creek Lane, St. Michaels, MD; 410-745-2529; www.turtlecovestudios.com) to see the gorgeous locally created inlaid items from wall art to benches and tables to mirrors. Open Sat from 11 a.m. to 4 p.m. or by appointment.

Now set out for the artsy town of **Easton,** less than a twenty-minute drive east from St. Michaels along MD 33. In recent years, the face, economy, and social dynamics of Talbot County seem to change as swiftly as the tides. To preserve the area's legacy, the **Historical Society Museum** (25 South Washington St., Easton, MD; 410-822-0773; www.hstc.org) exhibits furnishings, pictures, paintings, and memorabilia that span pre-Revolutionary to modern times. Open Mon through Sat, 10 a.m. to 4 p.m.; free. The society also offers guided "Craftsmen and Collector House" tours of an 18th century cabinet-makers cottage, the Federal townhome of one of the wealthiest families in the area and the reconstruction of a colonial home called "The Ending of Controversie." Colonial restoration Tues through Sat for $5.

AFTERNOON

LUNCH **Mason's,** 22 South Harrison St., Easton, MD; (410) 822-3204; www.masonsgourmet.com. Start with the meatball/vegetable "country soup," then move on to a po' boy sandwich made with local oysters, or Baja pizza with blackened chicken and refried beans on lavash bread. Open for dinner, too. Call for seasonal hours. $–$$.

Downtown Easton, on and around Dover Street, the main thoroughfare, is a treasure trove of artists' studios and galleries. Start out at the **Academy Art Museum** (106 South St., Easton, MD; 410-822-2787; www.academyartmuseum.org) with its permanent collection of prints from 1850 to present, drawings, photography, and plein air paintings plus rotating exhibitions of works representing a variety of media from national and regional galleries around the country. Hours are Mon and Fri 10 a.m. to 4 p.m. extended hours Tues through Thurs, Sat until 3 p.m. Admission is free.

At **Troika Gallery** (9 South Harrison St., Easton, MD; 410-770-9190; www.troikagallery.com), you can visit the three resident painters and browse through their works and those of more than thirty other artists from around the world. Open Mon to Sat around 10 a.m. to 5:30 p.m. Inside a restored Victorian home, **South Street Art Gallery** (5 South St., Easton, MD; 410-770-8350; www.southstreetartgallery.com) showcases mostly contemporary representational oil and plein air paintings many by artists from the mid-Atlantic and Eastern Shore areas. If you visit the former kitchen, you're likely to see painter/co-owner Nancy Tankersley at work. Hours are Thurs to Mon 10 a.m. to 5 p.m. Landscape painter, David Grafton, shares space with three other artists specializing in pastels and marine-scapes and creatures at **Grafton Galleries** (32 East Dover St., Easton, MD; 410-822-8922; www.graftonart.com). Call for hours.

EVENING

DINNER **Latitude 38° Bistro & Spirits**, 26342 Oxford Rd., Oxford, MD; (410) 226-5303; www.latitude38.org. Hand-painted murals and candlelight set the stage for some delightful dining. Meat, poultry, and seafood accented—but never overwhelmed—by creative sauces and sides. All entrees are available in half-portions. $–$$. Open Tues through Sun; call for seasonal hours.

Since you are heading back to Philadelphia from Easton following the most straightforward route, it should only take you a little more than two-and-a-half hours to get home. Go west on US 50 for about 20 miles until you come to US 301. Take US 301 north for 52 miles to I-95. Head north on I-95 into Philadelphia.

There's More . . . .

By the Water. Lady Patty, Knapps Narrows Marina, Tilghman's Island, MD; (410) 886-2215; www.sailladypatty.com. Two-hour excursions aboard a 1935 classic bay ketch. Day sales are $35 per person, champagne sunset sails are $35.

Tilghman Island Marina, 6140 Mariners Ct., Tilghman Island, MD; (410) 886-2500; www.tilghmanmarina.com. Watercraft rentals, including fishing and crabbing boats, 15-foot sailboats, wave runners, jet boats, kayaks, and canoes.

Cinemas. **Avalon Theatre,** 40 East Dover St., Easton, MD; (410) 822-0345; www.avalontheatre.com. A restored 1921 Art Deco movie/vaudeville palace that now features musical concerts, plays, films, and other wonderful stuff year-round. Ticket prices vary widely per performance.

Full-service Spas. **Five Gables Spa** at the **Five Gables Inn,** 209 North Talbot St., St. Michaels, MD; (410) 745-0100; www.five gables.com. Aveda spa. Try the Caribbean Therapy Body Treatment or the Rosemary Mint Awakening Body Wrap.

Linden Spa at the **Inn at Perry Cabin,** 308 Watkins Lane, St. Michaels, MD; (410) 745-2200; www.perrycabin.com. Signature treatments include the Linden Intensive Massage, Five Flowers Solace, and St. Michaels Tri-Crystal Experience.

Golf. **The Easton Club,** 28449 Clubhouse Dr., Easton, MD; (410) 820-9800; www.eastonclub.com. Eighteen-hole, beautifully landscaped course open to the public.

Hog Neck Golf Course, 10142 Old Cordova Rd., Easton, MD; (410) 822-6079; www.hogneck.com. Eighteen-hole and nine-hole executive public courses in wooded setting. $57 weekdays, $67 weekends.

Museums & Tours. **St. Mary's Museum,** off Talbot Street between Chestnut and Mulberry, St. Michaels, MD; (410) 745-9561; www .stmichaelsmuseum.com. A 19th-century waterman's family home and former town lockup/mortuary/barbershop have been joined together and furnished with personal possessions of local families during the period. Open May to Oct, Sat and Sun 10 a.m. to 4 p.m., Mon until 1 p.m. Admission is $3 adults, $1 children.

Music. **Night Cat,** 1 Goldsborough St., Easton, MD; (410) 690-3662; www.hair-o-the-dog.com. Intimate venue for wine and live music. Tickets from $10.

Shops. **Claiborne Ferry Furniture,** 603 Talbot St., St. Michaels, MD; (410) 745-5219; www.ferryfurn.com. Restoring old attic treasures is one thing, turning it into almost-animated functional furniture is another, so make sure you stop in at and see the magic that artists Robert and Susan Murphy create from castaways. Call for seasonal hours.

Wine & Spirits. **Eastern Shore Brewing,** tasting room and brewery are located in a historic old mill at 605 S. Talbot St., St. Michaels, MD; (410) 745-8010; www.easternshorebrewing.com. Taste small batch brews including St. Michaels Ale, Lighthause Ale, and Knot So Pale. Call for seasonal hours.

St. Michael's Winery, 605 South Talbot St. #6, St. Michaels, MD; (410) 745-0808; www.st-michaels-winery.com. Boutique winery producing all-Maryland dry white Long Slice and Cabernet Sauvignon. Pair with local Chapel's Creamery cheese, also available. Tours and tastings Mon to Fri noon to 6 p.m., Sat until 7 p.m., Sun until 4 p.m.

Special Events . . . .

MARCH

Annual Antiques Show and Sale, Waterfowl Festival Building, 40 South Harrison St., Easton, MD; (410) 822-0444; www.mhamdes .org. Appraisals, too. Benefits the Mental Health Association of Talbot County. $10.

Fourth International Chesapeake Chamber Music Competition, Avalon Theatre, 40 East Dover St., Easton, MD; (410) 819-0380; www .chesapeakechambermusic.org, www.avalontheatre.com.

JUNE

Tilghman Island Seafood Festival, www.tilghmanmd.com. Steamed crabs, hard shell crab races, music.

JULY

Plein Air-Easton, (410) 822-7297; www.pleinaireaston.com. Stop at the Coffee Cat (corner of Goldsborough and Washington Streets) for a program for this competition.

OCTOBER

Tilghman Island Day, on the harbor; www.tilghmanmd.com. Crab-picking and oyster-shucking contests, rowboat and work boat races, lots of seafood.

NOVEMBER

Annual Waterfowl Festival, Easton, MD; (410) 822-4567; www .waterfowlfestival.org. More than 400 of the nation's premier wildlife artists and exhibitors present paintings, sculpture, carvings, photos, decoys, sporting gear. Also wine tasting and World Championship Calling Contest.

Other Recommended Restaurants and Lodgings . . . .

EASTON

Inn at 202 Dover, 202 East Dover St.; (866) 450-7600; www.innat
202dover.com. In this gorgeous c. 1874 mansion, one room and
four suites are tastefully themed and equipped with every imagin-
able amenity. $$$. The on-site Peacock Restaurant & Lounge is the
epitome of elegance. $$$. Open for dinner Thurs to Mon from 5:30
p.m. Afternoon tea, too.

Washington Street Pub, 20 North Washington St.; (410) 822-
9011; www.wstpub.com. This local favorite serves hot and cold
sandwiches with names like the Barnyard Brawl and the Sly Fox.
Seasonal raw bar. Serves lunch and dinner. $–$$. Call for hours.

ST. MICHAELS

Bistro St. Michaels, 403 South Talbot St.; (410) 745-9111; www
.bistrostmichaels.com. This casual Parisian-style restaurant serves
a lively marriage of Eastern Shore specialties and classic French
bistro fare. Open for dinner Thurs through Mon at 5:30 p.m. $$.

Foxy's Marina Bar, 125 Mulberry St.; (410) 745-4340; www.foxys
stmichaels.com. Burgers, grilled sandwiches, steamed seafood. $.

Inn at Perry Cabin, 308 Watkins Lane; (410) 745-2200; www
.perrycabin.com. Built right after the War of 1812, this splendid
English-style country house on 25 manicured acres overlooking
Chesapeake Bay is considered the height of luxury on the Eastern
Shore. $$$. On-site white tablecloth restaurant, Sherwood Landing,
serves luxurious breakfasts, lunches, dinners, and afternoon teas.
Ask about Chef Mark Salter's fabulous tasting menus. $$–$$$.

Key Lime Café, 207 North Talbot St.; (410) 745-3158; www.key lime-cafe.com. Also serves breakfast, lunch, and brunch. Interesting international treatments of American staples in a cozy, intimate setting. Dinner $$–$$$. Open for breakfast Fri and Sat 8 a.m. to 11:30 a.m., lunch Mon to Sat 11 a.m. to 2:30 p.m., Sunday brunch 8 a.m. to 2 p.m., dinner Mon to Sun 5:30 to 9 p.m.

St Michaels Harbour Inn, Marina & Spa, 101 N. Harbor Rd.; (410) 745-9001; www.harbourinn.com. Mostly waterfront suites, some with two-person Jacuzzi, balconies. Outdoor pool and hot tub. $$$.

TILGHMAN ISLAND
Lazyjack Inn Bed & Breakfast, 5907 Tilghman Island Rd. on Dogwood Harbor; (410) 886-2215; www.lazyjackinn.com. Two rooms, two suites, full breakfast with a water view. Children age 12 and over welcome. $$–$$$.

Tilghman Island Inn, 21384 Coopertown Rd.; (410) 886-2141; www.tilghmanislandinn.com. Bright and airy water- or garden-view rooms in an easy-going, yet upscale setting. Pet friendly. $$$. Ask about special dinner and continental breakfast packages. At the on-site restaurant Isabel's, inn co-owner and chef David McCallum creates "trendy American" cuisine featuring fresh ingredients from local growers and watermen. $$–$$$. On Sat nights five-course prix-fixe tasting dinners are available for around $60; there's also a champagne brunch on Sun. The cafe offers more casual fare from burgers to mussels in white wine over linguini. $. Lunch is served Mon, Tues, Thurs, Fri, Sat, and Sun noon to 4 p.m.; dinner weekdays 6 to 9 p.m., weekends until 10 p.m. Sunday brunch noon to 3 p.m., dinner 5 to 9 p.m.

For More Information . . . .

Easton, Maryland; www.eastonmd.org.

Maryland Office of Tourism Development; (800) 634-7386 or (800) MD–IS–FUN; www.mdwelcome.org.

St. Michaels Maryland Business Association, P.O. Box 1221, St. Michaels, MD 21663; (800) 808-76222; www.stmichaelsmd.org.

Talbot County Visitor Center, 11 South Harrison St., Easton, MD 21601; (410) 770-8000; www.tourtalbot.org.

Town of Oxford; www.oxfordmd.net.

BETWEEN & BEYOND
ESCAPES

BETWEEN & BEYOND ESCAPE *One*

Lancaster County, Pennsylvania
BACK ROADS THROUGH LONG AGO/2 NIGHTS

> Horses and Buggies
> Howlin' with the Wolves
> Twisting Trial
> Beloved Buds

Along US 30, the main road that goes straight through the heart of Lancaster, you'll see lots of neon lights, a Pennsylvania Dutch-themed amusement park, just about every outlet store you can think of, and horse-drawn buggies filled with waving tourists. This **Lancaster** often surprises visitors who have come to experience a different culture, a more basic way of life, and a quieter getaway.

However, you can still find the Lancaster you seek, tucked away on green and rolling back roads and in small towns with names like Mount Joy, Lititz, Intercourse, and Bird-in-Hand that virtually radiate from the relative metropolis called Lancaster City. If you choose to take these back roads, you will find a whole other world, where black-clad Amish families tend their fields, windmills generate power, and horses and buggies share the roads with cars, motorcycles, and "Englisher" neighbors and visitors.

It might surprise you to know that there is also a sophisticated side to Lancaster County, filled with fine art, international cuisine, contemporary cool accommodations, and cultural venues. One destination, multiple diverse experiences, it doesn't get any better than **Pennsylvania Dutch** country.

DAY 1/MORNING

It takes an hour-and-a-half to get to **Lititz** and you'll want to leave early so you can have an authentic Pennsylvania Dutch breakfast

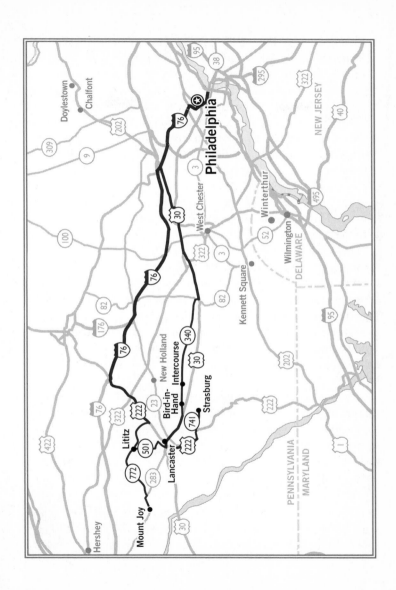

at a little, off-the-beaten-path restaurant that is a favorite of mine. Start out on I-76 west toward Valley Forge and drive for 58 miles, then take exit 286 toward US 222/Reading/Lancaster. Merge onto US 222 south via the ramp on the left, then follow for 9 miles. Take the 772 exit toward Browstown/Rothsville, then turn right onto PA 772/Newport Road and follow it for 6 miles. You'll see the **Lititz Family Cupboard** (12 West Newport Rd., Lititz; 717-626-7602). The food is homey and plentiful and includes local specialties such as baked oatmeal and scrapple. $. Hours are Mon to Sat 6 a.m. to 8 p.m., closed Sun. Be sure to stop at the restaurant's bakery next door to pick up one of the best shoo-fly pies.

Head to Landis Valley Museum. To get there, take a slight right onto Furnace Hills Pike/PA 501 and follow that for a little over 5 miles. Turn left onto Valley Road, which will become Landis Valley Road after about 1 mile. Turn left onto Kissel Hill Road. On your right, you'll see **Landis Valley Museum** (2451 Kissel Hill Rd., Lancaster; 717-569-0401; www.landisvalleymuseum.org), a more than 100-acre, seventeen-building living history village and farm with 18th- and 19th-century-focused costumed interpreters, craftspeople, and artifacts. Open Mon through Sat 9 a.m. to 5 p.m., Sun noon to 5 p.m. Admission is $12 for adults, $10 for seniors, $8 for children 6 to 17.

Okay, you know you've always wanted to know how it feels to ride in an Amish horse-drawn buggy. And since you're trying to soak in the local culture as much as possible, you can chalk it up to research. (Not to mention that it's fun.) You can catch one in the town of Intercourse. It takes about fifteen minutes to get there from Landis Valley. Start out by turning left onto Landis Valley Road, the right onto Oregon Pike/PA 272; follow for 2 miles until you can merge onto US 30 via the ramp on the left toward US 222 north. In a little over 3½ miles, take the PA 340 exit, then turn left onto 340/Old Philadelphia Pike. After 3 miles, you'll see **Abe's Buggy**

Rides (2596 Old Philadelphia Pike, Bird-in-Hand; 717-392-1794) on your right. Choose from a 2- to 5-mile back roads ride in your own private buggy. Abe's is open year-round; rides begin at $10.

AFTERNOON

LUNCH **Stoltzfus Restaurant and Deli,** 14 Center St., Intercourse; (717) 768-7287. Head east on Old Philadelphia Pike for 4½ miles, then turn right on Center Street., on the right hand side you'll see the restaurant. The Stoltzfus family has been making sandwiches for more than fifty years. Open Tues to Fri from 6 a.m. to 6 p.m., Mon and Sat until 5 p.m.

Get some background on the Amish culture before you take a tour with local families at work and at home. It all begins at **The Amish Experience** (3121 Old Philadelphia Pike, Bird-in-Hand; 717-768-3600, ext. 210; www.amishexperience.com). Every hour, this center's F/X Theater presents *Jacob's Choice,* a film that depicts one Amish boy's struggle to decide whether he wants to join the faith or live in the modern world, as well as an exploration of the culture's four-century history. Next, you can take a guided tour of the nine-room Amish Country Homestead, the only Amish house designated a Heritage Site by Lancaster County to further explore their lifestyle and traditions. You can purchase tickets to each attraction separately, but you'll save by purchasing a combined pass for $16 for adults, $11 for children.

EVENING

The center's **Amish V.I.P. Tour (Visit in Person)** is a three-hour evening excursion to visit and chat with an Amish farm family. Groups are small to allow for a more relaxed, personal experience. Tours are available mid-June to Oct Mon to Fri; tickets are $45. An alternative is an **Underground Railroad Tour,** available from July to Oct, for the same price.

DINNER **Haydn Zug's Restaurant,** 1987 State St., East Petersburg; (717) 569-5746; www.haydnzugs.com. Start with the rich and creamy veggie cheese chowder. My favorite entree is the grilled lamb tenderloin Dijonnaise, my husband's is the grilled Louisiana shrimp. Half portions are available. $$–$$$. Open Mon to Sat for lunch 11:30 a.m. to 4 p.m., dinner 4:30 to 9 p.m.

LODGING **Speedwell Forge B&B,** 465 Speedwell Forge Rd., Lititz; (717) 626-1760; www.speedwellforge.com. A twenty-minute drive away, go east on State Street/PA 722, the turn left onto South Main/PA 72. After 5½ miles, turn right onto East High Street, which becomes Doe Run Road in less than half a mile. After 2 miles, turn left onto Elm Road; continue 2 miles, then turn slight right onto Speedwell Forge Road. Follow Speedwell Forge for almost 2 miles; the bed-and-breakfast will be on your right. This 18th-century former ironmaster's mansion situated right next to the Pennsylvania Wolf Sanctuary. Most of the inn rooms and both of the private cottages have fireplaces and whirlpool tubs. On its own the inn is a worthy destination whether you stay in the main house or one of the cottages, includes three-course breakfast and afternoon refreshments. $$–$$$.

DAY 2/MORNING

BREAKFAST Speedwell Forge B&B.

It's been over a century since the last wild wolf was seen in Pennsylvania. But you can see more than forty of these magnificent creatures that are unable to live in their natural habitat. Tours of the **Wolf Sanctuary of Pennsylvania** (www.wolfsancpa.com) are available June to Sept on Sat and Sun at 10 a.m., Oct to May at noon. Cost is

$7 for adults, $6 for seniors, $5 for children (add $5 per camera). Full-moon tours, limited to ages 16 and up, are available for $20.

Its small-town look and feel, historic architecture, and mom-and-pop-boutique-lined Main Street belie Lititz's (www.venture lititz.com) big business background. This more than 250-year-old town is the home and headquarters of Wilbur Chocolate, which has been in operation since the mid-19th century and introduced its famous Wilbur Buds and the Julius Sturgis Pretzel Bakery, founded in 1861, America's first commercial pretzel bakery. While you can't tour the Wilbur factory, you can watch the confectioners make fudge and hand-dip all kinds of goodies, get a historic perspective on candy-making, and satisfy your biggest cravings at the **Wilbur Chocolate Candy Store & Museum** (48 N. Broad St., Lititz; 717-626-3249; www.wilburbuds.com). Admission is free, hours are Mon to Sat 10 a.m. to 5 p.m. During your tour of the **Julius Sturgis Pretzel Bakery** (219 E. Main St., Lititz; 717-626-4354; www.juliusturgis.com) you can try your hand at twisting with a little coaching from the pros. Call for seasonal hours; tours are $3 for adults, $2 for children.

The furniture and home decor items at **Cherry Acres** (23 E. Main St., Lititz; 717-626-7557; www.cherryacres.com) is beautifully handcrafted from rescued barn wood. Hours are Mon to Sat 10 a.m. to 5 p.m., Sun noon to 4 p.m. Walk past Sturgis Pretzel and keep going east even though there aren't any shops on the street and at 521 East Main St. you'll run into **North Star of Lititz** (717-625-1945, http://thenorthstaroflititzstudioandgallery.com), where artisans craft glass in the flame working studio, and the shelves are filled with decorative and gift items created by glassmakers from all over the country. Mon through Sat 10 a.m. to 5 p.m. Around the corner—turn right at the second light on Main Street—at **Pots by de Perrot** (201 South Locust St., Lititz; 717-627-6789; www.potsbydeperrot.com), Steve de Perrot makes stoneware functional pottery and tile tables, trivets, platters, and other items. Call for hours.

AFTERNOON

LUNCH   **Café Chocolate of Lititz,** 40 E. Main St.; Lititz; (717) 626-0123; www.chocolatelititz.com. You can't miss the chocolate fondue fountain in the window at this cute little cafe with a globally- and chocolaty-inspired menu that includes chili con chocolate, and South African babouti meatloaf or fruit-filled crepes. Finish with fondue ($20 brings enough for up to four people) or grab some chocolate-dipped fruits or madeleine to take across the street to **Lititz Springs Park** (North Broad Street, Lititz), an unexpected oasis where the town's Welcome Center sits in a replica of an 1884 train station at the entrance and ducks swim peacefully in the waters. $. Hours are Sun to Thurs 11 a.m. to 5 p.m., Fri to Sat 9 a.m. to 9 p.m. Admission is free.

Ask the pros at **Country Roads Scooter and Motorcycle** (220 North Ronks Rd., Bird-in-Hand; 717-598-3191; www.countryroadscoot ers.com) to develop a personal "insider's" itinerary for you, then hit the road on one of their rentals. You need only a driver's license to rent a scooter. Rates are $30 for two hours, $50 for four; ask about mid-week discounts. If you're a covered bridge enthusiast, Lancaster County has twenty-nine, so ask to include some of them on your itinerary.

EVENING

DINNER   **Bube's Brewery,** 102 North Market St., Mount Joy; (717) 653-2056; www.bubesbrewery.com. This is a very cool complex in a rejuvenated Victorian-era brewery (it's turning out great small-batch beer again). Its restaurants range from bottling works/outdoor biergarten to white tablecloth classy to stone-walled vault catacombs 43 feet below. It's about a half-hour drive to get there from Intercourse. Head west on Old Philadelphia Pike/PA 340 west/PA 772 west; continue to follow PA 340 west for 4½ miles. Make a slight right onto the ramp to York/Harrisburg, then merge onto US 30 west. Take a slight left at PA 283 west (sign says Harrisburg) and continue for 7 miles. Exit onto East Main Street/PA 230 west toward Mount Joy, follow 3½ miles, then turn right onto North Market Street. Bube's will be on your left. Prices range from $–$$ for the Bottling Works/Berggren. Open 7 days for lunch Mon to Sat starting at 11 a.m., Sun at noon; for dinner starting at 5 p.m. $$$. Stop for an appetizer or dessert prix-fixe dinner at upscale **Alois** (Fri and Sat 6 to 10 p.m.) or in the **Catacombs** (dinner seven nights from 5:30 p.m. weekdays, 5 p.m. weekends). Try to catch one of the themed dinners (e.g. Murder Mysteries, Medieval Feasts).

LODGING	Speedwell Forge B&B.

DAY 3/MORNING

BREAKFAST	Speedwell Forge B&B.

Spend the morning exploring the city of Lancaster, about a half-hour drive away. From Speedwell Forge Road, turn slight left onto Lake View Drive. After 1 mile, turn left onto W. Brubaker Valley Road. Continue for 1 mile, then turn right onto PA 501, which you will follow for 10 miles (it will become PA 272). Turn right onto US 222 south and, after a mile-and-a-half, left onto West King Street/PA 462 east. On your left, you will see the **Heritage Center Museum** (5 West King St., Lancaster; 717-299-6440; www.heritagecenter museum.com) where you can explore Lancaster County history and culture through locally-crafted decorative arts and other items. Admission is free. A three-minute walk away is the sister facility,

Lancaster Quilt & Textile Museum (37 Market St., Lancaster; 717-299-6440; www.quiltandtextilemuseum.com). Admission is $6 for adults. Hours for both museums are Mon to Sat 9 a.m. to 5 p.m., Sun 10 a.m. to 3 p.m.

If you're in the area on a Tues, Fri, or Sat, don't miss **Central Market** (23 North Market St., Lancaster; 717-735-6890, www.centralmarketlancaster.com), where more than sixty local vendors bring everything from farm-fresh produce to Amish and international specialty foods.

AFTERNOON

LUNCH **Rachel's Cafe and Creperie,** 309 N. Queen St., Lancaster; (717) 399-3515. This is cute, casual, and serves any kind of savory or sweet crepe creation that you can imagine. $. Hours are Tues to Fri 7 a.m. to 8 p.m., Sat from 9 a.m., Sun 9 a.m. to 3 p.m.

For railroad enthusiasts, the little village of Strasburg is a must-see. To get there, pick up US 222 in Lancaster and drive south for 5 miles until you reach PA 741; take PA 741 east for 4 miles into Strasburg. Make your first stop the **Railroad Museum of Pennsylvania** (PA 741 about a mile east of downtown; 717-687-8628; www.rrmuseumpa.org) to see locomotive and train exhibits, operate a simulator, and watch restoration activities. Open Apr to Oct Mon to Sat 9 a.m. to 5 p.m., Sun noon to 5 p.m., closed Mon Nov to Mar. Admission is $10 for adults, $9 for seniors, $8 for kids.

The National Toy Train Museum (300 Paradise Lane, between US 30 and PA 741, Ronks; 717-687-8976; www.nttmuseum.org) allows you to help operate five huge large model train layouts of different gauges and different periods from the 19th century to present and see push-, pull- and ride-on toys from the past. Call for seasonal hours. Open weekends in Apr, Nov, and Dec 10 a.m. to 5 p.m.; daily May 1 through Oct 31. Admission is $6 for adults, $5 for seniors, $3 for children; ask about family discounts.

EVENING

DINNER **"Lee E. Brenner" Dining Car,** on the Strasburg Rail Road, 301 Gap Rd., Ronks; (717) 687-7522; www.strasburgrailroad.com/dining-on-the-train.php. Board the elegantly restored Victorian dining car on an authentic steam locomotive for a forty-five-minute ride, upscale dinner (prime rib or crabmeat-stuffed flounder), and live entertainment. Dinner trains run Apr to Dec; prices are $50 for adults, $30 for children. Lunch and rides without meals in open-air, coach, or first-class cars are available at prices ranging from $13 to $20 for adults, $7 to $14 for children.

For your return trip to Philadelphia, take PA 896 north about 3 miles to US 30. Retrace your trail home going east on US 30 until you reach the Schuylkill Expressway (I-76). The entire trip should take about 1½ hours.

There's More . . . .

Amusement Parks. **Dutch Wonderland,** 2249 US 30 east, 4 miles east of Lancaster; (717) 291-1888; www.dutchwonderland.com. Family-friendly amusement park with rides, shows, and water play activities for all ages. Call for seasonal ticket prices and hours.

Ballooning. **The U.S. Hot Air Balloon Team,** (800) 763-5987; www.ushotairballoon.com. Offers sunrise and sunset flights all year. $199 per person.

Camping. **Flory's Cottages & Camping,** 99 N. Ronks Rd., Ronks; (717) 687-6670; www.floryscamping.com. RV campsites with hookups, comfy guesthouse, and one- to three-bedroom cottages. $–$$.

Museums & Tours. **DeMuth House,** 120 East King St., Lancaster; (717) 299-9940; www.demuth.org. Former home and studio of early-20th-century American modernist Charles DeMuth displays his paintings and drawings and visiting exhibits. Tues to Sat 10 a.m. to 4 p.m., Sun 1 to 4 p.m. Closed Jan. Donations are welcome.

Hands-on House, 721 Landis Valley Rd., Lancaster; (717) 569–KIDS; www.handsonhouse.org. Eight play-and-learn areas including a corner grocery, a factory, a farm, and a spaceship designed for youngsters from ages 2 to 10 and their parents to explore together. Open Labor Day to Memorial Day Mon to Wed and Sat 10 a.m. to 5 p.m., Fri until 8 p.m., Sun noon to 5 p.m. Admission is $7 for children and adults.

Kitchen Kettle Village, PA 340, Intercourse; (800) 732-3538; www.kitchenkettle.com. Visit the kitchen and see jams, jellies, bakery products, and other goodies being made. Shop the village for all kinds of items from leather products, colonial punched tin decor, toys, and locally quilted pillows. Open year-round Mon to Sat 9 a.m. to 5 p.m.; May to Oct until 6 p.m. For overnighters, deluxe rooms ($–$$) and suites ($$–$$$) are available. Kling House Restaurant serves Pennsylvania Dutch fare for breakfast and lunch. $.

Lancaster Museum of Art, 135 North Lime St., Lancaster; (717) 394-3497; www.lmapa.org. A contemporary art gallery with a global perspective. Open Tues to Sat 10 a.m. to 4 p.m., Sun noon to 4 p.m. Free.

Wheatland, PA 23, 1120 Marietta Ave., Lancaster; (717) 392-8721; www.wheatland.org. Built in 1828, this carefully restored example of Federal architecture was the home of James Buchanan,

15th president of the United States. Call for seasonal hours and admission prices.

Music. **Fulton Opera House,** 12 North Prince St., Lancaster; (717) 397-7425; www.thefulton.org. Magnificently restored Victorian structure, the nation's oldest theater in continuous operation showcased Sarah Bernhardt and Al Jolson. Home to the Lancaster Symphony Orchestra, Fulton Academy Theatre, and the Lancaster Opera Company. Call for performance schedules and prices (generally between $20 to $55).

Shops. **Eldreth Pottery,** 246 North Decatur St. at PA 896, Strasburg; (717) 687-8445; www.eldrethpottery.com. Salt-glazed pottery handcrafted and fired using a 500-year-old German process. Hours are Mon to Sat 9 a.m. to 5:30 p.m., Sun noon to 5 p.m.; July to Dec 9:30 a.m. to 8 p.m.

Special Events . . . .

LATE FEBRUARY TO EARLY OCTOBER
Mud Sales, www.padutch.com. Auctions and sales of everything from horses and buggies, home furnishings, farm equipment, and crafts to benefit community fire departments. Various locations.

MAY
Annual Rhubarb Festival, Kitchen Kettle Village, PA 340, Intercourse; (800) 732-3538; www.kitchenkettle.com. Celebrate spring and pay homage to this noble plant and food source at a fun-filled festival featuring food, music, family festivities, and games—all centered around rhubarb.

AUGUST TO OCTOBER

Pennsylvania Renaissance Faire, Mount Hope Estate & Winery, 2775 Lebanon Rd., Manheim; (717) 665-7021; www.parenfaire .com. Royal revelry, jousting, human chess game, and Shakespeare in an Old English shire.

SEPTEMBER

Long's Park Arts & Crafts Festival, 1441 Harrisburg Pike, Lancaster; (717) 735-8883, www.longspark.org. Four-day showcase for more than 200 artists and artisans from the U.S. and Canada.

OCTOBER

Lititz Chocolate Walk; Lititz; http://lititzchocolatewalk.org. One ticket entitles you to enjoy a variety of chocolate treats from twenty different stops throughout the town.

NOVEMBER

Pennsylvania Guild's Holiday Fine Craft Fair, Manheim Township High School, School Road, Lancaster, PA; (717) 431-8706; http://pacrafts.org. More than 140 local, regional and national artisans display one-of-a-kind decorative and functional home décor items, clothing, jewelry and furniture.

Other Recommended Restaurants and Lodgings . . . .

BIRD-IN-HAND

Plain & Fancy Farm Restaurant, 3121 Old Philadelphia Pike (PA 340); (800) 669-3568; www.plainandfancyfarm.com. Farm-to-fork Amish fare served family-style or a la carte. $–$$.

GORDONVILLE

Beacon Hollow Farm, 130 Centerville Rd.; (717) 768-8218. Two-bedroom cottage (with electricity) with full country breakfast on a working Amish dairy farm. $. Cash or travelers checks only.

LANCASTER

Lancaster Arts Hotel, 300 Harrisburg Ave.; (717) 299-3000; www.lancasterartshotel.com. Posh rooms and suites decorated with locally created art and furnishings. $$$. **John J. Jeffries,** (717) 431-3307; www.johnjjeffries.com. On-site restaurant serves creative, organic, locally-sourced seasonal fare.

LEOLA

Inn at Leola Village, 38 Deborah Dr., PA 23; (717) 656-7648; www.theinnatleolavillage.com. Posh rooms and suites and spa. $$–$$$. **Restaurant Mazzi,** (717) 656-8983; www.restaurantmazzi.com. On-site dining, open every night for dinner. $$$.

MARIETTA

Josephine's Restaurant, 324 West Market St.; (717) 426-2003; www.josephinesrestaurant.net. Short ribs in grapefruit pomegranate reduction and house-made ice cream—yum. Situated in an 18th-century log home. $$$. Open Wed to Sat 5 to 9 p.m.

Olde Fogie Farm B&B, 106 Stackstown Rd.; (717) 426-3992; www.oldefogiefarm.com. Traditional bed-and-breakfast rooms or family suites with kitchen on a hands-on-optional working farm. $.

STRASBURG

Red Caboose Motel, 312 Paradise Lane, Ronks; (717) 687-5000; www.redcaboosemotel.com. Real train cars have been converted into motel rooms for couples and families. $–$$. On-site restaurant. $.

Strasburg Country Store & Creamery, 1 West Main St., Centre Square; (717) 687-0766; www.strasburg.com. Wake up and smell the waffle cones being made for the homemade ice cream. Sandwiches, too. $

For More Information . . . .

Lancaster County Reservation Center, (866) 220-8824. Last minute trip without a reservation? Call here for help!

Pennsylvania Dutch Country Information; www.padutch.com.

Pennsylvania Dutch Convention and Visitors Bureau, 501 Greenfield Rd.; Lancaster, PA 17601; (717) 299-8901; www.padutch country.com.

BETWEEN & BEYOND ESCAPE *Two*

Harrisburg and Hershey, Pennsylvania

STATE CAPITAL, WORLD CAPITAL/2 NIGHTS

Only 13 miles apart in central Pennsylvania lie two capitals— one built on handshakes, the other on kisses. On weekdays, Harrisburg is a sea of serious suits focused on the goings-on of government. And, as everyone knows, the town of

> Urban Island
> Moonlight Floats
> Wild Rides
> Chocolate, Chocolate,
> Chocolate

Hershey was built specifically for the business of making chocolate. Yet, as industrious as both these state and world chocolate capitals are, that doesn't mean that they're all work and no play. No matter what time of year you visit, there's never a lack of fun, whether your idea of a good time is riverside recreation, sky-high amusement rides, dining diversity, or sports on the green, diamond, or rink.

DAY 1/MORNING

Harrisburg is nearly two hours due west of Philadelphia. To get there, take the Schuylkill Expressway (I-76) west to the Pennsylvania Turnpike. You'll be on the turnpike for about 81 miles when you'll come to I-283. Go north on I-283, then north again on I-83 for a total of about 6 miles. Then go west on US 22 for about 3 miles into Harrisburg.

You can't miss the **State Capitol Building** (Third and State Streets, Harrisburg; 800-868-7672; www.pacapitol.com), the magnificent Italian Renaissance-style structure on top of the hill. Begin at the Welcome Center, with its interactive displays on how laws are made and passed. This Capitol building is a must-visit site not only

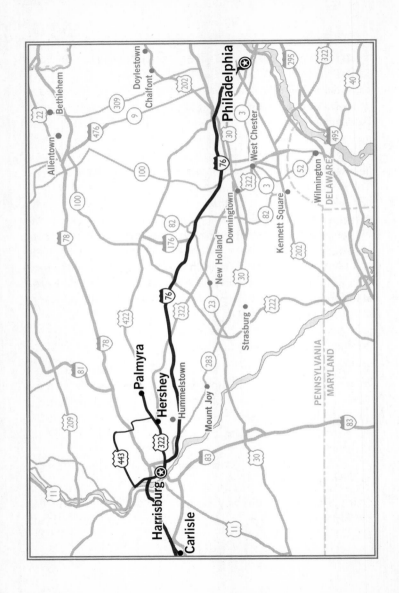

because of its significance as Pennsylvania's seat of government, but also because it is, as President Theodore Roosevelt called it, "the handsomest building I ever saw," with its soaring 272-foot-high vaulted domes modeled after St. Peter's Basilica in Rome and its sweeping staircase inspired by the one at the Paris Opera. There are also splendid collections of art and sculpture, including dramatic wall murals and ceramic tiles, created by Doylestown's Henry Mercer, depicting Pennsylvania history and symbols. Free forty-minute guided and self-guided tours encompassing the rotunda, senate, house, and supreme court are available weekdays every half-hour and weekends 9 and 11 a.m. and 1 and 3 p.m.

You don't have to be an Einstein to have a great time at the **Whitaker Center for Science and the Arts** (222 Market St., Harrisburg; 717-214-2787; www.whitakercenter.org). Even mathematics and physics can be fun at the Harsco Science Center where more than 200 interactive exhibits and theatrical performances demonstrate the down-to-earth dynamics of human movement, weather, and the environment. The center also has an IMAX theater (admission is separate) that features entertaining and educational 2- and 3-D films. Science Center admission is $14 for adults, $12 for seniors, students, and children. Hours are Tues through Sat 9:30 a.m. to 5 p.m., Sun 11:30 a.m. to 5 p.m.

AFTERNOON

LUNCH Get ready for some really good, really authentic Mexican food at **El Sol** (18 S. Third St., Harrisburg; 717-901-5050; www.elsolmexicanrestau rant.com). In addition to the requisite burritos, tacos, fajitas, and enchiladas, El Sol offers signature seafood, steak and grilled *specialties*. Be sure to try one of the fruity and floral *aguas frescas* $–$$. Open Mon through Thurs 11 a.m. to 10 p.m., Fri until 11p.m., Sat 4 p.m. to 11 p.m.

After lunch, stop in for a free guided tour and tasting at **Tröegs Brewing Company** (800 Paxton St., Harrisburg; 717-232-1297; www.troegs.com). In addition to the five year-rounders such as classic pale ale and Trögenator" double bock, there are seasonals including summery Sunshine Pils and holiday Mad Elf Ale. Ask about the latest brew in Tröegs experimental scratch beer series. Tasting room hours are Mon through Fri 10 a.m. to 5 p.m., Sat noon to 4 p.m.; tours are Sat 1:30 p.m., 2 p.m., and 2:30 p.m.

In the spring, summer, and fall, the place to be on a beautiful afternoon is **City Island,** Harrisburg's playground located just offshore (1,000 yards) from the downtown area accessible by car over the Market Street Bridge or by foot or bike over the Walnut Street Bridge. Play eighteen holes of mini **Water Golf** (717-232-8533) from Apr through Oct, $6 for adults, $5 for children. Ride the antique carousel, scaled-down Civil War Era-style steam train or horse-drawn carriage. Rent a paddleboat, canoe, bicycle, or take a guided tour or full moon float from **Susquehanna Outfitters** (717-503-0066; www.susquehannaoutfitters.com), call for seasonal hours and prices. Board the *Pride of the Susquehanna* (717-234-6500; www.harrisburgriverboat.com), an authentic paddlewheel riverboat that offers forty-five-minute scenic cruises and two-hour dinner cruises from May to Oct. Cost for the forty-five-minute day or sunset cruises are $5 for adults, $3 for children 3 to 12, free for children 2 and under. Special fall foliage, murder mystery, Italian festival, and other dinner cruises cost $42 to $50.

Take a swing at the batting cages at **Riverside Stadium** (717-231-4444, http://harrisburg.senators.milb.com), home of the Harrisburg Senators Class AA minor league baseball team that plays from Apr to Sept. General admission is $6 for adults, $4 for children.

EVENING

DINNER **Bricco,** 31 South Third St., Harrisburg; (717) 724-0222; www.briccopa.com. The Mediterranean-style food is excellent and the ambience comfortable contemporary, but even better is the fact that the restaurant is a collaboration of the Olewine School of Culinary Arts at Harrisburg Area Community College and Harrisburg Hotel Association to help future chefs and restaurateurs perfect their skills. Don't miss the strozzapretti (short ribs, baby spinach, and truffle cream) or sage pappardelle (braised duck, red wine, and pancetta ragout). $$–$$$. Open for lunch 11:30 a.m. to 2:30 p.m., dinner Mon through Fri 5:30 to 10 p.m., Sun 3 to 8 p.m.

LODGING **Felicita Garden Resort & Spa,** 2201 Fishing Creek Valley Rd., Harrisburg; (717) 599-5301; www.felicitaresort.com. Less than twenty minutes northeast. To get there, start driving southeast on South Third Street toward Chestnut Street; turn left onto Chestnut then right onto South Fourth Street. South Fourth Street becomes Mulberry Street. Turn left onto South Cameron Street and follow for 2 miles at which point it becomes US 22 west. After a little over 4 miles, take the PA 443 exit toward Fishing Creek. Turn right onto Fishing Creek Valley Road/PA 443 north. After a little under 4 miles, look for Felicita on your right. Situated on 750 acres with magnificent gardens and surrounded by miles of state park game lands and the Blue Mountains, this resort, which bears a name that means "great happiness" in Italian, has a wide open feeling that carries you far from the city. You can choose from a California Mission style-furnished room at one of the lodges with a private balcony or porch for view-admiring or a room in the inn set in a spacious converted barn. $–$$. With its garden-themed eighteen-hole golf course, full-service spa, and elegant on-site restaurant, Felicita could be a multiple-day getaway spot all by itself.

DAY 2/MORNING

If you want to include a visit to **Hershey** on this quick escape, then get going early so you can have breakfast in **The Circular Dining Room** at the **Hotel Hershey** (100 Hotel Rd., Hershey; 717-533-2171; www.hersheypa.com). It's a half-hour drive, beginning by heading east on Fishing Creek Valley Road/PA 443. Follow 443 for just over 8 miles until it becomes Mandala Gap Road. Stay on Mandala Gap Road for about 2 miles, then turn left onto Jonestown Road. In less than half a mile, turn sharp right onto Sand Beach Road; after 5 miles turn right onto Front Street, then right onto 1 Hotel Rd., which will be on your right-hand side.

BREAKFAST The **Circular Dining Room** has long been renowned for its super-opulent Sunday brunch buffet, which, for $40 for adults, $19.50 for children, features a huge seafood bar, prime rib carving station, and tables filled with all kinds of scrumptious breakfast/lunch/dinner offerings. For a more moderate price any day Mon through Sat, go for the breakfast-only buffet, complete with omelet and waffle stations, for $18, $8.50 for children. After breakfast, take a few minutes to visit the **Jeweler at the Hotel Hershey,** (717) 534-8830; www.thehotelhershey.com. See or, better yet, try on some limited edition, Australian chocolate (it's their real color!) diamonds.

Even now, the engineers at **Hersheypark** (100 Hersheypark Dr., Hershey; 717-534-3900; www.hersheypark.com) are developing some new demonic device to add to their lineup of roller coasters (including Fahrenheit, with its super-scream-inducing 97-degree plunge). For kiddies, there are plenty of just-the-right-size-and-speed rides. And the Boardwalk offers a wide array of ways to get wet from easy-riding on a river raft, to surfing some wild waves, and taking on one of the world's tallest splash-down rides. To give your traumatized tummy a time-out, take in one of the live musical performances, parades, or seal, dolphin, and sea lion shows. One admission price (call for seasonal options and hours) covers all park attractions including the Boardwalk and **ZooAmerica,** where you can get up-close-and-personal with more than 200 North American animals. If you want to visit just the zoo, located across a walking bridge from the park and open year-round, tickets are $9 for adults, $7.50 for seniors and children. If you want to get a fresh point of view on the zoo, take the two-hour, behind-the-scenes, guided, after-hours tour and animal interaction. Apr through Sept, Wed and Sat 8 to 10 p.m., Oct through Mar 6 to 8 p.m. Admission is $35 per person.

AFTERNOON

LUNCH **Chocolate Avenue Grill,** 114 W. Chocolate Ave., Hershey; (717) 835-0888; www.chocolateavenuegrill.com. One of the hot new casual eateries in town serves fun food including salads with hot sauce-tossed buffalo shrimp, coconut-breaded chicken, or grilled filet mignon. The signature "Noah" sandwich has double stacks of turkey, bacon, avocado, and melted provolone. $–$$. Mon through Sat 11 a.m. to 10 p.m.

After the wild rides of Hersheypark, it's a good time to seek a little serenity at **Hershey Gardens** (170 Hotel Rd., Hershey; 717-534-3492; www.hersheygardens.org), a 23-acre Eden with themed gardens, including an extensive and highly imaginative area designed specifically for children, more than 7,000 roses and more than twenty-five varieties of butterflies in an outdoor abode. Admission is $10 for adults, $9 for seniors, and $6 for children. Call for seasonal hours and winter discounts.

If you think chocolate facials and body treatments are simply a gimmick to promote the town's predominant product, reserve judgment until you try the cocoa massage, chocolate fondue wrap, or the multi-layered cocoa facial experience at **The Spa at the Hotel Hershey** (100 Hotel Rd., Hershey; 717-520-5888; www.chocolate spa.com)—talk about non-caloric nirvana! Service hours begin at 9 a.m. and prices range from $45 to $170.

DINNER   **What If . . . of Hershey,** 845 East Chocolate Ave., Hershey; (717) 533-5858; www.whatifdining.com. Straightforward steaks and linguini with white clam sauce share the menu with interesting combinations such as shrimp gnocchi, tenderloin medallions with eggplant parmesan, and chicken with wild mushrooms and sweet chestnuts. $$–$$$. Hours are Mon through Thurs 11 a.m. to 10 p.m., Fri and Sat until 11 p.m., Sun 4 to 10 p.m.

Hershey may be a small town, but it's a big center for the performing arts. For an evening's entertainment, check out whether it's a Broadway musical, classic drama, concert, or dance performance taking center stage at the **Hershey Theatre** (15 Caracas Ave., Hershey; 717-534-3405; www.hersheytheatre.com). This is a dazzling venue, complete with formal arches, sculpted ceilings, marble walls, and Italian lava rock floors required a $3 million-dollar renovation to restore it to its early 1930s glory. Call for performance schedules and ticket prices.

LODGING   **Annville Inn,** 4515 Hill Church Rd., Annville; (717) 867-1991; www.annvilleinn.com. While Hershey can get somewhat hectic in peak season, this inn offers an oasis of tranquility only a fifteen-minute drive east on US 422. Situated on three acres of lush landscaping, including gorgeous gardens created by co-owner Craig George, director of Hershey Gardens, the huge home features five guest rooms and suites, some (including the very cool "Secret Room") with year-round fireplaces and some with Jacuzzis. Amenities include an outdoor swimming pool, high definition movie theater with stadium seating, game room with pool table, and a full breakfast prepared by innkeeper, Rosalie George. $$–$$$.

DAY 3/MORNING

....

| BREAKFAST | Annville Inn. |

Hershey is renowned for its premier collection of golf courses, two of which are open to the public. Overlooking the city, the eighteen-hole **Hershey Links** (101 Hanshue Rd., Hummelstown; 717-533-0890; www.hersheylinks.com), an eight-minute drive west on US 322, provides a challenge to golfers of all skill levels. Peak season rate is $115 for eighteen holes, $55 for nine holes. If you want to give the kids an opportunity to get out on the greens, **Spring Creek Golf Course** (450 E. Chocolate Ave., Hershey; 717-533-2847; www.springcreekhershey.com), which was the first course in the U.S. open to players under age 18, offers nine (or eighteen) holes of family fun. Rates for eighteen holes are $21 for adults, $18 for juniors weekdays, $25/$21 weekends; nine holes are $13/$10.

AFTERNOON

....

| LUNCH | **Hershey Pantry,** 801 East Chocolate Ave., Hershey; (717) 533-7505; www.hersheypantry.com. An über-popular local breakfast and lunch spot where you can build your own half-pound burger or savor a cut-above sandwich such as grilled ham and smoked gouda on a pretzel roll. If you want to really relax, order a full soup to dessert British-style afternoon tea. $. Open Mon through Sat 6:30 a.m. to 9 p.m. |

Before you head for home, take a few hours to do a little antiquing. You'll find dozens of dealers selling everything from housewares to homespun quilts, table settings, and toys in the two-story parabolic barn that houses **Crossroads Antique Mall** (825 Cocoa Ave., Hershey, Intersection of PA 743 & US 322; 717-520-1600; www

.crossroadsantiques.com). Hours are Thurs through Mon 10 a.m. to 5:30 p.m.; daily in June, July, and Aug. For more treasures, visit the seventy-five dealers at **Zieglers Antiques** (2975 Elizabethtown Rd., Hershey; 717-533-1662; www.zieglersantiques.com). Hours are Thurs through Mon, 9 a.m. to 5 p.m. For furniture, go to the **Hershey House Antiques Co-op** (289 Hershey Rd., Hummelstown; 717-566-6042; www.hersheyhouse.net). Hours are Sat and Sun 10 a.m. to 5 p.m.

EVENING

DINNER Harvest; (717) 534-8800). The latest dining spot at the Hotel Hershey features locally-sourced all-American classics such as buttermilk fried chicken, crispy pork shank, and braised beef short ribs. Be sure to start out with the restaurant's signature she-crab soup. $$. Lunch is served daily 11:30 a.m. to 5 p.m., dinner from 5 to 10 p.m.

To return to Philadelphia, travel east on US 322 for 14 miles until you come to PA 72. Go south on PA 72 for 2 miles until you come to the Pennsylvania Turnpike. Take the turnpike going east for 61 miles until you get to the Schuylkill Expressway (I-76); then head east on the expressway for 22 miles into Philadelphia.

There's More . . . .

Camping. **Hershey Highmeadow Camp,** 1200 Matlock Rd., Hummelstown; (717) 566-0902; www.hersheypa.com. Nearly 300 open and shaded sites and rental cabins on 55 beautiful acres with many amenities. Prices vary by time of year and type of camping facility.

Golf. **Felicita Golf Course,** 511 Lakewood Dr., Harrisburg; (717) 599-5028; www.felicitaresort.com. Eighteen-hole, garden-themed, championship, public course, $59 weekdays, $79 weekends, discounts are available for seniors and juniors.

Museums & Tours. **Antique Auto Museum,** Antique Automobile Club of America, 161 Museum Dr., Hershey; (717) 566-7100; www.aacamuseum.org. Vintage cars and trucks spanning almost a century of American transportation history. Don't miss the 1895 Chicago Motor Benton Harbor, two 1917 Pierce Arrows, and 1941 Valentine diner. Hours are 9 a.m. to 5 p.m. daily. Admission is $10 for adults, $9 for seniors and $7 for children.

Fort Hunter Mansion and Park, 5300 North Front St., Harrisburg; (717) 599-5751; www.forthunter.org. Restorations, exhibits, and demonstrations bring the 19th century to life at this plantation complex situated on 40 acres on the banks of the Susquehanna River. Mansion tours are available from May through Dec from Tues through Sat 10 a.m. to 4:30 p.m., Sun noon to 4:30 p.m. Admission is $5 adults, $4 seniors, and $3 students.

The Hershey Story, 111 West Chocolate Ave., Hershey; (717) 534-3439; www.hersheystory.org. The name says it all—interactive exhibits, mini-theaters, artifacts, and first-hand stories trace the history of the entrepreneur as well as the company, the town and the school that bear his name. Admission is $10 for adults, $9 for seniors, $7.50 for children. Open every day, hours vary by month. Stop in at Café Zooka for a Countries of Origin Chocolate Tasting ($9.95) and participate in a hands-on Chocolate Lab. Call for ticket prices.

Hershey's Chocolate World, 251 Park Blvd., Hershey; (717) 534-4900; www.hersheys.com. At this visitor center, you'll find all things chocolate from the free theme-park-ridelike "factory tour" (complete with singing cows); multimedia chocolate tasting adventure ($9.95 for adults, $9.45 for seniors, $7 for children); 3-D animated musical extravaganza ($6 for adults, $5.45 for seniors, $5 for children); Trolley Works (717-533-3000; www .hersheytrolleyworks.com), which offers a tour of the town on an old-fashioned trolley complete with singing conductor. Tickets are $13 for adults, $12 seniors, $6 for children. Open seven days a week year-round from 9 a.m. to 5 p.m. or until 9 p.m., depending on the time of year.

National Civil War Museum, One Lincoln Circle at Reservoir Park, Harrisburg; (717) 260-1861; www.nationalcivilwarmuseum .org. Multimedia exhibits, life-size tableaux, and more than 4,000 artifacts show the human side of war from the perspectives of a wide range of people from slaves to civilians to Northern and Southern soldiers. Hours are Mon, Tues, and Thurs through Sat 10 a.m. to 5 p.m., Wed until 8 p.m., Sun noon to 5 p.m. Call for winter hours. Prices are $9 for adults, $8 for seniors, $7 for students.

The State Museum of Pennsylvania, 300 North St., Harrisburg; (717) 787-4980; www.statemuseumpa.org. Four floors of exhibits, many interactive, tracing the state's history from prehistoric to modern times. For a broader perspective don't miss the multimedia planetarium. Open Tues through Sat 9 a.m. to 5 p.m., Sun noon to 5 p.m. Admission is $3 for adults, $2 for seniors and children.

Susquehanna Art Museum, 301 Market St., Harrisburg; (717) 233-8668; www.sqart.org. The Doshi Gallery focuses on the works of international and regional, established, and up-and-coming contemporary artists. Hours are Tues, Wed, Fri, and Sat 10 a.m. to 4 p.m.; Thurs until 8 p.m., Sun 1 to 4 p.m. Admission is $5 for adults, $3 for seniors, students, and children.

ZooAmerica–The Falconry Experience, 30 Park Ave., Hershey; (717) 534-3900; www.zooamerica.com. There's no feeling in the world that compares to having one of these magnificent birds fly to your arm. Admission includes a sixty-to-ninety-minute presentation and one-to-one interaction with these winged wonders. Admission is $85 for adults, $70 for children age 13+; sessions are offered at 9 a.m., 11:30 a.m., and 2 p.m. Wed through Sun from Memorial Day to Labor Day and on Sat and Sun in Apr, May, Sept, and Oct.

Music. **Sunoco Performance Theater at the Whitaker Center for Science and the Arts,** 222 Market St., Harrisburg; (717) 214-2787; www.whitakercenter.org. A major showcase for national headliners and professional regional talent from all genres of music and dance. Call for performance schedule and ticket prices.

Spas. **Felicita Spa,** Felicita Resort, 2201 Fishing Creek Valley Rd., Harrisburg; (717) 599-7615; www.felicitaresort.com. Signatures at this full-service spa include a remineralizing body polish and European rose mud treatments. Services range from $60 to $150.

Spectator Sports. **The Hershey Bears,** Giant Center, 950 West Hersheypark Dr., Hershey; (717) 534-3911; www.hersheybears.com. One of the nation's oldest continuously operating American Hockey League teams plays from Oct through mid-Apr. Tickets range from $16 to $22.

Special Events . . . .

JANUARY
Pennsylvania Farm Show, Farm Show Complex, Harrisburg; (717) 787-2905; www.farmshow.state.pa.us. Since 1851, this annual five-day showcase of farm animals, equipment, food, agricultural demonstrations, and hundreds of exhibits has been drawing visitors from all over the East Coast. Free.

FEBRUARY

Chocolate-Covered February, Hershey; www.hersheypa.com. A month filled with hundreds of chocolate-themed events, activities, meals, wine pairings, and demonstrations.

JULY

American MusicFest, City Island, Harrisburg; (717) 255-3020; www.harrisburgevents.com. Four days of international music, dance, food, and culture. July 4th weekend.

SEPTEMBER

Kipona Celebration, City Island, Harrisburg; (717) 255-3020. Fishing, karate, and soccer competitions; chili cook-off; Native American pow-wow; arts and crafts, live music, and amusement rides. Labor Day weekend.

OCTOBER

Pennsylvania National Horse Show, Farm Show Complex, Harrisburg; (717) 770-0222; www.panational.org. Over 1,000 horses and top international riders compete for prestigious titles and large cash awards.

MID-NOVEMBER TO LATE DECEMBER

Christmas in Hershey; www.hersheypa.com. Hersheypark Christmas Candylane, selected rides, entertainment, live reindeer, and a million twinkling lights. Admission is $11. Hershey Sweet Lights, 2-mile drive-through display featuring nearly 600 illuminated, animated displays. $20 per carload.

Other Recommended Restaurants and Lodgings . . . .

CARLISLE

Pheasant Field Bed & Breakfast, 150 Hickorytown Rd., Carlisle; (717) 258-0717; www.pheasantfield.com. Well worth the half-hour drive from downtown Harrisburg, this eight-guestroom (including one suite) charmer is situated in a historic brick farmhouse. Some rooms have whirlpool tubs. It is so pet friendly that it even offers overnight accommodations for your horse. $$–$$$.

HARRISBURG

Passage to India, Comfort Inn, 525 South Front St.; (717) 233-1611. Tandooris, vegetarian creations, and mango-lassi shakes. The ten-course lunch buffet is a real bargain. $. Lunch hours are noon to 2:30 p.m.; dinner is Mon through Sat 5 to 10 p.m., Sun until 9 p.m.

Raspberries, Hilton Harrisburg, 1 North Second St.; (717) 233-6000; www1.hilton.com. Casual Italian-accented bistro menus. $$. Open for breakfast Mon through Fri 6:30 to 11:30 a.m., Sat 7 a.m. to 1 p.m., Sun until 11 a.m.; lunch Mon through Fri 11:30 a.m. to 2 p.m.; brunch Sun 11 a.m. to 2 p.m.; dinner Mon through Sun 5 to 10 p.m.

Stocks on 2nd, 211 North Second St.; (717) 233-6699; www.stocksonsecond.com. Harrisburg's first martini bar serves up sophisticated fare such as the signature "Stockyard" grilled steak with gorgonzola bread pudding. Serving lunch Mon through Fri from 11:30 a.m., dinner every day from 6 p.m. Live music on weekends. $$–$$$.

HERSHEY

1825 Inn Bed & Breakfast, 319 South Lingle Ave., Palmyra; (717) 838-8282; www.1825inn.com. Charming inn guest rooms and suites in a peaceful residential area 8 miles east of downtown Hershey. $$–$$$.

Breads N' Cheese of Hershey, 243 West Chocolate Ave.; (717) 533-4546; www.breadsandcheese.com. This cozy European-style bakery and cafe serves great homemade soups, sandwiches, and pastries every day plus an Italian menu dinner on Wed. Take home some of the twenty-five styles of freshly baked breads, international cheeses, and pâtés. And did I mention pastries? Inexpensive. Hours are Tues 7:30 a.m. to 6 p.m., Wed and Fri until 8 p.m., Sat until 4 p.m.

Hershey Entertainment and Resorts Company Properties. Three full-service resort accommodations with distinctive personalities and multiple casual and upscale restaurants.

Hershey Lodge, 325 University Dr.; (717) 533-3311; www.hershey lodge.com. Contemporary cozy with a wide array of family-friendly activities.

Hotel Hershey, Hotel Road; (717) 533-2171. Exquisite Old World-style ambience. $$$.

Milton Motel, 1733 East Chocolate Ave.; (717) 533-4533. This clean, comfortable family-run operation has a heated pool and many other amenities. $$ for rooms, $$$ for suites.

New Woodside Cottages at the Hotel Hershey, part of the company's recent $67 million "Grand Expansion," provides flexible accommodation options in a private setting.

For More Information . . . .

Hershey Harrisburg Regional Visitors Bureau, 17 South Second St., Harrisburg, PA 17101; (717) 231-7788; www.hersheyharris burg.org.

Harrisburg, Hershey and Central Pennsylvania Welcome Center; www.visithhc.com.

Hershey Information; (800) HERSHEY (437-7439); www.hershey pa.com.

BETWEEN & BEYOND ESCAPE *Three*
Gettysburg, Pennsylvania
BEYOND THE BATTLEFIELD/1 NIGHT

War and Peace
Antique Capital
Gardens of Garlic
Elephants on Parade

It was a chance encounter that brought General Robert E. Lee's 75,000-man Army of Northern Virginia and General George Meade's 97,000-man Army of the Potomac together at Gettysburg for three days of pitched battle that would decimate both forces and prove to be the turning point of the Civil War. Since then, the town has dedicated its efforts to preventing those events and the people they affected from being relegated to dusty history books.

But, a century-and-a-half after the battle, **Gettysburg** is a also a place of peace, surrounded by the quiet Adams County countryside with its mile upon mile of farms and orchards. Adams County is the number one apple-producing area in the state and number five in the country. Whatever your interests, you'll find everything from more than 200 antique dealers, fifteen golf courses, visual and performing arts, flaming foliage, old-fashioned agricultural festivals, miniature horses, and even a few lions, tigers, cougars, and coatimundis. Historic hideaways on the outskirts of town offer cozy accommodations and cuisine that runs the gamut from homespun to haute. You might even come to view the battlefield itself from a new perspective.

Peak tourist months for Gettysburg are Apr through Oct; it is quietest in Jan and Feb. Locals suggest coming in Nov, when most sites are open and a number of special annual events take place.

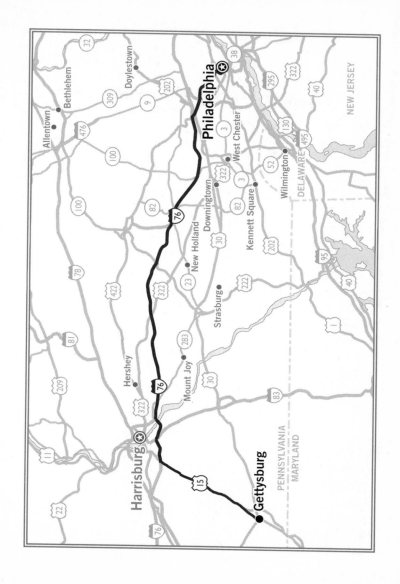

DAY 1/MORNING

It takes about two-and-three-quarter hours to get to Gettysburg from Philadelphia. The quickest way is to take the Schuylkill Expressway (I-76) 22 miles west to the King of Prussia entrance to the Penn-sylvania Turnpike. Travel west on the turnpike for about 92 miles to exit 236 (Gettysburg/US 15); go south on US 15 until you come to US 30 west. Take US 30 west for about 2 miles into Gettysburg.

BREAKFAST   **Avenue Restaurant,** 21 Steinwehr Ave., Gettysburg; (717) 334-3235; www.avenuerestaurant.net. Yes, they serve the expected egg dishes, but go for the yummy sweet potato pancakes with brown sugar sour cream topping at this half-century-old local landmark. $. Lunch and dinner, $–$$.

If you think you've already seen **Gettysburg National Military Park,** I suggest that you look again, this time as a miles-long magnificent and meaningful outdoor sculpture gallery. Hire a **Licensed Battle-field Guide** ($50 for two hours in your own car; 717-337-1709; www.gettysburgtourguides.org) to take you to the bronze statue of Major General John Sedgwick on his horse, Handsome Joe, one of the nation's most finely detailed and studied examples of equestrian art. There's also the North Carolina Monument (one of the few representing the South), featuring the work of Gutzon Borglum, best known as the man behind Mount Rushmore. You can also construct your own art tour with the help of the book, *Gettysburg: Stories of Men and Monuments*, published by the Association of Licensed Battlefield Guides, and available at the **Gettysburg National Military Park Visitor Center** (241 Steinwehr Ave., Gettysburg; 717-337-1709; www.gettysburgtourguides.org). Battlefield hours are Apr to Oct 6 a.m. to 10 p.m. Nov to Mar until 7 p.m. Call for winter hours.

But first, stop in **The Museum and Visitor Center at Gettysburg National Military Park** to experience one of the most impressive works of art anywhere. After a massive five-year conservation effort, **The Cyclorama,** a 360-degree, 377-foot-around, 42-foot-high painting in the round that creates a 3-D effect to give you the illusion that you are in the thick of Pickett's Charge. First unveiled in 1884, this is one of the last remaining artworks of its kind left in the world. Open Nov to Mar 8 a.m. to 5 p.m., Apr to Oct until 6 p.m. Purchase tickets ($10.50 for adults, $9.50 for seniors and active military, $6.50 for youths) online at www.gettysburgfoundation.org and save $1 per ticket. Your ticket also entitles you to view the film *A Birth of Freedom* and the museum's twelve exhibit galleries.

If want to plan an entire battle-focused getaway, I have listed a number of other sites to visit and activities to do in the "There's More" part of this chapter. But I also want to emphasize the other attractions that make Gettysburg a place to get away just for the fun of it.

AFTERNOON

LUNCH **Gettysburg Eddie's,** 217 Steinwehr Ave., Gettysburg; (717) 334-1100; www.gettysburgeddies.com. More than a fun little burger and sandwich eatery, it's also a tribute to a native son who earned a place in the Baseball Hall of Fame in 1946 for being the National League's first lefty lobber to win 300 games. Try the signature Eddie's House Hero or interesting salmon BLT. $. Open for dinner, too. $–$$. Open 11 a.m. to 10 p.m.

Antique seekers will find an abundance of early Americana in **New Oxford** (717-624-7787; www.newoxfordantiques.com), a tiny community located about 9 miles east of Gettysburg on US 30. Brick sidewalks, landscaped streets, and well-persevered 18th- and 19th-century homes provide the perfect setting for more than 500 dealers offering everything from furniture to folk art and textiles to toys.

Two of the largest multi-dealer complexes are **New Oxford Antique Center** (333 Lincolnway West, New Oxford; 717-624-7787; www .newoxfordantiquecenter.com) and **Golden Lane Antique Gallery** (11 North Water St., New Oxford; 717-624-3800). Each has seventy dealers and both are open daily 10 a.m. to 5 p.m.

One of the most highly regarded golf courses in the area is the challenging, European-style **Links at Gettysburg** (601 Mason Dixon Rd., Gettysburg; 717-359-8000; www.thelinksatgettysburg .com) with its fast sloping greens, multiple water hazards, and red-rock canyons and formations. In-season (Apr to Oct) rates are $58 weekdays, $90 weekends.

If the kids are along, you might opt for a visit to **Land of Little Horses** (125 Glenwood Dr., Gettysburg; 717-335-7259; www .landoflittlehorses.com). Animal lovers will be enchanted by these eensy-weensie equines and their furred and feathered friends. Find more than one hundred miniature horses and other fuzzy and furry friends as they play, perform, and nuzzle up for some petting. Hand-on activities include goat-milking and horse grooming and bathing. Call for off-season hours. Admission is $13.50 for adults, $12 for kids. Call or check the Web site for seasonal days, hours, and activity schedules.

EVENING

DINNER **Fairfield Inn,** 15 West Main St., 8 miles west of Gettysburg on PA 116, Fairfield; (717) 642-5410; www.thefairfieldinn.com. A local landmark for more than 250 years, the oldest inn in Gettysburg and one of America's oldest continuously operated inn has hosted many famous guests including Patrick Henry, Robert E. Lee, and the Eisenhowers. Its **Mansion House Restaurant** has long been lauded for its chicken n' biscuits and Lord Baltimore's rack of lamb. $$–$$$. Indoor fireplace and outdoor patio seating are available in season. Lunch ($) and three-course prix-fixe Sunday brunch ($$) are available. The restaurant is open seven days for overnight guests; to the public Tues to Sat 5 to 9 p.m., Sun 3 to 8 p.m. for dinner; Fri and Sat 11 a.m. to 4 p.m. for lunch, and Sun 11 a.m. to 3 p.m. for brunch. On Tues through Sat evenings at 7 p.m. and Sun at noon, you can even get a show with your dinner as illusionist and storyteller "Professor Kerrigan" gives period-inspired performances including magic, ghost stories, and a high-spirited séance. Price with dinner is $40 for adults, $20 for children.

LODGING **The Fairfield Inn.** Owners Joan and Sal Chandon have restored its six rooms and suites to their pre-Civil War elegance, uncovering early architectural accents and adding their own antique furnishings. Continental breakfast is included. $$–$$$.

DAY 2/MORNING

BREAKFAST The Fairfield Inn.

It's only a little more than a mile west on West Main Street/PA 116, then a left onto Jacks Mountain Road and right onto Zoo Road to get to the **East Coast Exotic Animal Rescue** (320 Zoo Rd., Fairfield; 717-642-5229; www.eastcoastrescue.org), an 85-acre sanctuary for large and small refugees from unsuitable homes, zoos, and research labs. Current residents include lions, tigers, cougars, coatimundis, monkeys, parrots, and alligators. This nonprofit refuge is no petting zoo, but it is a powerful educational experience. Admission is $7 for adults, $5 for children. Hours are May to Oct, Sat and Sun 10 a.m. to 6 p.m.

Treat your senses to a visit to **Willow Pond Farm Herbs and Everlastings** (145 Tract Rd., Fairfield; 717-642-6387; www.willow pondherbs.com), a family-owned, organic certified oasis of fragrant and flavorful flora, including two acres planted with one hundred species of its namesake herb, as well as edible and decorative products that showcase them. Check out the lavender-filled "dream pillows" and silver lockets. You can also just enjoy a beautiful spring or summer day wandering through the farm's five-acre wildflower meadow or butterfly garden. Apr 1 to Christmas, Thurs to Sat, 9 a.m. to 5 p.m.; mid-Apr to mid-June and Nov to Dec., Sun noon to 5 p.m.

AFTERNOON

LUNCH **Dunlap's Restaurant and Bakery,** 90 Buford Ave., Gettysburg; (717) 334-4816; www.dunlapsrestaurant.com.You could make an entire meal from the deep-fried pickles, corn chip pie with chili, and signature cream of crab soup. But if you're in the mood for something a little less exotic, you'll also find plenty of burgers, wraps, melts, and clubs. Open for breakfast and dinner. $. Hours are Sun 6:30 a.m. to 8 p.m., Fri and Sat until 9 p.m.

Downtown Gettysburg has some unique little shops including **Abraham's Lady** (25 Steinwehr Ave., Gettysburg; 717-338-1798; www.abrahamslady.com), where you can outfit yourself from head to toe, corset to cape, bonnets to buttons in historically correct Civil War-era garb. Call for seasonal hours. The works of local women artisans are on display at the **Spirited Ladies Shoppe** (45 Chambersburg St., Gettysburg; 717-688-0588; www.thespiritedladies.blogspot.com). Look for handcrafted items such as painted chairs; hand-sewn, knitted, and embroidered clothing and decorative items; jewelry; and greeting cards. Tues to Sat 10 a.m. to 8 p.m., Sun 11 a.m. to 4 p.m., Mon 10 a.m. to 1 p.m. At Gettysburg's artist-in-residence, **Dale Gallon's** eponymous gallery (9 Steinwehr Ave., Gettysburg; 717-334-8666; www.gallon.com), you'll find this world-renowned painter's prints depicting the Civil War and other historical periods. Hours are Mon to Thurs 10 a.m. to 5 p.m., Sun noon to 4 p.m.

Three wineries have sprung up in the Gettysburg area and three are located in the tiny town of Orrtanna. It's close to 11 miles west of Gettysburg, close to ten of which are along US 30. Turn right onto Orrtanna Road, drive 1 mile then turn right onto Scott School Road then right again onto Peach Tree Road. On your left you will see **Adams County Winery** (251 Peach Tree Rd., Orrtanna; 717-334-4631; www.adamscountywinery.com). Best-sellers include Tears of Gettysburg, a Niagara white blend, and Rebel Red, a semi-sweet Concord and Niagara blend. Hours are 10 a.m. to 6 p.m. daily. **Reid's Orchard & Winery** (2135 Buchanan Valley Rd., PA 234, Orrtanna; www.reidsorchardwinery.com) produces a wide variety of reds, whites, and blends from European varietals and native American grapes, as well as easy-drinking fruit wines including a refreshing hard cider. Tasting room hours are Thurs and Fri noon to 5 p.m., Sat 11 a.m. to 6 p.m., Sun noon to 5 p.m.

Elephants in Orrtanna? You'll see more than 6,000 of them in all shapes and sizes (an elephant potty seat?) at **Mister Ed's Elephant Museum** (6019 Chambersburg Rd., US 30, Orrtanna; 717-352-3792; www.mistereds.com), one of the largest collections in the world. Kids will be delighted by the life-size water-spewing Commander Robert Eli and the adorably animated Miss Ellie Phant. If you develop a sudden craving for peanuts, try the ones prepared in Ed's antique roasters. Admission is free; hours are every day from 10 a.m. to 5 p.m.

EVENING

DINNER Historic Cashtown Inn, 1325 Old Route 30; (717) 334-9722; www.cashtowninn.com. To get there follow US 30 east for a little less than 5 miles.

Commandeered by Confederate General A. P. Hill as his headquarters during the battle, this 1749 inn now serves such specialties as orange- and maple-crusted duck and panko-crusted crab cakes. $$–$$$. Lunch is served Tues to Sat 11:30 a.m. to 2 p.m., dinner beginning at 5 p.m. Stay the night if you dare ($$–$$$)—the bar isn't the only place where spirits have been sighted.

Spend the evening taking in a live theatrical, musical, or dance performance or independent, classic, or foreign film in the splendid surroundings of downtown **Gettysburg's Majestic Theater** (25 Carlisle St., Gettysburg; 717-337-8200; www.gettysburgmajestic .org). Following a recent $16.5 million restoration, this 1925 colonial revival-style vaudeville and movie house with its pressed tin ceilings, hand-stenciled walls, plush seats, grand staircase, and stained glass chandeliers has regained its stellar style and standing as a cultural hotspot. Call for performance schedules and ticket prices.

LODGING	The Fairfield Inn.

DAY 3/MORNING

BREAKFAST	The Fairfield Inn.

Head to the **Gettysburg National Military Park Visitor Center**, approximately 1 mile south of town on Taneytown Road (SR 134) and Steinwehr Avenue (US 15 business route) to catch the shuttle to the **Eisenhower National Historic Site** (717-338-9114 ext. 10; www.nps.gov/eise), where, during his two terms as president, Dwight D. Eisenhower and wife, Mamie, came for weekend retreats and where they retired. Furnishings and personal belongings offer insight into the lives of this renowned couple. Call for seasonal hours.

Built in 1914, **The Round Barn,** located just 8 miles west of downtown Gettysburg right off of US 30 (298 Cashtown Rd., Biglerville; 717-334-1984; www.roundbarngettysburg.com) is one of the last remaining structures of its kind and remains a thriving market selling fruits and veggies grown on its own and neighboring farms. Hours are late Apr to Oct 9 a.m. to 5 p.m. daily, early Nov to mid-Dec Fri and Sat. If you would prefer to pick your own, head for the family-owned **Hollabaugh Brothers, Inc. Farm & Fruit Market** (545 Carlisle Rd., Biglerville; 717-677-9494; www.holla baughbros.com).

AFTERNOON

LUNCH The Inn at Herr Ridge, 900 Chambersburg Rd., Gettysburg; (717) 334-4332; www.innatherrridge.com. Best known for its cream of crab with corn soup and pastrami Reuben (get the soup and sandwich combo so you can have both). $. Also open for dinner ($$$) and offers upscale overnight accommodations ($$–$$$).

Save room because you're going to another tasting, but it's not wine this time—it's garlic. At **Hacienda Shiloh Herb Farm** (327 Knox Rd., Gettysburg; 717-642-9161), Marda Mattox grows twenty-five varieties of garlic, ranging from mild Mediterranean to "volcanic" Bavarian, from around the globe. Although it has a Gettysburg address, the farm is actually located about 5 miles south of downtown. To get there, drive northwest on US 30 toward Herr's Ridge Road for about 1 mile, then turn left onto Knoxlyn Road and continue for 2½ miles before you turn right onto Knoxlyn Orrtanna Road. In one-half mile, turn left onto Knox Road and in about a mile, you'll see it on the right. Aside from the brazen, breathtaking bulbs, you'll find those hard-to-find herbs (fenugreek, epazote) you've been seeking along with more than 200 custom-blended teas, peppercorn blends, and spiced-up salts. Call for seasonal hours.

Pop a breath mint and hit the road for the two-and-one-half-hour drive back home to Philadelphia. Begin by going east on Knox Road to Carr Hill Road, then, after about a mile-and-a-half, turn left onto Fairfield Road/PA 116. Continue 6 miles before you make a slight left onto York St./US 30/Lincoln Highway and follow for 2 miles. Merge onto US 15 north toward Harrisburg and stay on for about 30 miles. Merge onto I-76 east/PA Turnpike toward Philadelphia exits 242–359 and drive for 91 miles, then merge onto I-76 via exit 326 toward US 202/I-476/Philadelphia/Valley Forge. After 18 miles, keep left to take the Vine St. Expy/I-676 E/US 30 east via exit 344 toward Central Philadelphia.

There's More . . . .

Biking Tours. Gettysbike, 241 Steinwehr Ave., Gettysburg; (717) 752-7752; www.gettysbike.com. Three-hour guided bicycle tours with licensed battlefield guides. $61 for adults, $30 for children.

Camping. Artillery Ridge Camping Resort, 610 Taneytown Rd., Gettysburg; (717) 334-1288; www.artilleryridge.com. Tent and RV accommodations with hookups, free 24-hour hot showers, laundry room. Base rate for tents $34 for family of four, with water and electric $42, log cabins $60–$83.

Horse Riding Tours. Battlefield Horseback Tour, National Riding Stable, Artillery Ridge Camping Resort, 610 Taneytown Rd., Gettysburg; (717) 334-1288; www.artilleryridge.com. Two- and four-hour guided horseback battlefield tours. $40–$70 per person.

Museums & Tours. **The David Wills House,** 8 Lincoln Sq., Gettysburg; (717) 334-2499; www.davidwillshouse.org. Five museum galleries and two recreated rooms, including the one where Lincoln revised his famous address, depict the town's post-war period. Admission is $6.50 for children, $5.50 for seniors, $4 for children. Call for seasonal hours.

General Lee's Headquarters and Museum, 401 Buford Ave., Gettysburg; (717) 334-3141; www.civilwarheadquarters.com. Seminary Ridge home where General Robert E. Lee made his battle plans, and Confederate and Union military and medical equipment and artifacts are on display. Open mid-Mar through mid-Nov, daily 9 a.m. to 5 p.m.; extended summer hours. Admission is $3 for adults, $1 for children.

Gettysburg National Cemetery, 97 Taneytown Rd., adjacent to the National Park Service Information Center; (717) 334-1124. Here rest nearly 7,000 of Gettysburg's esteemed dead spanning two centuries, the Civil War and subsequent wars. Open dawn to dusk.

Hall of Presidents and First Ladies, 789 Baltimore St., Gettysburg; (717) 334-5717; www.gettysburgbattlefieldtours.com. Wax figures of all the American presidents, beginning with George Washington, tell, in their own words, the nation's story. Also see America's First Ladies, dressed in reproductions of their inaugural gowns. Open spring and fall daily 9 a.m. to 5 p.m., summer until 7 p.m. $7 for adults, $3.50 for children.

Lincoln Train Museum, 425 Steinwehr Ave., Gettysburg; (717) 334-5678; www.gettysburgbattlefieldtours.com. Collection of more than 1,000 toy trains from the 1800s to present. Take a simulated ride to Gettysburg with Abe Lincoln. Open daily spring and fall 9 a.m. to 5 p.m., until 7 p.m. in summer. Admission is $7 for adults, $3.50 for children.

Shriver House, 309 Baltimore St., Gettysburg; (717) 337-2800; www.shriverhouse.org. Restored and authentically furnished family home that was occupied by Confederate sharpshooters. Open Apr to mid-Nov 10 a.m. to 5 p.m., Sun noon to 5 p.m.; Dec Sat 10 a.m. to 5 p.m., Mar Sat 10 a.m. to 5 p.m., Sun until 2 p.m. Admission $7.50 for adults, $7 for seniors, $5 for children.

Soldiers National Museum, 777 Baltimore St., Gettysburg; (717) 334-4890; www.gettysburgbattlefieldtours.com. Miniature dioramas of ten major Civil War battles, life-size narrated Confederate encampment, artifacts, and memorabilia. Open spring and fall daily 9 a.m. to 5 p.m., summer until 7 p.m. $7 for adults, $3.50 for children.

***Shops.* Gettysburg Village Factory Stores,** 1863 Gettysburg Village Dr., Gettysburg; (717) 337-9705. Bargain shopping meets entertainment at this seventy-plus name brand store complex modeled after a 19th-century "Main Street." Call for seasonal hours.

Special Events . . . .

(Unless otherwise indicated, the contact telephone number for the following events is 800-337-5015.)

MAY AND AUGUST
Annual Gettysburg Spring and Summer Bluegrass Festivals, Granite Hill Campground, 6 miles west of Gettysburg on PA 116; (717) 642-8749. Nonstop music from some of the country's best bluegrass music performers in a beautiful country setting.

MAY

Annual Gettysburg Outdoor Antique Show, downtown Gettysburg. More than 175 dealers from thirteen states line the downtown streets.

Annual Memorial Day Parade and Ceremonies. One of the oldest (more than 130 years) Memorial Day observances in the United States with a parade and ceremony in Gettysburg National Cemetery.

JULY

Battle Reenactments, call for specific locations; (717) 338-1525. Encampments and battles, period music, and domestic arts demos.

Other Recommended Restaurants and Lodgings . . . .

GETTYSBURG

Dobbin House Tavern, 89 Steinwehr Ave.; (717) 334-2100; www .dobbinhouse.com. Authentically decorated and outfitted 1776 former private home/Civil War hospital serving hearty helpings of classic American fare. $$–$$$. Tavern and deli lunches and dinner, too ($–$$).

Historic Farnsworth House Restaurant & Inn, 401 Baltimore St.; (717) 334-8838; www.farnsworthhouseinn.com. Authentically restored ca. 1810 dining room with photos by Mathew Brady specializing in period fare such as game pie, peanut soup, and spoon bread. $$. Overnight accommodations (some haunted) are also available. $$.

Inns of the Gettysburg Area; (800) 587-2216 or (717) 624-1300. This bed-and-breakfast association is composed of twenty of the area's historic accommodations, all located within minutes of the battlefield. You tell them your specifications, they'll offer a variety of choices and let you know which ones are available on the dates you specify.

James Gettys Hotel, 27 Chambersburg St.; (717) 337-1334. This restored two-century-old hotel offers eleven amenity-filled suites. $$.

For More Information . . . .

Gettysburg Convention and Visitors Bureau, 8 Lincoln Sq. (inside The David Will's House), Gettysburg, PA 17325; (717) 334-2499; www.gettysburg.travel.

Gettysburg National Military Park, 1195 Baltimore Pike, Suite 100, Gettysburg, PA 17325; (717) 334-1124; www.nps.gov/gett.

Gettysburg.com, 89 Steinwehr Ave., Gettysburg, PA 17325; (717) 334-2100.

BETWEEN & BEYOND ESCAPE *Four*
Washington, D.C.
FROM FREE TO SHINING FREE/2 NIGHTS

You might not normally think of Washington, D.C., as a free-and-easy kind of town. But it can be if you know where to look—and how to get around.

Monumental Decisions
Island Picnic
Boating the City
Night Lights

Free—as in no charge—is the admission price for visiting a wide range of Washington's top attractions, including the National Zoo, Air and Space Museum, National Gallery of Art, U.S. Holocaust Memorial Museum, and a slew of Smithsonians. Now that doesn't mean you can leave the credit cards at home. D.C.'s outstanding hospitality of the food-and-lodging variety is far from free. But with all of the money you save on attractions, you can afford a little luxury without breaking your budget.

DAY 1/MORNING

Washington, D.C., is a little over 140 miles south of Philadelphia. That should take about 2¾ hours, but you will be driving on the outskirts of several heavily trafficked cities, so expect to be on the road about three hours. Take I-95 south about 110 miles, then merge onto MD 295 south via exit 52 toward BWI Airport. Follow 295 for 30 miles, then merge onto US 50 W/NY Ave. NE toward Washington and continue for about 5 miles to downtown D.C. Once in the city, a good focal point is the National Mall.

HELPFUL HINTS: As in many other major downtown areas, parking in D.C. can be a pain in the neck. To save yourself time,

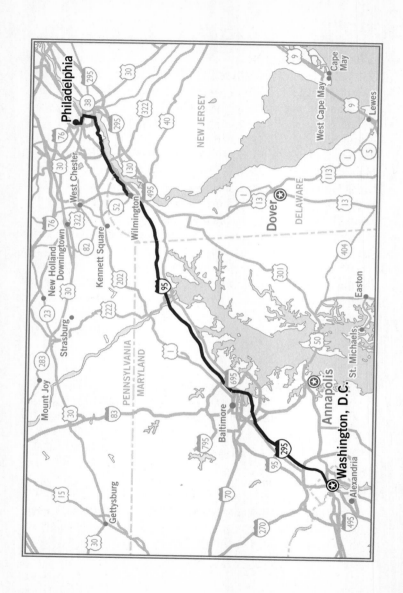

aggravation, and more than a few bucks, use the **Metro Rail, Metro Bus,** and **D.C. Circular** as your main means of transportation. You can find schedules and prices on the Web at www.wmata.com and www.dccirculator.com. They are all convenient, clean, safe, and save you the aggravation of trying to figure out if—and when—streets are one-way and wasting gas or fuming in your car as you crawl along during peak traffic times. The Metro operates Mon to Fri 5 a.m. to midnight, Fri until 3 a.m., Sat 7 a.m. to 3 a.m., Sun to midnight. For the best deal, purchase a one-day ticket for under $8 and ride as many times as you'd like after 9:30 a.m. weekdays and all day weekends. The Circulator costs $1 per trip (transfers are free) and has numerous interconnecting routes to main attractions. Public transportation maps are available at all stops and other locations throughout the town.

If you insist on driving, keep in mind that radiating out from the Capitol are four quadrant designations. The divider streets are North Capitol, South Capitol, East Capitol Streets, and the National Mall. Numbered streets run north-south, with addresses getting higher the farther away you go from the Capitol; east-west streets are named for letters in alphabetical order.

Now for your parking options:

- Free parking: Now don't get too excited. While there are some free spaces on the National Mall along Madison and Jefferson Drives in front of the Smithsonians, they fill quickly so you can't count on finding an open one. If you do find one, your time is usually limited to two hours and parking is restricted during morning and evening rush times.

- Paid parking lots: **Center City Lot,** 900 Ninth St., NW, Corner of Ninth and New York Avenue; maximum price $20 weekdays, $5 weekends; open Sun to Thurs 6 a.m. to midnight, Fri and Sat until 2 a.m. **Union Station,** 50 Massachusetts Ave.

NE; maximum $16; open 24/7. **Ronald Reagan Building and International Trade Center,** 1300 Pennsylvania Ave. NW; $22 maximum; open 5 a.m. to 2 a.m.

AFTERNOON

LUNCH The Eastern Market, 225 Seventh St., SE, Washington, D.C.; (202) 698-5253; www.easternmarketdc.com. Completed in 1873, the market is a popular shopping spot for the Capitol Hill community. It's also a great place to grab some lunch (or breakfast if you get there early enough) and do a little browsing. In the market's South Hall you'll find the legendary **Market Lunch** with its heavenly "blue-buck" (blueberry buckwheat) pancakes (only for breakfast) and crab cake sandwiches. $. **Canales Delicatessen**—the lines are long and the service some-times snarky, so you might opt for a rosemary prosciutto sub or panini, $. For dessert go to **Fine Sweet Shop** for a yummy cupcake, or fruit from **Calomiris** produce. South Hall hours are Tues to Fri 7 a.m. to 7 p.m., Sat until 6 p.m., Sun 7 a.m. to 5 p.m. On Sat and Sun only there's a giant outdoor flea market and arts and crafts market (both 9 a.m. to 6 p.m.) and a produce-packed farmers market (7 a.m. to 4 p.m.). The weekend is also the only time to go to **Crepes at the Market,** where you can build-your-own sweet or savory creation. Many of the vendors in the market accept cash only.

Although the big-draw **Smithsonian Museums** (the **National Air and Space Museum** (www.nasm.si.edu) is the number one most visited museum in America) can never be considered been-there-done-that sites, you might want to visit one or two of them. I know the government buildings, monuments, and major Smithsonian museums are the biggest draws in D.C., so, for the sake of this chapter, I'm going to assume you are already familiar with them and make some suggestions for some other, perhaps lesser-known, ones that might not be top-of-mind. To explore all of your options, start at the aptly named ca.-1855 **Castle** (1000 Jefferson Dr. SW, 202-633-1000; www.si.edu; hours: 8:30 a.m. to 5:30 p.m.), the official visitor center for the Smithsonian, to find out about your options and pick up brochures and maps. At the same time, ask about any Smithsonian After Five evening activities that may be scheduled during your visit or you can find them on the www.si.edu Web site.

Choosing from among the nineteen Smithsonian Museums and Galleries, ten of which are located on the National Mall within a 1-mile span from Third to Fourteenth Streets between Constitution Avenue and Independence Avenue, is almost as difficult as finding a place to park in D.C. All, including the **National Zoo** (http://nationalzoo.si.edu) are free and open every day of the year except Christmas. Among my favorite Smithsonian museums on the National Mall are the **Freer Gallery of Art** (Jefferson Drive at Twelfth Street, SW; www.asia.si.edu) and **Arthur M. Sackler Gallery** (1050 Independence Ave., SW; www.asia.si.edu). Connected by an underground exhibition space, the museums focus on Near and Far Eastern art and culture. The **National Museum of African Art** (950 Independence Ave., SW; http://africa.si.edu) features African visual arts. The **National Museum of the American Indian** (Fourth Street & Independence Avenue, SW; www.nmai.si.edu), exhibits art and artifacts exploring the lives of American Indians across the country and from archeological digs in South America and Mexico. All the museums are open from 10 a.m. to 5:30 p.m. Don't miss the museums' stores for items you won't find anywhere else.

For an overview of the offerings, begin at the information Center (called the **Castle**) at 1000 Jefferson Dr., SW; (202) 633-1000; www.si.edu.

AFTERNOON

LUNCH   **Art and Soul DC**, 415 New Jersey Ave., NW, Washington, D.C.; (202) 393-7777; www.artandsouldc.com. Located nearby in Capitol Hill, celebrated chef Art Smith lends his own touch to Southern style cooking. Try the picnic basket hoecake with pulled pork, baked beans, and the trimmings; the Chesapeake Bay Fry; or the Maryland fried chicken and buttermilk mashed potatoes. $$. Open for breakfast Mon to Fri 6:30 to 10:30 a.m. Sat and Sun 7:30 to 10:30 a.m.; lunch 11:30 a.m. to 2:30 p.m.; dinner 5:30 to 10:30 p.m. Mon to Thurs and Sun, to 11 p.m. Fri and Sat. brunch is served Sat and Sun.

Get a rental at **Tidal Basin Pedal Boats** (1501 Maine Ave., NW; 202-479-2426; www.tidalbasinpaddleboats.com) and have some fun floating in the shadow of the Thomas Jefferson Memorial. Pedal boats are available mid-Mar to Labor Day 10 a.m. to 6 p.m. seven days a week; after Labor Day to Columbus Day Weekend Wed to Sun. Rental rates are $10 for a two-person boat, $18 for a four-person one. Columbia Road, NW, between Sixteenth and Eighteenth Streets.

If monuments could talk . . . of course, they can't, but the wise and witty licensed guides of the free **D.C. By Foot** tours (1740 Eighteenth Street, NW, Suite 304; Washington, D.C.; 202-370-1830; www.dcbyfoot.com) are happy to tell you the inside scoop, offer anecdotes that bring history to life, share entertaining tidbits and inside secrets, and conduct good-natured trivia contests as they lead you on a 1-mile walk through the National Mall and visit key monuments. Free tours of Arlington National Cemetery and fee-based excursions exploring the various aspects of the Abraham Lincoln assassination ($10) and the Ghosts of Georgetown ($12) are available. Call or check the Web site for tour schedules and meeting places. (*NOTE:* Be sure to tip generously—these guides deserve it.)

EVENING

Catch the Metro to **Adams Morgan** (www.culturaltourismdc.org), a neighborhood filled with international sights, sounds, and flavors resulting from the combination of African, Asian, and Central American cultures. Located where Eighteenth Street and Columbia Road meet, 2 miles from the White House, Adams Morgan is a feast for the eyes with colorful wall murals, Victorian town houses, luxurious Sixteenth Street embassies, and boutique shops selling everything from garb made in Ghana to silver accessories from Peru.

DINNER The Grill from Ipanema, 1858 Columbia Rd. NW, Washington, D.C.; (202) 986-0757; www.thegrillfromipanema.com. If the name doesn't make your taste buds start to samba, the Brazilian menu surely will. If you're up to it, sample the native, kick-you-in-the-butt sugarcane liquor called cachaça or have it in a lime and sugar mellowed caipirinha. If you don't want alcohol, get a Guarana, a soft drink made with berries from the Amazon. A must-try is the feijoada, the national dish of Brazil, which is a rich stew of black beans and a quartet of meats. $$. Open Mon to Thurs 4:30 to 11 p.m., Fri until midnight, Sat and Sun noon to midnight. Sat and Sun three-course, champagne Brazilian brunch is $19, noon to 4 p.m.

Any Fri or Sat evening, you can enjoy the wry topical insights of a group of former congressional staffers-cum-musicians/political-satirists called the **Capitol Steps** in the Amphitheater of the **Ronald Reagan Building and International Trade Center** (1300 Pennsylvania Ave., Washington, D.C.; 202-312-1555; www.capsteps.com). Performances Fri and Sat at 7:30 p.m. year-round. Tickets are $35 and can be purchased in advance through Ticketmaster.

LODGING D.C. Guesthouse, 1337 Tenth St., NW, Washington, D.C.; (202) 332-2502; www.dcguesthouse.com. The four owners' extensive and eclectic personal art collection, which spans continents, cultures, and centuries, should be recognized as a D.C. attraction all by itself. Each of the seven guest rooms in this double Federal-style town house is decorated with the same artistic sense and attention to detail. But there's nothing museumlike about the ambience. The owners have created a warm and welcoming getaway spot; sipping wine in the common room is sheer heaven. Full breakfast in the elegant dining room included. Another bonus is the off-street parking; you can leave your car and catch the Metro only 2 blocks away. $$$.

DAY 2/MORNING

| BREAKFAST | D.C. Guesthouse. |

Head to Georgetown for a guided tour of the ca.-1765 **Old Stone House** (3051 M St., NW, Washington, D.C.; 202-426-6851; www .nps.gov/olst), the oldest standing building in D.C., which is furnished as it might have been in the late 1700s. Be sure to check out the beautiful English-style garden. Open Wed to Sun noon to 5 p.m. Admission is free.

Right next door is **Rock Creek Park,** where you can rent a canoe or kayak at **Thompson Boat Center,** (2900 Virginia Ave. NW, Washington, D.C.; 202-333-9543; www.thompsonboatcenter.com). This is the best (and one of the only) means of transportation for getting to **Theodore Roosevelt Island,** a beautiful 88-acre wilderness preserve in the Potomac between Georgetown and Virginia dedicated to one of America's most ardent environmentalists. Wandering the 2 miles of footpaths, you may very well find yourself alone (except for the 17-foot bronze statue of our 26th president) to commune at will with the abundant trees, wildflowers, and wildlife. Canoes are $8 per hour/$22 per day, single sit-in kayaks are $8 per hour/$24 per day. Thompson also rents double kayaks by the hour or day, Sunfish sailboats by the hour only, and bicycles. Call for seasonal hours.

BEFORE LUNCH   **TJ's Deli,** 1025 Thomas Jefferson St., NW, Suite 135 (it's in an office building), Washington, D.C.; (202) 333-3370. Picnicking is permitted at Theodore Roosevelt Island if you don't mind eating on a bench or bringing along a blanket to spread out on the grass. Before you take out the boat, pick up lunch to go at TJ's Deli, renowned for its gigantic deli sandwiches. $. Also stop in at **Baked and Wired** (1052 Thomas Jefferson St., NW, between 30 and 31 Streets and K and M Streets, Washington, D.C.; (202-333-2500; http://bakedandwired.com) for some cookies, brownies or other portable dessert. $.

When you return from the island, stay in Georgetown to take a tour of the architecturally intriguing, yellow stucco, **Tudor Place** (1644 Thirty-first St., NW, 2 blocks east of Wisconsin Avenue between Q and R Streets, Washington, D.C.; 202-965-0400; www.tudorplace .org), built in 1816 for George Washington's granddaughter, Martha Custis, and her husband Thomas Peter, son of Georgetown's first mayor. Inside, you'll see many personal furnishings and possessions, including an impressive porcelain collection, as well as artifacts from George and Martha. Admission is $8 for adults, $6 for seniors, $3 for children and students—reservations are suggested. Call for seasonal hours. The fee includes a self-guided tour of the lovely English-style garden (garden tour alone is $3) with its heirloom roses and Japanese tea house.

Catch the Metro to DuPont Circle to see more than twenty abandoned fire and police call boxes that have been transformed by local painters into traditional and contemporary works of art, **Art on Call** (202-661-7581). Art on Call is a city-wide effort led by Cultural Tourism D.C. to restore Washington D.C.'s abandoned police and fire call boxes as neighborhood artistic icons. The reinvented call boxes range in style from the traditional to the avant-garde. Police and fire call boxes were installed throughout the capital starting in the 1860s. They began to become obsolete with the introduction of the 911 emergency call system in the 1970s, and the working electronic components were all removed by 1995. Yet the call boxes remained, too large and heavy to remove and subject to deterioration from weather and vandalism. *NOTE:* There are more in Capitol Hill.

Also in the DuPont neighborhood is the **Phillips Collection** (1600 Twenty-first St., NW, Washington, D.C.; 202-387-2151; ww.phillipscollection.org), housed in a former home and adjacent buildings, this almost-hidden gem has a permanent collection that includes nearly 3,000 works by American and European artists including Degas, Cézanne, Van Gogh, Picasso, O'Keeffee, Renoir (luncheon of the boating party is here), Matisse, Rothko, and more. Hours are Tues to Sat 10 a.m. to 5 p.m., Sun 11 a.m. to 6 p.m. Fifteen-minute spotlight tours are offered Tues to Fri at noon; full introduction tours every Sat at noon. The museum also hosts Sun concerts at 4 p.m. Oct to May; included in museum admission. Tues to Fri admission is by donation, Sat and Sun visitors pay the special exhibition fee or, when none is scheduled, $10 for adults, $8 for seniors and students.

EVENING

....

DINNER **Founding Farmers,** 1924 Pennsylvania Ave, NW, IMF Head-quarters 2, 3 blocks west of the White House, Washington D.C.; (202) 822-8783; www.wearefoundingfarmers.com. You can have your choice of a family-size communal table, silo-shaped booth, or table for two. Sustainable ingredients from family farms go into the creation of small plates (candied bacon lollis, seafood volcano) or entrees such as signature rustic pot pie, farmhouse mixed grill, or lobster mac and cheese. $–$$. Open for breakfast Mon to Fri 8 to 11 a.m.; lunch and dinner Mon to Wed11 a.m. to 10 p.m., Thurs and Fri until 11 p.m.; Sat 2 to 11 p.m., Sun until 9 p.m.

Every evening year-round at 6 p.m., you can see a free hourlong live musical and/or dance performance at the **Millennium Stage** in the grand foyer of the **Kennedy Center for the Performing Arts** (2700 F St., NW, Washington, D.C.; 202-467-4600; www.kennedy-center .org). No tickets are required.

| LODGING | D.C. Guesthouse. |

DAY 3/MORNING

| BREAKFAST | D.C. Guesthouse. |

Within easy walking distance of the bed-and-breakfast is **Logan Circle/U Street/Shaw,** a Victorian-era-built neighborhood with a roller coaster history. Almost twenty years before Harlem took the spotlight as the nation's African-American cultural center, D.C.'s northwest U Street corridor (roughly the area from Ninth to Sixteenth Streets) aka the "Shaw neighborhood," was widely renowned as "Black Broadway," the epicenter of social life, the place to see and be seen, and a mecca for musicians, particularly jazz musicians. Duke Ellington was born here, and everyone from Louis Armstrong to Billie Holiday played in its numerous clubs. Beginning with the 1968 riots that followed the assassination of Dr. Martin Luther King, the neighborhood was decimated and remained in virtual ruins until a major revitalization effort was launched in the mid-1990s. Today, the community is once again a lively entertainment and shopping destination, its streets lined with music clubs (including the original Crystal Caverns—now named the Bohemian Caverns—where the early jazz greats performed) and quirky boutique shops. One of the most exciting is **Dekka** (1338 U St., NW, 2nd Floor, Washington D.C.; 202-986-1370; www.dcafam.com), which features art, clothing, music, and home decor created by local designers. Open Tues to Fri 1 to 7:30 p.m., Sat to Sun 10 a.m. to 7:30 p.m.

AFTERNOON

You can't visit the U corridor without chowing down on a chili dog or chili half-smoke (a regional specialty that's like a big, more textured, spicy hot dog) and chili fries at **Ben's Chili Bowl** (1213 U St., NW; 202-667-0909; www.benschilibowl.com), a local landmark and legend since 1958. Although founder Ben Ali has passed away, two of his sons are carrying on the tradition. $. Open Mon to Thurs 6 a.m. to 2 a.m., Fri until 4 a.m., Sat from 7 a.m. to 4 a.m., Sun from 11 a.m. to 11 p.m. There's a breakfast menu Mon to Sat, but you can get your chili dog or half-smoke fix any time.

Another well-known snack spot is **Love Café** (1501 U St., NW, Washington, D.C.; 202-265-9800; www.cakelove.com), the small eat-in sweet spot opened by Warren Brown (host of Food Network's Sugar Rush). Settle in with an espresso drink and a signature Crunchy Foot (mini, bundt-shaped pound cakes with crunchy edges) or Bedroll (walnut cake rolled up with cream cheese icing and sprinkled with cinnamon). $. Open Mon and Tues 11 a.m. to 9 p.m., Wed and Thurs from 9 a.m., Fri and Sat until 10:30 p.m., Sun until 9 p.m.

To return to Philadelphia, take I-495 north to I-95. I-95 north will take you all the way home. The trip should take about three hours.

There's More . . . .

D.C. Attractions. **Washington Monument.** National Mall at Fifteenth Street NW, Washington, D.C.; (202) 426-6841; www.nps.gov/

wamo. Free, but ticket required available at the Washington Monument Lodge along Fifteenth Street, open 8:30 a.m. for same-day, timed tickets. To save time, you may reserve tickets online at www .recreation.gov or by calling (877) 444-6777 (there's a $1.50 service charge per ticket).

White House, 1600 Pennsylvania Ave., NW, Washington, D.C. To visit, you must submit your request to your state Congressman up to six months in advance of the desired date. Tours are usually scheduled Tues through Sat 7:30 to 11:30 a.m. Seasonal White House Garden Tours may also be offered. Even if you haven't scheduled a tour, you can get a glimpse via the numerous exhibits at the White House Visitor Center, Fifteenth and E Streets; (202) 456-7041; open daily 8 a.m. to 4 p.m.

U.S. Capitol, Capitol Hill, First Street between Constitution and Independence Avenues; (202) 226-8000; www.visitthecapitol.gov. Advance tickets are necessary to join one of the Mon to Sat guided tours of the Capitol; reserve online. No ticket is necessary to visit the Capitol Visitor Center, with its large exhibition hall featuring original documents, artifacts, interactive displays, and films explaining the workings of Congress. Mon to Sat 8:30 a.m. to 4:30 p.m.

Golf. **National Park Service Historic Golf Courses;** www.golfdc.com.

Langston Golf Course, 2600 Bennington Rd, NE, Washington D.C.; (202) 472-3873. $22 for eighteen holes Mon to Thurs, $30 Fri to Sun. Senior and junior discounts are available.

Rock Creek Golf Course, 6100 Sixteenth St., NW, Washington, D.C.; (202) 882-7332. $20 Mon to Thurs, $25 Fri to Sun. Senior and junior discounts are available.

Museums & Tours. **Bureau of Engraving and Printing (The Mint),** Fourteenth and C Streets, SW, Washington D.C.; (202) 874-3019; www.moneyfactory.gov. Free forty-minute tours; first-come, first-served tickets available from the Visitor Center open daily 8:30 a.m. to 3:30 p.m. in Mar, until 7:30 p.m. Apr to Aug; tours go from 9 a.m. to 2 p.m. No tickets are required Sept to Feb.

Ford's Theater, 511 Tenth St., NW, Washington, D.C.; (202) 347-4833; www.fords.org. Daytime tours are free, but require tickets. Order in advance via Web site or phone. Includes museum with artifacts and interactive exhibits as well as visit to Petersen House across the street where Abraham Lincoln died. Both attractions are open year-round 9 a.m. to 5 p.m.

International Spy Museum, 800 F St., NW, Washington, D.C.; (202) 393-7798; www.spymuseum.org. Only public museum in U.S. dedicated to global espionage featuring the largest collection of spy-related artifacts anywhere as well as interactive displays and films. Check out the museum store, too. Admission is $18 for adults, $17 seniors and military/intelligence community, $15 children. Check for seasonal hours and special programs.

National Aquarium, Fourteenth St. & Constitution Avenue, NW; (202) 482-2825; www.nationalaquarium.org. Nation's oldest aquarium with more than 250 species and animal feedings. $7 for adults, $6 for seniors and military, $3 for children. Cash or check only. Open daily 9 a.m. to 5 p.m.

National Museum of American History, Fourteenth St. & Constitution Avenue, Washington, D.C.; (202) 633-1000.

Tourmobile Sightseeing, (202) 554-5100; www.tourmobile .com. For a single ticket price ($27 for adults, $13 children), you can hop on and off all day at twenty-five stops convenient to more than forty major historic sights and attractions (including Arlington National Cemetery).

Theater. **Saturday Morning at the National Theatre,** 1321 Pennsylvania Ave., NW; (202) 628-6161, Washington D.C.; www.national theatre.org. Free performances of puppet and magic shows, music, and ballet. Tickets are available thirty minutes prior to performance. Check Web site for performance schedule.

Ticket Passes. **Washington D.C. Power Pass,** (800) 490-9330, www .visitticket.com. One-, three-, or five-day one-price passes cover more than twenty top fee-based attractions and tours. Prices start at $26.

Special Events . . . .

LATE MARCH TO MID-APRIL
Cherry Blossom Festival, various locations; (877) 44BLOOM; www .nationalcherryblossomfestival.com. The blooming of 6,000 Japanese cherry trees is celebrated with a parade, crowning of the Cherry Blossom Festival Queen, sports activities, and arts-and-crafts shows. Free.

APRIL
Annual White House Easter Egg Roll, White House South Lawn and Ellipse; www.whitehouse.gov. Children of all ages are invited to participate in this day of fun and entertainment.

JUNE
National Capital Barbecue Battle; www.bbqdc.com. Home cooks and pros compete; everyone else eats. Mid-June to mid-Aug.

Washington Craft Show; www.craftsamericashows.com. A gathering of almost 200 of the nation's leading craft artists.

LATE JUNE TO EARLY JULY
Smithsonian Folklife Festival, www.festival.si.edu. Song, dance, cooking, storytelling, and more from around the world.

DECEMBER

National Christmas Tree Lighting, www.thenationaltree.org. The celebration includes seasonal music and caroling. Nightly choral performances and special programs until New Year's Day. Free.

Other Recommended Restaurants and Lodgings. . . .

WASHINGTON, D.C.

The Diner, 2453 Eighteenth St., NW; (202) 232-8800; www .trystdc.com. Breakfast, lunch, and dinner 24/7. $.

Georgetown Inn, 1310 Wisconsin Ave., NW; (888) 587-2388; www.georgetowninn.com. Historic accommodations with colonial warmth, European style. $$$.

Hotel Harrington, 436 Eleventh St., NW; (202) 628-8140; www .hotel-harrington.com. Centrally-located; simple, yet comfortable; family-owned and -operated since 1914. $$.

Kinkead's, 2000 Pennsylvania Ave., NW; (202) 296-7700; www .kinkead.com. Adapting international dishes to American ingredients and taste is the hallmark of this very popular restaurant. $$$. Lunch $–$$.

Latham Hotel, 3000 M St., NW, Georgetown; (202) 726-5000; www.thelatham.com. Elegantly appointed rooms. $$$.

Martin's Tavern, 1264 Wisconsin Ave., NW; (202) 333-7370; www .martins-tavern.com. A Georgetown staple since 1933, serving numerous oyster- and crab-centric specialties, burgers, and breakfast. $–$$. Open Mon to Fri 11 a.m., Sat and Sun 9 a.m.; Sun to Thurs until 1:30 a.m., Fri and Sat until 2:30 a.m.

Morrison-Clark Historic Inn, 1015 L St., NW; (202) 898-1200; www.morrisonclark.com. Beautiful, gracious, romantic—this ca.-1864 boutique hotel comprises two separate historic town houses. It is also the only inn located in the nation's capital to be listed on the National Register of Historic Places. $$$.

Old Ebbitt Grille, 675 Fifteenth St., NW; (202) 347-4800; www .ebbitt.com. D.C.'s oldest saloon (1856) has fed numerous presidents and is a regular haunt of White House staffers. The menu features good crab cakes, mussels, and an oyster bar paired with oyster-friendly wines. $$. Breakfast and lunch, $. Mon to Fri 7:30 a.m. to 1 a.m., Sat and Sun 8:30 a.m. to 1 a.m.

Veranda, 1100 P St., NW; (202) 234-6870; www.verandaonp.com. Friendly neighborhood spot serving great Greek and Italian food. Serving dinner Mon to Thurs 5 to 10 a.m., Fri and Sat until 11 a.m., Sun until 9 p.m. $$. Brunch, too.

For More Information . . . .

Destination D.C.; (202) 789-7000, http://washington.org. Also for advance reservations for and discounts on many tours.

Washington, D.C., Chamber of Commerce Visitor Information Center, 1213 K St., NW, Washington, D.C. 20005; (202) 638-7330; www.dcchamber.org. Open Mon to Fri 9 a.m. to 4:30 p.m.

www.dcpages.com, check out this site for more parking locations.

BETWEEN & BEYOND ESCAPE *Five*

Alexandria and Mount Vernon, Virginia

GEORGE PARTIED HERE/2 NIGHTS

> Torpedo Factory
> Foodie Forays
> Nifty Neighborhoods
> VIP Treatment

George Washington may have slept in a lot of places, but he always came home to his "beloved Alexandria." Who could blame him? For more than 250 years this lovely city on the Potomac has been capturing the affections of Americans with its timeless beauty and vibrant personality.

In Old Town **Alexandria,** today and yesterday happily coexist—sometimes in a single building. On gas-lantern-lit cobblestone streets named for international and American royalty, you can admire three centuries of architecture ranging from the modest to the magnificent. Then only a block or two away, find yourself in a modern mecca of top-shelf shopping and dining.

There has rarely been a dull moment here from its days as a busy 18th-century seaport to its role as a tinderbox for revolution and a somewhat reluctant defender of the capital during the Civil War. You can immerse yourself in all of that history by day. After dark, however, Alexandria becomes a real party town, proving every night that the place where George used to kick back is still a pretty happening spot.

DAY 1/MORNING

It's a two-and-one-half hour (152-mile) drive from Philadelphia to Alexandria. Take the Schuylkill Expressway (I-76) to I-95; go south on I-95 for 95 miles to I-895. Take I-895 through the Harbor

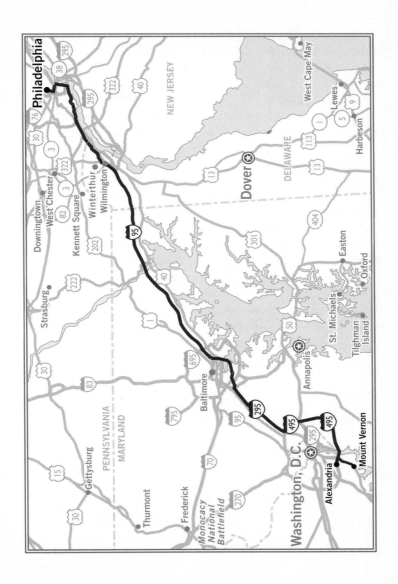

Tunnel and continue for 12 miles until you come to I-295 (the Baltimore–Washington Expressway). Take the Expressway for 29 miles to the Anacostia Freeway and stay on that for 21 miles. Get on I-495 (the Capital Beltway) and drive south for 2 miles into Alexandria.

If you want to skip downtown Alexandria's parking meter madness, make your first stop the **Ramsay House Visitor Center** (221 King St., Alexandria, VA; 703-746-3301; http://visitalexandriava .com). The nice folks of this lovely city will issue you a 24-hour Parking Proclamation, entitling you to park free at any two-hour meter. Tell them if you're staying for more than one day, you'll need a separate Proclamation for each day of your visit. Also, consider purchasing an **Alexandria Key to the City** ($12), which gives you free admission to nine historic sites and many discounts on shopping and dining. The visitor center is open daily 9 a.m. to 5 p.m.

If you're planning to shop or dine anywhere along King Street (the heart of Old Town), you can hop on and off the free King Street Trolley, which makes twenty stops between the Monorail Station and Potomac River waterfront.

AFTERNOON

LUNCH **Old Town Alexandria Tasting and Historical Walking Tour;** www.dcmetrofoodtours.com. Taste while you tour on a three- to three-and-a-half hour excursion through centuries of the city's culinary past and present. In addition to providing an ongoing narration regarding the history, character. and culture of each Old Town neighborhood, your guide will take you to historic restaurants and family-owned and artisan-specialty shops to sample a wide range of regional foods, including the jelly cake that has been an Alexandria staple for more than a century. Tours are available Thurs through Sun 1 to 4 p.m. Tickets are $50; order in advance online.

To continue your historical hike, head to **The Lyceum** (201 South Washington St., Alexandria, VA; 703-838-4994; http://oha.alex andriava.gov). In this 1839 Greek Revival former private home and Civil War hospital, you can trace Alexandria's history from its founding in 1749 to the present through archaeological finds, furniture, textiles, original art, and photos by famous photographers such as Mathew Brady, tools, toys, and other artifacts. The silver and potter collections are particularly impressive. Admission is $2. Hours are Mon to Sat 10 a.m. to 5 p.m., Sun from 1 p.m.

One of the things that makes Alexandria's waterfront so exciting is the fabulous art center known as the **Torpedo Art Factory,** 105 North Union St., Alexandria, VA; 703-838-4565; www.torpedo factory.org. Once used for the manufacture of weapons of war—there's a torpedo on display on the first floor—this huge building now houses studios for more than 165 visual artists as well as six galleries and the Alexandria Archaeology Museum. Although not all the work spaces are active at the same time, you can always find sculptors, painters, photographers, printmakers, jewelers, and other talented residents at work. The galleries showcase the works of national and international artists. The **Alexandria Archaeology Museum** (703-838-4399; http://oha.alexandriava.gov), a working laboratory where you can watch the pros piece together the city's past through rescued artifacts. Admission to the Torpedo Factory and Archaeological Museum are free. Ask about family dig days ($5 per person for one-and-one-hours). The Torpedo Factory is open daily 10 a.m. to 5 p.m.; the Archaeology Museum is open Tues through Fri 10 a.m. to 3 p.m., Sat until 5 p.m., and Sun 1 to 5 p.m.

A popular spot to river- and boat-watch is **Founders Park** (400 North Union St., Alexandria, VA; 703-838-4343), particularly at the City Marina at the park's southeast tip. The waterfront is also a favorite open-air stage for a variety of colorful street performers. And you never know when one of those magnificent tall ships will happen to dock nearby.

EVENING

DINNER　　**Columbia Firehouse,** 109 S. St. Asaph St., Alexandria, VA; www.columbiafirehouse.com. With almost 140 restaurants, deciding where to eat in Old Town can be a mind-boggling experience. One of the new (and very good) kids on the block is Columbia Firehouse, named for the ca.-1880 building in which it is housed. It's a great place for steaks. Add a crab cake for an extra $12 and start off with a kettle of mussels prepared in one of three exotic ways. $$–$$$. Also open for lunch ($–$$) and weekend brunch ($–$$). Hours are Tues to Sun 11 a.m. to 3 p.m., dinner 5:30 to 10 p.m., brunch 11 a.m. to 3 p.m.

After dinner, take in some of Alexandria's vibrant nightlife. One must-go is the **Birchmere** (3701 Mount Vernon Ave., Alexandria, VA; 703-549-7500; www.birchmere.com), a 500-seat, dinner-theater-style venue that presents headliner musicians and comedians. Tickets generally range from $25–$45. Call or check the Web site for the schedule.

LODGING　　**216: A City B&B,** 216 S. Fayette St., Alexandria, VA; (703) 548-8118; www.216bandb.com. You literally get a home away from home here: Instead of just a room or even a suite, you get an entire three-story, three-bedroom historic town house located only a block away from the heart of Old Town. Innkeepers Kathryn and Charlie Huettner have thought of everything from cold beer with chilled mugs and wines to fresh fruit and pastries. Generous private continental breakfast is included. $$$.

DAY 2/MORNING

BREAKFAST   216: A City B&B.

Opened in 1792, the **Stabler–Leadbeater Apothecary Shop** (105–107 South Fairfax St., Alexandria, VA; 703-836-3713; http://oha.alexandriava.gov) was the place where George and family, Daniel Webster, and Robert E. Lee bought everything from medicine to house paint. When the Depression caused the shop to close in 1933, the doors were simply locked and everything left as it was. Now this amazingly well preserved collection speaks volumes about the theories and tools that were the basis of medical care in early America. Admission is $5 for adults, $3 for children. Hours are Mon through Sat 10 a.m. to 4 p.m., Sun 1 to 5 p.m.

George Washington attended many balls and, in fact, held more than one of his own birth-night celebrations at what is now **Gadsby's Tavern Museum** (134 North Royal St., Alexandria, VA 22314; 703-838– 4242; http://oha.alexandriava.gov). Today Gadsby's has been restored to its 18th-century splendor as a museum furnished in period tavern style. Admission is $5 for adults, $3 for children. Open Apr through Oct, Tues through Sat 10 a.m. to 5 p.m., Sun and Mon 1 to 5 p.m.; Nov through Mar, Wed through Sat 11 a.m. to 4 p.m., Sun 1 to 4 p.m.

Take a stroll (or a trolley cruise) along King Street to browse the boutique and antiques shops. Jewelry designer David Martin will create a one-of-a-kind piece for you at his **Gold Works** (1400 King St., Alexandria, VA; 703-683-0333; www.goldworksusa.com). **Imagine Artwork** (1124 King St., Alexandria, VA; 703-548-1461; www.imagineartwear.com) features American-crafted clothing, jewelry, and accessories. **Pink & Brown** (1212 King St., Alexandria, VA; 703-684-1050; www.pinkandbrownboutique.com) sells 100-percent organic cotton designer children's clothing and other furnishings and accessories. You can get everything for your home bar (except the liquor) at **The Hour Shop** (1015 King St., Alexandria, VA; 703-224-4687), including vintage and contemporary designer glasses, shakers, and accoutrements.

AFTERNOON

LUNCH   **Fontaine Caffee & Creperie,** 119 S. Royal St., Alexandria, VA; (703) 535-8151; www.fontainecaffe.com. Pick a sweet or savory crepe. The menu includes veggie and gluten-free selections—filled with local and seasonal ingredients. Order a *boule* de cidres (a bowl of sparkling hard cider) to go with your meal. $.

If you haven't succumbed to the siren call of a dessert crepe, take a short seven-minute drive northwest to Mount Vernon Avenue, the main drag that goes through the historic and eclectic neighborhood of Del Ray. If you have a sweet tooth, I dare you not to find something to satisfy it with artisan offerings such as the hot chocolate drinks so rich they're named after Old Hollywood divas at **ACKC: Artfully Chocolate/Kingsbury Confections** (2003A Mt. Vernon Ave., Alexandria, VA; 703-635-7917, www.thecocoagallery.com) and Wisconsin-style frozen custard (super-smooth and creamy like frozen crème anglaise) and seasonal sorbet selections at **Dairy Godmother Frozen Custard & Nostalgic Treats** (2310 Mount Vernon Ave., Alexandria, VA; 703-683-7767; www.thedairygodmother.com), once visited by President Obama and his daughters.

Seven miles west of downtown Del Ray is **Fort Ward Museum and Historic Site** (4301 West Braddock Rd., Alexandria, VA; 703-838-4848; http://oha.alexandriava.gov). Immediately after Virginia's official secession in 1861, Union troops occupying Alexandria and nearby Arlington built sixty-eight earthwork forts known to protect Washington. The best-preserved is Fort Ward, which is situated within a more than 45-acre park and has a period furnished reconstructed officers' hut displaying a broad range of Civil War artifacts, videos, and themed exhibits exploring Civil War military and civilian life and medicine of the time. Tours of the park are self-guided, but you can arrange for a guide for a modest fee if you make a reservation in advance. The museum and park are open daily Tues to Sat 9 a.m. to 5 p.m., Sun noon to 5 p.m. Both the park and museum are free. Check the online events calendar for special living history programs such as soldier-led tours, July's Civil War Camp Day & Skirmish, Revolutionary Reenactments and Civil War Christmas in Camp.

DINNER   **Bilbo Baggins Global Wine Café and Restaurant,** 208 Queen St., Alexandria, VA; (703) 683-0300; www.bilbobaggins.net. For *Lord of the Rings* fans, this cafe is like a Middle Earth oasis with its literary-inspired murals, stained-glass windows, and whimsical wood-and-brick-cabin-in-the-woods charm. There's also a lively bar that serves draft beer on tap. The menu shows imagination as well, from homemade tortellini stuffed with salmon, to gourmet pizzas to andouille sausage- and jalapeño cheese-stuffed chicken breast. There are also extensive wine (many by the glass) and microbrew offerings. $–$$. Lunch ($) and Sunday brunch ($), too. Open Mon to Sat 11:30 a.m. to 10:30 p.m., Sun 11 a.m. to 9:30 p.m., light fare 2:30 to 5:30 p.m.

In a town with as tumultuous a history as Alexandria, you can be sure there will still be some restless spirits from the past floating (flying? walking?) around. You can hear some of their stories—and perhaps even experience your own sighting—on the one-hour, 6-block, lantern-lit guided **Alexandria's Original Colonial Ghost and Graveyard Tour,** (703-370-0185; www.alexcolonialtours.com); $10 for adults, $5 for children (tour is appropriate for ages 9 and up); reservations are suggested.

LODGING   216: A City B&B.

DAY 3/MORNING

BREAKFAST   216: A City B&B.

You can't possibly leave George Washington country without paying a visit to the place he cherished most in the world, **Mount Vernon** (3200 Mount Vernon Memorial Hwy., Mount Vernon, VA; 703-780-2000; www.mountvernon.org). The 8-mile trip south takes only about twenty minutes by car along the scenic George Washington Memorial Parkway, but a much more fun and scenic way to travel there is to cross the Potomac on the *Miss Christin* (703-684-0580; www.potomacriverboatco.com), which sails Tues through Sun at 10:30 a.m. and returns at 5:30 p.m. Round-trip ticket, which include admission to Mount Vernon, are $38 for adults, $21 for children.

At Mount Vernon, start at the orientation center for an introductory video and numerous exhibitions of more than 500 original artifacts. From there, go on to tour the mansion house, with many of the original furnishings and possessions, that Washington built between 1735 and 1787. Then take a walk through the close to 450-acre estate to see the four gardens, four-acre working farm, more than a dozen outbuildings including slave quarters and greenhouse, the burial tomb of George and Martha, and the Slave Memorial and Burying Ground. Admission (if you don't come by boat) is $15 for adults, $14 for seniors, $7 for children.

LUNCH   **Mount Vernon Inn,** adjacent to the mansion; www.mountvernon.org. Served on a first-come, first-served basis. I am always wary of dining establishments associated with major attractions because all too often they are merely bastions of mediocre food and so-so service hiding behind a stellar name. But this was a delightful surprise. The dining rooms, of course, are pure colonial, tastefully accented with wood beams and fireplaces and the menus show true respect for Southern cooking. You can start with a bowl of Virginia peanut and chestnut soup, then move on to salmon corn cakes, Southern pulled-pork barbecue, or colonial turkey "pye" with homemade buttermilk biscuit crust. $.

After docking back in Alexandria, return to Philadelphia by reversing the route from day one. The drive home should take about two-and-one-half hours.

There's More . . . .

(Web site for attractions is http://oha.alexandriava.gov unless otherwise indicated.)

The Arts. **Athenaeum,** 201 Prince St., Alexandria, VA; (703) 548-0035; http://nvfaa.org. Northern Virginia Fine Arts Association exhibits works of regional artists and performances by renowned musicians and actors. Gallery hours Thurs, Fri, and Sun noon to 4 p.m., Sat from 1 p.m.

Museums & Tours. **Alexandria Black History Museum,** 902 Wythe St., Alexandria, VA; (703) 838-4356. Art, photographs, documents, and thousands of artifacts trace the history and achievements of African Americans from 1749 to present in Alexandria. The Alexandria African American Park, part of the complex, has a preserved 19th-century cemetery and sculptures throughout. Tues to Sat 10 a.m. to 4 p.m. $2.

    Christ Church, 118 North Washington St., Alexandria, VA; (703) 549-1450; www.historicchristchurch.org). Still-active house of worship regularly attended by George Washington (his pew has been preserved) and Robert E. Lee provides docent-led tours. Donations are welcome. Call for days and hours.

Lee-Fendall House Museum and Garden, 614 Oronoco St., Alexandria, VA; (703) 548-1789; www.leefendallhouse.org. Built in 1785, this home to thirty-seven members of the Lee family is furnished with their own heirlooms and period reproduction pieces to reflect their early-Victorian-era life. Guided tours Wed to Sat 10 a.m. to 4 p.m. and Sun 1 to 4 p.m. $5 for adults, $3 for children.

Sailing. **Mariner Sailing School,** Belle Haven Marina, Alexandria, VA; (703) 768-0018; www.saildc.com. Daylong sailing lessons for adults and children 8 years old and up. Adult weekdays $275, weekends $325; kids $165. Also rentals of 19-foot Flying Scot ($46–$54), 14-foot Sunfish ($30–$35 for two hours), canoe or single kayak ($20), double kayak ($30). C & C sloop with captain, $90 per hour. Hours are weekdays 9:30 a.m. to 8 p.m., weekends 9 a.m. to 6 p.m.

Special Events . . . .

(Web site for events is http://oha.alexandriava.gov unless otherwise specified.)

FEBRUARY
George Washington's Birthday Celebration, throughout Alexandria; (703) 991-4474. Parade, birth-night banquet and ball, reenactments.

MARCH
Annual Antiques in Alexandria, Episcopal High School's Flippin Fieldhouse, 3900 W. Braddock Rd., Alexandria, VA; (703) 548-

7469; www.antiquesinalexandria.net. More than sixty dealers at one of the mid-Atlantic's most respected shows.

APRIL

Annual House and Garden Tour, Old Town Historic District, Alexandria, VA; (703) 746-3301; www.thetwig.org. Visit seven of Old Town's most prestigious private homes.

MAY

Annual Memorial Day Jazz Festival; (703) 883-4686; www.alexandriava.gov. Musical performances all day.

JUNE

Annual Alexandria Red Cross Waterfront Festival, www.waterfrontfestival.org. Entertainment, amusement rides, 10K and 5K runs, tall ship, fine arts and crafts, children's hands-on activities.

JULY

Annual Virginia Scottish Games and Festival, Episcopal High School; 3901 West Braddock Rd., Alexandria, VA; (703) 912-1943; www.alexandriava.gov. U.S. National Highland Heptathlon, dancing competitions, bagpipe parades, and a British antique automobiles show.

SEPTEMBER

Alexandria Festival of the Arts, King Street, from Union to Washington Streets, Alexandria, VA; (703) 746-3301; www.artfestival.com. More than 200 juried artists display and sell their creations.

Other Recommended Restaurants and Lodgings . . . .

ALEXANDRIA

219 Restaurant, 219 King St. (next to the visitor center); (703) 549-1141; www.219restaurant.com. Innovative French food. Lunch ($), dinner ($–$$), brunch ($–$$).

The Fishmarket, 105 King St.; (703) 836-5676; www.fishmarket va.com. Family-owned and -operated since 1950, this restaurant is known for its simply prepared fresh seafood. $ for lunch or dinner portions. Actual fish market and Pop's ice-cream parlor on the premises, too.

Gadsby's Tavern, 138 North Royal St.; (703) 548-1288; www .gadsbystavernrestaurant.com. Quite good colonial American fare including George Washington's Favorite Duck. $$. Lunch ($), Sun brunch ($).

King Street Blues, St. Asaph Street South (1 block from King Street); (703) 836-8800; www.kingstreetblues.com. Southern comfort, especially ribs. $–$$.

Morrison House Hotel, 116 South Alfred St.; (703) 838-8000; www.morrisonhouse.com. Grand manor house-style boutique hotel with every amenity imaginable. Pet-friendly. On-site fine dining restaurant. $$$.

Raw Silk Indian Restaurant & Lounge, 719 King St.; (703) 706-5701, www.rawsilkalexandria.com. Authentic Indian food and belly-dancing show on Thurs evenings. Lunch and dinner. $.

BETHESDA

Alexandria & Arlington Bed & Breakfast Network; 4938 Hampden Lane, Suite 164; (703) 549-3415; www.aabbn.com. Free reservation service featuring accommodations in Old Town Alexandria.

For More Information . . . .

Alexandria Convention & Visitors Association, 221 King St., Alexandria, VA, 22314; (703) 746-3301; http://visitalexandriava.com.

Alexandria Transit Company's DASH system bus service; (703) 370-DASH (3274); www.dashbus.com.

Virginia Tourism Corporation; (800) 847-4882; www.virginia.org.

BETWEEN & BEYOND ESCAPE *Six*

Baltimore, Maryland

CITY OF FIRSTS/2 NIGHTS

Harbor Happenings
The Other Mount Vernon
Star-Spangled Site
Got Games

The history of **Baltimore** is filled with so many firsts, including the first use of an umbrella in the United States (1772) and the establishment of the first umbrella factory (1828). The Charm City also claims the building of the first passenger railroad train ("Tom Thumb" in 1830), the invention of the Ouija board, and the manufacture of such necessities of life as canned corn (1839) and ice cream (1851). It is also a city of first-class historical, recreational, and cultural attractions. Ringing its lively harbor are some of the finest—and some of the funkiest—museums, shops, and dining spots you'll ever find in one place. Adding to entertaining atmosphere is the plethora of street performers, including magicians, dancers, jugglers and musicians, who regularly hang out at the Inner Harbor. On Fri, Sat and Sun evenings beginning 7 p.m. from Memorial Day to Labor Day, the Harborplace Amphitheater also offers free musical performances.

But don't stop there. Beyond the waterfront are the city's 250 distinctive neighborhoods, each with its own colorful personality, individual history, particular style of hospitality, and delicious flavors.

DAY 1/MORNING

Baltimore is about a two-hour drive from Philly. The most straightforward route for getting there is to take the Schuylkill Expressway

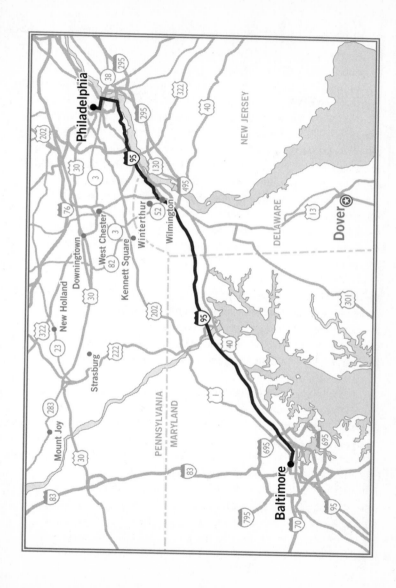

(I-76) to I-95. Travel south on 95 for 87 miles to I-895 south and the Harbor Tunnel. From the tunnel, take US 40 west straight into Baltimore. There are plenty of places to park in garages and open lots around the Inner Harbor. You can find an interactive map on www.baltimorecity.gov.

If you're able to plan your visit in advance, sign up at www.bal timorefunguide.com to have special half-price discounts to attractions, restaurants, entertainment venues, and shops e-mailed to you every Thurs morning. Also, if after you arrive in Baltimore you need directions or additional information on what's up throughout the city, look for a volunteer Certified Tourism Ambassador (CTA). **Baltimore's Water Taxi** (www.thewatertaxi.com), the only service of its kind in the country, offers all-day, unlimited, on-off service to more than thirty attractions and neighborhoods for $9 for adults, $4 for kids.

BREAKFAST	

BREAKFAST   **Miss Shirley's Café,** Inner Harbor, 750 East Pratt St., Baltimore, MD; (410) 528-5373; www.missshirleys.com. Miss Shirley's offers Southern-style specialties with surprise twists (think sweet corn cake eggs Benedict or coconut cream-stuffed French toast with brûléed bananas). $–$$. Open for lunch, too. Open Mon to Fri 7 a.m. to 3 p.m., Sat and Sun 7:30 a.m. to 3:30 p.m.

With its Chesapeake Bay-centric culture, Baltimore is a great place to expand your nautical knowledge. Begin by touring the **Historic Ships in Baltimore** (Pier 1, 301 E. Pratt St., Baltimore, MD; 410-539-1797; www.historicships.org), four military ships from time periods spanning the mid-19th century to the mid-1980s plus a ca.-1856 Chesapeake lighthouse, one of the only structures of its kind left in existence. Uniformed crewmembers and an audio tour offer details about topics of particular interest. Ticket pricing is structured so you can visit one ($10 for adults, $8 for seniors, $5 for children) or all four ($16 for adults, $13 for seniors, $7 for children) of the ships. If you just want to see the lighthouse, it's free and the view of Baltimore Harbor is spectacular. Call for seasonal hours.

The Inner Harbor and the Camden Yard neighborhood about a mile-and-a-half northwest are also home to a number of other highly unusual, super-cool museums. One of the newest is **Geppi's Entertainment Museum** (301 W. Camden St., Baltimore, MD; 410-625-7060; www.geppismuseum.com) where eight themed galleries take you time-traveling through generations of popular culture. Open Tues to Sun 10 a.m. to 6 p.m. Tickets are $10 for adults, $9 for seniors, $7 for students; all admissions are half-price every Tues and Thurs. My all-time favorite building to browse is the **American Visionary Art Museum** (800 Key Hwy., Baltimore, MD; 410-244-1900; www.avam.org). The 55-foot-high, multicolored whirligig outside should be your tip-off that this is not your traditional art museum. Exhibits inside its six themed galleries and sculpture barn showcase the works of self-taught artists—ordinary people from farmers to housewives to the homeless who express themselves in media ranging from painting and sculpture to tattoos and toothpicks. Look for great handcrafted gifts at the museum store. Open 10 a.m. to 6 p.m. Tues to Sun. Admission is $14 for adults, $12 for seniors, $8 for children. The outdoor wildflower/ sculpture garden with its fragrant flora and hand-built wood meditation chapel is the perfect place to just relax and chill out—best of all it's free.

AFTERNOON

To get an overview of some of Baltimore's nearest neighborhoods, take a free, ninety-minute, 1½-mile, guided **Heritage Walk** (443-514-5900; www.heritagewalk.org) which leaves from Baltimore's

Inner Harbor Visitor Center Apr through Oct. Call for seasonal hours. If you would rather tour on your own, you can download a self-guided walking map at the same Web site. Make sure you head for **Hampden,** a 19th-century blue-collar community in the northern part of town that's now best known as the home of the "hon" (big hair, cat's-eye glasses, and ample attitude), the queen of "Bawlmer" (Baltimore-speak for their beloved city) kitsch, and a cafe named in her honor.

LUNCH **Café Hon,** 1002 W. Thirty-sixth St., Baltimore, MD; (410) 243-1230; www.cafehon.com. An anything-but-understated 30-foot-tall flamingo marks the entrance. Here the meatloaf is "better than mom's," you can "platter" your burger with fries and slaw, and you can have the signature "Bawlmer Omelet" stuffed with cheesy crab dip, provolone, and more crab meat. $. Open for breakfast, dinner, and brunch, too. Hours are Mon to Thurs 7 a.m. to 9 p.m., Fri until 10 p.m., Sat 9 a.m. to 10 p.m., Sun 9 a.m. to 8 p.m.

About 3 miles south of Hampden is the neighborhood of **Mount Vernon** and the nation's oldest antique district, dating from the 1840s. You could spend an entire day—and a big part of your budget—popping in and out of the close to forty shops along Baltimore's Antique Row, which actually spans the 800 block of North Howard Street and the 200 block of West Read Street (www.shop antiquerow.com), where you'll find an astounding array of items from period English and continental to arts and crafts, Mission oak furniture, clocks, chandeliers, and toys and doll houses from the 19th- to the mid-20th centuries. Check out the more than twenty-diverse-dealer **Antique Row Stalls** (809 North Howard St., Baltimore, MD; 410-728-6363; www.antiquerowstalls.com). Hours are 11 a.m. to 5 p.m. every day except Tues. There's also **Anne Smith Antiques and Toy Museum** (222 West Read St., Baltimore, MD; 410-230-0580), Thurs to Sat 11 a.m. to 4 p.m.

At North Charles and Mt. Vernon Place, you will see the 178-foot-high white marble column that was the first architectural monument (built in 1829) erected to honor George Washington. While at over 555-feet the "other" Washington Monument may be taller, it's more than half-a-century younger. **Baltimore's monument** has a ground-floor museum and, for a $1 donation, you can climb the 228 steps to the top for a fabulous view of the city. Open Wed through Sun 10 a.m. to 4 p.m.

Aside from the monument, this urban oasis of 19th-century homes and beautifully landscaped parks called Mount Vernon is also a renowned cultural destination. The exciting global galaxy of exhibits at the **Walters Art Museum** (600 North Charles St. at Mount Vernon Square, Baltimore, MD; 410-547-9000; http://thewalters .org) includes ancient Egyptian and Roman sarcophagi, European and Japanese armor, Art Deco jewelry, and Old Masters' paintings. Open Wed through Sun 10 a.m. to 5 p.m. Admission is free.

While you're in the neighborhood, you may want to check if there are concert, opera, or other special events scheduled at the world-famous **Peabody Conservatory of Music** (1 East Mt. Vernon Place, Baltimore, MD; 410-234-4500; www.peabody.jhu.edu). Ticket prices range from $15 to $35 for adults, discounts for seniors and students. Box office is open Mon to Fri 10 a.m. to 4 p.m. and one hour prior to all ticketed events.

The Lyric Opera House (140 W. Mt Royal Ave., Baltimore, MD; 410-685-5086; www.lyricoperahouse.com) offers Broadway shows, ballet, popular and classical music, comedy, and, of course, opera. Ticket prices vary. Box office is open Mon to Fri 10 a.m. to 5 p.m., performance days until show time. Or see if the **Baltimore Symphony Orchestra** is playing at the **Joseph Meyerhoff Symphony Hall** (1212 Cathedral St., Baltimore, MD; 410-783-8000; www .bsomusic.org). Ticket prices vary; $20 unreserved seats (there are no unobstructed views). Mon through Fri, 10 am to 6 pm, and Sat and Sun, noon to 5 pm. The ticket office window is also open one hour before concerts and through intermission.

EVENING

DINNER **The Brewer's Art,** 1106 N. Charles St., Baltimore, MD; (410) 547-6925; www.thebrewersart.com. You might not expect to find such an intriguing menu at a brewery, but Brewer's Art is a pleasant surprise with such selections as eighteen-hour braised pork and Kobe pot roast. $$. Open Mon to Sat 4 p.m. to 2 a.m., Sun 5 p.m. to 2 a.m., full dinner service starting at 5:30 p.m.

LODGING **Inn at 2920,** 2920 Elliott St., Baltimore, MD; (410) 342-4450, www.theinnat2920.com. This contemporary boutique hotel in a late 19th-century Baltimore-style row home (once a brothel!) is located in a quiet residential community 2 blocks from the water taxi and 1 block to a local bus, both of which will take you to Baltimore's Inner Harbor. High ceilings, large windows, and thoughtfully restrained decor make the three rooms and one suite bright and airy; most have Jacuzzi tubs. $$$.

DAY 2/MORNING

BREAKFAST **Inn at 2920** for a full hot breakfast. Special dietary restrictions from allergies to vegan are cheerfully accommodated.

At the heart of the revitalized industrial community of **Canton** (www.cantoncommunity.org) is **O'Donnell Square.** This 4-block urban park is bordered by an eclectic collection of restaurants, bars, and shops. Visit the **2910 on the Square** boutique (2910 O'Donnell St., Canton, MD; 410-675-8505; www.2910onthesquare.com; call for seasonal hours) for Baltimore and Ravens memorabilia, Judaica, handmade crafts, and other fun stuff. The **Canton Gallery** (2935 O'Donnell St., Baltimore, MD; 410-342-6176; www.cantongallery .com) has local art and antique maps. Open Tues to Fri 10 a.m. to 8 p.m., Sat until 5 p.m. On some of the side streets you'll see examples of traditional folk art paintings on metal wire mesh window screens.

Two miles west of Canton (right on Boston Street, 1 mile then left onto Aliceanna Street) is another historic community, **Fell's Point** (www.fellspoint.us), known for its cobblestone streets, hundreds of examples of 18th- and 19th-century architecture, art galleries, antique and specialty shops, excellent restaurants, and outdoor recreational opportunities. A couple of really interesting shops are **Caviar & Cobwebs** (724 S. Broadway, Baltimore, MD; 410-276-2828; www.caviarandcobwebs.com) for designer wearables. Mention their Web site for a discount; call for hours. **Polish Treasures** (429 South Chester St., Baltimore, MD; 410-563-8760; www.polishtreasures.com) offers an assortment of art and gift items from Poland, including traditional hand-painted Easter eggs, pottery, tapestry, wooden folk art sculptures, and pictures. Hours are Mon, Wed and Fri 10 a.m. to 6 p.m., Tues until 8 p.m., Thurs until 3 p.m., Sat until 5 p.m., Sun until 1 p.m.

AFTERNOON

LUNCH   **John Steven Ltd. Five Points Tavern**, 1800 Thames St., Fell's Point, Baltimore, MD; (410) 327-5561; www.johnstevenltd.com. If the weather permits, have your meal al fresco in the courtyard of one of Charm City's most charming dining spots. Have the Maryland crab soup and oyster po' boy. $. Open for dinner ($$) and Sunday brunch, too. Hours are Sun to Thurs 11 a.m. to 10 p.m., Fri and Sat until 11 p.m.

A shorter voyage across the harbor in a water taxi will take you back to the Inner Harbor and the **National Aquarium in Baltimore** (Pier 3, 501 East Pratt St., Baltimore, MD; 410-576-3800; www.aqua .org), where more than 16,000 creatures are on display in natural-istic habitats representing environments ranging from Maryland's own mountain ponds to the Atlantic coral reef to a tropical rain for-est. There's a new dolphin show and 4-D Immersion Theater (that includes smell, mist, and wind) that brings a wide array of films to life. Call for seasonal hours. Admission is $30 for adults, $29 for seniors, $20 for children for the "Total Experience Package"—in my opinion this is the best deal. Lower priced packages including general admission with either the dolphin show or 4-D Theater are also available.

Make the most of your water taxi pass and visit the **Fort McHenry National Monument and Historic Shrine** at the end of Fort Avenue, Baltimore, MD (2400 East Fort Ave., Baltimore, MD; 410-962-4290; www.nps.gov/fomc). Even if the flag flying over its ramparts hadn't stirred Francis Scott Key to pen our national anthem, this star-shaped brick fortress, originally built during the Revolution and in use through World War II, would be a site worth seeing. Admission is $7 for adults, free for children 15 and under. Open daily 8 a.m. to 4:45 p.m.

EVENING

DINNER **Chiapparelli's Restaurant,** 237 South High St., Baltimore, MD; (410) 837-0309; www.chiapparellis.com. Just east of Inner Harbor (a ten-minute walk or quick water-taxi ride away) is the picturesque neighborhood known as Little Italy. While not the fanciest eatery in the area, it has been a local favorite for more than seventy years, beloved for its warm ambience and homemade pasta. $$. Open for lunch, too (yum, fresh dough pizzas). $. Hours are Sun to Thurs 11:30 a.m. to 9 p.m., Fri to Sat until 11 p.m.

DAY 3/MORNING

BREAKFAST Inn at 2920.

Take a three-hour cruise in Baltimore's inner harbor on the 41-foot *Catawampus II* racing sailboat (410-428-1711, www.harborsail .com). If it's a Tues or Thurs evening, you'll get a bird's-eye view of the sailboat races. Day or evening sails start at $300 for up to four passengers. If you would rather break out the rod and reel, try **Captain Don's Fishing Charters** (Henderson's Wharf Marina, 1001 Fell St., Baltimore, MD; 410-342-2004; www.fishbaltimore.com) and head out on the Lady Luck for a three-hour fishing (June to Sept) or crabbing (July to Oct) excursion for $260.

Of Baltimore's six public markets, the original and still most famous is **Lexington Market** (400 West Lexington St., Baltimore, MD; 410-685-6169; www.lexingtonmarket.com). Founded in 1782 and the world's largest, continuously running market, Lexington is home to more than 150 merchants that sell all kinds of fresh produce, baked goods, and fresh meat and fish. Mon through Sat 8:30 a.m. to 6 p.m.

AFTERNOON

LUNCH **John W. Faidleys Seafood,** Lexington Market, 201 North Paca, Baltimore, MD; (410) 727-4898; www.faidleyscrabcakes.com. Some of the best and most celebrated crab cakes are the handmade, all-lump crab cakes at

Faidleys which has been family-owned and -operated since 1886. $–$$. Open Mon to Sat 9 a.m. to 5 p.m.

If a home game is scheduled, drive 1 mile north to **Orioles Park at Camden Yards** (333 West Camden St., Baltimore, MD; 410-685-9800; http://baltimore.orioles.mlb.com). Ticket prices vary according to seat location and opposing team. If you happen to miss baseball season, the **Baltimore Ravens** football team now has its own field at the nearby **M&T Bank Stadium** (1101 Russell St., Baltimore, MD; 410-261-7283; www.baltimoreravens.com).

To return to Philadelphia, head east on Pratt Street to Charles Street; turn right onto Charles and right again at Conway Street. Turn left in front of the ballpark, onto I-395. Stay toward the right; you'll be exiting almost immediately onto I-95 north. Pass through the toll tunnel and take I-95 north all the way back home. The trip should take about two hours.

There's More . . . .

Museums & Tours. **Baltimore Museum of Art,** 10 Art Museum Dr., North Charles Street at Thirty-first Street, Baltimore, MD; (410) 396-1700; www.artbma.org. More than 90,000 ancient to modern works including the world's largest Henri Matisse collection and one of the nation's African collections. Sculpture Garden, too. Free. Open Wed through Fri 10 a.m. to 5 p.m., Sat and Sun 11 a.m. to 6 p.m.

Maryland Science Center, 601 Light St. at Key Highway, Inner Harbor, Baltimore, MD; (410) 685-5225; www.mdsci.org. Huge array of hands-on activities, an IMAX theater and planetarium. Open 10 a.m. to 5 p.m. Tues through Thurs, until 6 p.m. Sat, 11 a.m. to 5 p.m. Sun. Total package admission (including exhibits, planetarium, demo stage, visiting exhibit and one IMAX film) is

$25 for adults, $24 for seniors, and $19 for children. Other pricing packages are available.

Port Discovery (35 Market Place, corner of Market and Lombard Streets, Baltimore, MD; (410) 727-8120; www.portdiscovery .org). "Kid-powered" interactive exhibits designed in collaboration with Walt Disney Imagineering to educate and entertain the entire family. Open Oct to Memorial Day 9:30 a.m. to 4:30 p.m. Tues to Fri, Sat 10 a.m. to 5 p.m., Sun noon to 5 p.m.; call for winter hours. Tickets are $13 for age 2 and above.

Travel Passes. **Baltimore Harbor Pass,** (877) BALTIMORE or Baltimore Visitor Center on the West the Inner Harbor's West Promenade. Four-day pass provides fifteen- to twenty-five-percent discounts on admission to five of the city's biggest attractions. Prices are $57 for adults, $38 day-of-visit, but you'll save the maximum amount if you order by phone at least three days in advance.

Zoos. **The Maryland Zoo in Baltimore,** 1875 Mansion Hill Dr., Druid Hill Park, Baltimore, MD; (410) 396-7102; www.marylandzoo.org. More than 1,500 animals from around the world in natural habitats. Open daily 10 a.m. to 4 p.m., extended summer weekend hours. Admission is $15 for adults, $12 for seniors and $10 for children.

Special Events . . . .

APRIL

Baltimore Waterfront Festival, (410) 752-8632. Boat races, nautical life presentations, seafood cooking demos.

MAY

The Preakness, Pimlico Track, (410) 243-5307. More than 130-year Triple Crown event. Also less well-known Preakness Crab Derby at Lexington Market (410-685-6169).

JUNE

HonFest, Hampden, www.honfest.net. Women with beehive hairdos in spandex pants vie for the coveted title of "Best Hon."

JULY

Artscape, (410) 396-4575, www.artscape.org. Nation's largest arts festival showcases local and regional literary, visual, and performing arts.

SEPTEMBER

Star-Spangled Weekend, Fort McHenry; (410) 962-4290, www.nps .gov/fomc. Commemoration of the bombardment and the writing of our national anthem includes military encampments and reenactments, weapons firings, parades, concerts, "bombardment" of fort, fireworks. Fees for most events; Fri night festivities are free.

Other Recommended Restaurants and Lodgings . . . .

BALTIMORE

Abacrombie Fine Food & Accommodations, 58 West Biddle St.; (410) 244-7227; www.badger-inn.com. Enchanting 1880s town house. $$. Continental breakfast. Also on-site fine dining restaurant. $$.

Admiral Fell Inn, 888 South Broadway, Fell's Point; (410) 522-7377; www.harbormagic.com. European-style inn with on-premises gourmet restaurant, and an English-style pub. $$$. On-site Meli Patisserie & Bistro—breakfast, lunch and dinner. $–$$.

Celie's Waterfront Inn, 1714 Thames St., Fell's Point; (410) 522-2323, www.celieswaterfront.com. Late-19th-century bed-and-breakfast offers boutique amenities. $$–$$$.

Jack's Bistro, 3123 Elliott St.; (410) 878-6542; www.jacksbistro .net. Intriguing mac and cheese plus chocolate appetizer, cassoulet, and sous vide short rib. $$. Wed to Sun 5 p.m. to 10 p.m.

Ryleighs Oyster Restaurant, 36 E. Cross St., Federal Hill; (410) 539-2093; www.ryleighs.com. Super-fresh seafood and popular Bloody Mary Sun brunch. $–$$. Open Mon to Sun 11 a.m. to 2 a.m.

Salt, 2127 E. Pratt St.; (410) 276-5480; www.salttavern.com serves real foodie fare with whimsical twists, $$–$$$. Mon to Sat from 5 p.m.; Sun from 4 p.m.

For More Information . . . .

Baltimore Visitor Center, 401 Light St., Baltimore, MD 21202; (877) BALTIMORE (225-8466); www.baltimore.org. Hours vary by season.

Greater Baltimore Cultural Alliance, www.baltimorefunguide.com— up-to-the-minutes news on events and performances.

Maryland Office of Tourism, (866) 639-3526, www.visitmaryland.org.

BETWEEN & BEYOND ESCAPE *Seven*
New York City, New York
DELICIOUS TO THE CORE/2 NIGHTS

> More than Trees
> Street Food
> Village Visit
> Surprise Savings

Like a friendly Great Dane, **New York City** can bowl you over with its expanse and unbridled energy. From the moment you merge into the crush of humanity that, day and night, flows up and down its sidewalks and its streets, you can't help but become swept up in that energy, too.

Although the brilliant, longtime marketing campaign has established Manhattan as "the Big Apple" in the minds of many, I think that "the Big Onion," a name used by a local tour company, is a more apt description. No matter how long you stay there you'll always find more zesty layers to peel away and enjoy, but start with a three-day getaway. It will be enough to whet your appetite for more.

By the way, if you think a visit to New York has to take a big bite out of your budget, you might be surprised at some of the inexpensive (even some free) attractions and economical eateries the city has to offer.

DAY 1/MORNING

Geographically, New York City is about a two-hour drive away. That is, if you make sure to leave home in time to avoid morning head-to-work hysteria. Quite frankly, the easiest and most efficient way to get to New York is by train, either on **Amtrak** (800–USA–RAIL, www .amtrak.com) or by bus on **Greyhound Bus** (800-231-2222, www

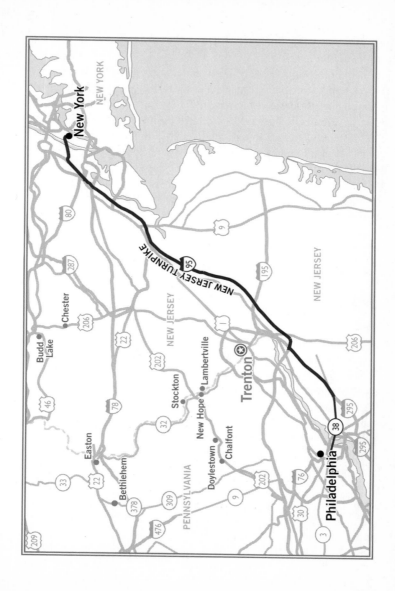

.greyhound.com). Once you arrive in the city, you can get around the way the locals do—on foot or via taxi (quick and reasonably priced) or by bus or subway (if you are comfortable with the routes). If you can't bear to be without your car, take I-95 north/New Jersey Turnpike north toward New York and stay on for about 79 miles to exit 16 E/Lincoln Tunnel/New York City. After nearly a mile, keep left to take I-495 east toward the Lincoln Tunnel, then a little more than 3½ miles later, take the exit on the left toward I-495 east/42 St./NY 9A/All Points, then right onto Forty-second Street and left onto Eighth Avenue. Enter the next roundabout and take the second exit onto W. Fifty-ninth Street. After a little less than a mile, turn left onto Park Avenue, then, about a mile-and-a-half later, right onto E. Eighty-sixth Street.

AFTERNOON

LUNCH **Papaya King**, 179 East Eighty-sixth St., corner of Third Avenue between Third and Lexington; New York, NY; (212) 369-0648; www.papayaking .com. This Upper East Side institution is a true American dream story, founded by a young Greek immigrant who came through Ellis Island without a penny to his name. $. While the franks may or may not be "tastier than filet mignon" as the company claims, they're pretty special. Pair them (or the spicy beef smoked sausage) with the Cajun curly fries, signature knish, and, of course, an all-natural, house-blended tropical drink or non-dairy smoothie. Hot dogs for breakfast? Yup, if that's what you're craving because it's open Sun through Thurs 8 a.m. to noon and Fri and Sat until 2 a.m. Papaya King also has a second location in Harlem at 121 West One-twenty-fifth St. between Lenox and Adam Clayton Powell.

With so much to do and see in New York, it's hard to know where to start. So, before you leave from home, make a reservation for a **Big Apple Greeter** (1 Centre St.; New York, NY; 212-669-8159; www

.bigapplegreeter.org), a volunteer New York resident who will take you on a two- to four-hour, private, individually designed insider's tour of the city and its neighborhoods, highlighting places and topics that suit your specific interests and explaining how to use the public transit system to make the rest of your visit easier and less expensive. A nonprofit organization founded in 1992 and the first program of its kind in the country, **Big Apple Tours** guide services are all free and there is a no tipping policy. If you have special language or physical disability needs, there are guides available to work with you.

With a little pre-planning, you can visit more than fifty of the city's most famous attractions such as the Statue of Liberty/Ellis Island, the Empire State Building Observation Deck, the Museum of Modern Art (MOMA), and Guggenheim Museum. Take the city's best tours, including the Circle Line River Cruise, Food on Foot, and NBC Studio Tours. Get discounts at numerous stores and restaurants and front-of-the-line privileges by purchasing a **New York Pass** (www.newyorkpass.com) online prior to your visit. This "smart card," which costs $75 for adults, $55 for children for one day; $99/$81 for two days.

With all those twinkling lights and architecturally compelling theater buildings, you simply can't ignore **Broadway's theater district**—the Great White Way between West Forty-first and West Fifty-fourth Streets where there are almost three dozen venues. If you don't have your heart set on a particular show, you can save up to fifty percent on some of the hottest ones at **TKTS Discount Booths** (www.tdf.org), which sells day-of-performance evening and matinee tickets TKTS has three locations: One is in Times Square "under the red steps" in Father Duffy Square on Broadway and Forty-seventh Street, open Mon, Wed, and Sat 3 to 8 p.m., Tues from 2 p.m., Sun 3 p.m. until one-half hour before the latest curtain time. The second is the South Street Seaport booth at the corner of Front and

John Streets, near rear of the Resnick/Prudential Building, 199 Water St., open Mon to Sat 11 a.m. to 6 p.m., Sun 11 a.m. to 4 p.m. The third is Downtown Brooklyn, 1 MetroTech Center at the corner of Jay Street and Myrtle Avenue Promenade, open Tues to Sat 11 a.m. to 6 p.m.

EVENING

DINNER **Carmine's Theater District,** 200 West Forty-fourth St., New York, NY; (212) 221-3800; www.carminesnyc.com. Carmin's is legendary for its authentic Italian specialties served in humungous portions made for sharing among four to six people. $$–$$$, but the per-person price usually comes out to $. Hours are Mon 11 a.m. to 11 p.m.; Tues, Thurs, and Fri until midnight; Wed and Sat 11 a.m. to midnight; Sun 11 a.m. to 11 p.m.

After the theater, it's time for dessert at **Serendipity3** (225 East Sixtieth St. between Second and Third Avenues; New York, NY; 212-838-3531; www.serendipity3.com). Try the cream de la crème cream cheese cake, dark double devil mousse, YuDuFunDu, one of their famous ice-cream sundaes (if you're feeling flush there's a $1,000 Golden Opulence selection) or signature hot or iced hot chocolate. $–$$. Hours are Sun to Thurs 11:30 a.m. to midnight, Fri until 1 a.m., Sat until 2 a.m.

LODGING **Dream,** 210 West Fifty-fifth St. in Midtown between Broadway and Seventh Avenue, New York, NY; (212) 247-2000; www.dreamny.com. There may be lower-priced accommodations in the city, but cool, contemporary Dream really captures its chic sophistication. There are four restaurants and lounges, including the rooftop Ava Lounge, plus a Chopra Center Ayurvedic Spa on site. $$$.

DAY 2/MORNING

BREAKFAST **Chelsea Market,** 75 Ninth Ave., between Fifteenth and Sixteenth Streets, New York, NY; www.chelseamarket.com. Still revered as the site where the first Oreo cookie was made, this ca.-1840 National Biscuit Company (Nabisco) factory is now home to a new generation of great cookie bakers as well as vendors of all kinds of other good stuff from artisanal cheeses to house-made gelato, Jacques Torres chocolates to Iron Chef Morimoto's masterpieces. And since the market opens early (hours are weekdays 7 a.m. to 10 p.m., weekends 8 a.m. to 8 p.m.), this is a great place to build your own breakfast feast. Start at **Ronnybrook Farm Dairy** (212-741-6455; www.ronnybrook.com) for some rich organic yogurt. Next stop, **Manhattan Fruit Exchange** (212-989-2444; www.manhattan fruitexchange.com) for some additional nutrients; and finally, **Amy's Bread** (212-462-4338; www.amysbread.com) for some oven-fresh scones, brioche, muffins, or a true Parisian repast of one-half baguette with butter, coffee or tea, and jam. $.

Central Park (212-310-6600; www.centralparknyc.org), the first park built in America, has 843 acres, twenty-one playgrounds (including jungle- and Wild West-themed ones) and just about every outdoor activity you can imagine.

Feeding time for the sea lions is only one of the many delights at the **Central Park Zoo** and **Tisch Children's Zoo** (East Side between Sixty-third and Sixty-sixth Streets; 212-439-6500; www .centralparkzoo.com). Here more than two dozen species of animals live and play in natural habitats. Admission is $8 for adults, $4 for seniors, $3 for children. Open seven days a week 10 a.m. to 4:30 p.m. You can also rent a rowboat for paddling ($12 first hour) or take a half-hour gondola ride ($30) at **Loeb Boathouse on the Lake** (Seventy-second and Fifth Avenue; 212-517-2233; www.thecentralparkboathouse.com), available Mar through Oct, 10 a.m. to 6 p.m., Wed 9 a.m. to 6 p.m. One dollar buys a ride atop one of the antique carved horses on the 1908 carousel (Mid-Park at Sixty-fourth Street, 212-879-0244).

From Nov to Mar, you can ice-skate on **Wollman Rink** (East Side between Sixty-second and Sixty-third Streets, 212-439-6900; www.wollmanskatingrink.com), $10 Mon to Thurs, $15 Fri to Sun. There's even a full amusement park, **Victorian Gardens** (East Side between Sixty-second and Sixty-third Streets, 212-982-2229; www.victoriangardensnyc.com) with one-of-a-kind rides, games, live interactive shows, face painting, balloon sculptors, and concession stands selling everything from caramel corn to cotton candy. Open May to mid-Sept, $6 weekday, $7 weekend, pay-as-you-go rides and games, or an all-inclusive unlimited wrist band $18/$21.

And we haven't even touched on all the free stuff you can do at the park such as enjoying the free warm weather concerts (212-360-3444) and following the age-old tradition of climbing Alice in Wonderland and Hans Christian Andersen, two of the twenty-one pieces of sculpture. Or you could opt for a guided two-hour ride through this urban oasis with **Central Park Bike Tours** (203 West Fifty-eighth St.; 212-541-8759; www.centralparkbiketour.com) for $49 for adults, $40 for children. Open year-round, seven days a week. Tours are scheduled 10 a.m., 1 p.m., 4 p.m., additional tours at 9 a.m. and 11 a.m. on summer weekends. Mon to Sun from 9 a.m. to 6 p.m., you can rent your own bike by the hour beginning at $20 or the day for $65.

AFTERNOON

Skip the regular restaurant routine and hoof it around town on one of the three-hour guided **Foods of New York Tours** (917-408-9539, 212-209-3370 [tickets], www.foodsofny.com). Each of the walking tours of Greenwich Village (daily), Chelsea Market/Meatpacking

District (Thurs to Sun), or Central Village/SoHo (Thurs to Sat) consists of seven sampling stops at mom and pop shops and other neighborhood eateries, including a sit-down tasting at one of them. Tickets are Mon to Fri $44 for adults, $20 for children, Sat and Sun $44 for all ages. More extensive Mon-only Explore Chinatown Tours and Saturday Sushi and Japanese Tapas events are $65 (add $10 for beer and sake with the sushi).

EVENING

After your culinary tour, you'll probably want to postpone dinner for a while. So there's no better time to visit one of the city's renowned museums. If you purchased a New York Pass, just choose any attraction from the list and get in for free. But if you're paying as you go, check out the "pay as you wish" days and times at various attractions. The **Museum of Modern Art**—aka MOMA (11 West 53 St.; New York, NY; 212-708-9400; www.moma.org) offers pay as you wish Fri 4 to 7:45 p.m. (regular admission is $20). At the **Guggenheim Museum** (1071 Fifth Ave. at Eighty-ninth Street, New York, NY; 212-423-3500; www.guggenheim.org) it is Sat 5:45 to 7:45 p.m. (regular admission is $18). For another of my favorites, the **Frick Collection** (1 East Seventieth St., New York, NY; 212-288-0700; www.frick.org) the donation day is Sun 11 a.m. to 1 p.m. (regular admission is $18). *TIP:* If an admission price is prefaced by the word "suggested," you can pay as you wish any time. For a full list of free or discounted museums, go to http://gonyc.about.com.

DINNER **DBGB Kitchen and Bar,** 299 Bowery between Houston and First Streets, New York, NY; (212) 933-5300; www.danielnyc.com. If you always wanted to dine in the domain of culinary luminary, Daniel Bouloud, but find his eponymous eatery too pricey, this more casual eatery offers a more economical alternative with an imaginative and playful menu that runs the gamut from matzo ball soup to a slew of exotic artisanal sausages to house-made tagliolini pasta. $$.

LODGING   Dream.

DAY 3/MORNING

Head to Washington Square Park and the Washington Arch, where a 77-foot-high statue of George himself welcomes you to **Greenwich Village.** Bordered by the Hudson River, Houston (pronounced How-stun) Street, West Broadway, and Fourteenth Street, the Village has been a gathering place for artists and rebels for more than one hundred years. You can still experience some of that electricity today in the galleries, shops, music clubs, and restaurants along Bleecker Street. But, unlike in the past, the Village is not exactly a place for starving artists. You have to really hunt to find a bargain, but, for visitors, that's part of the fun. Right next to the Village is **SoHo** (south of Houston), which runs from Broadway west to Sixth Avenue and Houston Street south to Canal Street, a more fashionable (i.e., even more expensive) neighborhood, where upscale chain stores and independently-owned boutiques predominate.

BRUNCH   **August,** 359 Bleecker St. between Charles & West Tenth, New York, NY; (212) 929-4774; www.augustny.com. Start your day in the warm, intimate ambience of August with its wood-fired oven and Mediterranean to Eastern European regional cuisine. Order one of the specialty wood-oven baked eggs en cocotte with bacon, onion, and crème fraiche; roasted potatoes, raclette cheese, and dill; tomato and mozzarella or chorizo and blistered peppers. $. Lunch and dinner, too. $–$$. Open Mon to Fri noon to 3:30 p.m. for lunch; Mon to Thurs 5:30 to 11 p.m., Fri to Sat 5:30 p.m. to midnight, Sun 5:30 to 10 p.m., for dinner; Sat and Sun 11 a.m. to 3:30 p.m. for brunch.

Über-designer **Marc Jacobs** (www.marcjacobs.com) has a large footprint on Bleecker Street—three shops: one for women (403–405 Bleecker St.; 212-924-0026), one for men (385 Bleecker St.; 212-924-6126), and one for kids (382 Bleecker St.; 212-206-6644). **Satya** (330 Bleecker St. between Christopher and West Tenth Streets; 212-243-7313, www.satyajewelry.com) offers yoga-inspired jewelry, including "healing" gemstones and home accents such as a traveling meditation altar and peace pillows. Hours are Mon to Sat 11 a.m. to 8 p.m., Sun noon to 6 p.m. **Bleecker Street Records** (239 Bleecker St.; 212-255-7899; www.bleeckerstreetrecords.com) specializes in vintage and rare vinyl and posters as well as used and new CDs. **Mxyplyzyk** (125 Greenwich Ave.; 800-243-9810; www.mxyplyzyk.com), named after the Superman villain, is a hoot featuring items such as *The Encyclopedia of Immaturity* and a purse that looks like a giant take-out coffee cup. Open Mon to Sat 11 a.m. to 7 p.m., Sun noon to 5 p.m.

In SoHo, **Pearl River** (477 Broadway between Grand Street and Broom; 212-431-4770; www.pearlriver.com) features Asian-inspired fashion and home furnishings. Open daily 10 a.m. to 7:20 p.m. (yes, that's 7:20). It's hard to choose from among the must-have merchandise at the **Museum of Modern Art Design Store** (81 Spring St. between Crosby and Broadway; 212-646-1367; www.momastore.org), which features all kinds of clothing, home accents, and even toys inspired by museum exhibitions and created by renowned international designers—prices begin at under $25. Hours are Mon to Sat 10 a.m. to 8 p.m., Sun 11 a.m. to 7 p.m.

Check out a few of the underdiscovered galleries in this area, including the **Ukrainian Museum in the West Village** (222 East Sixth St. between Second and Third Streets; 212-228-0110; www.ukrainianmuseum.org), where you'll explore Ukrainian culture through arts, woven and embroidered textiles, clothing, and the famous decorated Easter eggs. Admission is $8 for adults, $6 for seniors. Call for seasonal hours. The **Forbes Galleries** (lobby of the Forbes Building, 62 Fifth Ave. at Twelfth Street; www.forbesgaller ies.com) showcases more than 500 toy soldiers, 10,000 boats, the evolution of Monopoly, vintage jewelry, and photography. Open 10 a.m. to 4 p.m.

DINNER   **Balthazar Restaurant,** 80 Spring St. between Broadway and Crosby, New York, NY 10012; (212) 965-1414; www.balthazarny.com, features a sophisticated menu including selections such as duck shepherd's pie, moules frites, and homemade fettuccine. Be sure to leave room for the house-made desserts such as apple tart or homemade ice creams and sorbets. Open for dinner and after hours Mon to Thurs 5:45 p.m. to midnight, Fri and Sat until 1 a.m., Sun 5:30 p.m. to midnight. $$–$$. Serves breakfast ($–$$), brunch ($$), and lunch ($–$$), too.

It will take you almost two hours to get home. Take the Holland Tunnel (it becomes Fourteenth Street and then I-78 west/New Jersey Turnpike W). After 8 miles, get on I-95 S/Turnpike south exit, then merge onto New Jersey Turnpike south and continue for about 70 miles. Take the NJ 73 exit, exit 4 toward Camden/Philadelphia, merge onto NJ 73 north and stay on for about 1½ miles. Merge onto Kaighn Avenue/NJ 38 west toward Rt. 41/B Franklin BR/Haddonfield. After 6 miles, turn slight right onto Admiral Wilson Boulevard/US 30 west then continue 4 miles to I-676 west/US 30 west ramp.

There's More . . . .

***Ferries.* Statue of Liberty/Ellis Island Ferry,** (212) 269-5755. One round-trip ticket price for the ferry is $12 for adults, $10 for seniors, $5 for children. Includes access to statue pedestal and museum. Call for seasonal schedules.

Museums. **American Folk Art Museum,** 45 West Fifty-third St., New York, NY; (212) 265-1040; www.folkartmuseum.org. History-linked traditional arts from weathervanes to whirligigs, carousels to checkerboards. Admission is $9 for adults, $7 for seniors and children, free on Fri evenings. Hours are Tues to Sun 10:30 a.m. to 5:30 p.m., Fri 11 a.m. to 7:30 p.m.

American Museum of Natural History and **Rose Center for Earth and Space,** Central Park West at West Seventy-ninth Street, New York, NY; (212) 769-5100; www.amnh.org. A mind-boggling collection of more than forty-five permanent exhibitions that explore the evolution of all things animal, vegetable, and mineral. Open daily 10 a.m. to 5:45 p.m. Ask about free guided tours. Suggested basic admission is $16 for adults, $12 for seniors and students, and $9 for children; IMAX and Hayden Planetarium Space shows are extra; "supersaver" bundles for all attractions are available.

The Children's Museum of Manhattan, The Tisch Building, 212 West Eighty-third St. between Amsterdam Avenue and Broadway, New York, NY; (212) 721-1223; www.cmom.org. Kids learn about culture, health, history, and nature through play. Hours are Tues to Sun, 10 a.m. to 5 p.m., Fri free from 5 a.m. to 8 p.m. Admission is $10 for children and adults, $7 for seniors.

Madame Tussaud's, 234 West Forty-second St., New York, NY; (212) 512-9600; www.madametussauds.com. The name says it all! Open daily at 10 a.m.; call for seasonal closing times. $35 for adults, $32 for seniors, $28 for children. Purchase tickets online for substantial savings.

Ticket Passes. **City Pass** (www.citypass.com). One ticket good for admission to six attractions including MoMa, the Guggenheim, and Circle Line Sightseeing Cruises. $79.

Free Tickets to TV Shows, www.nytix.com.

Tours. **Big Onion Walking Tours,** 476 13th St., New York, NY; (212) 439-1090; www.bigonion.com. Two-hour guided weekend ethnic, neighborhood, and historic area walking tours. $15 adults, $12 seniors and students. Call for school schedules.

Circle Line Sightseeing Cruise, Pier 83, West Forty-second Street, New York, NY; (212) 563-3200; www.circleline42.com. Three-hour, full-island grand tour. Tickets for daily cruises cost $34 for adults, $29 for senior citizens, and $21 for children.

Special Events . . . .

JUNE, JULY, AUGUST

Shakespeare in the Park, Delacorte Theater, Central Park; (212) 539-8500; www.publictheater.org. Founded by Joseph Papp, these spectacular free summer productions of Shakespeare and other works are performed in an open-air amphitheater.

NOVEMBER

Annual Thanksgiving Day Parade. Begins at Central Park West at Seventy-seventh Street, continues down Broadway to Macy's Herald Square (Thirty-fourth Street), and finishes at Seventh Avenue.

DECEMBER

Ice-skating at Rockefeller Center, Fifth Avenue between Forty-ninth and Fiftieth Streets; (212) 332-7654. Daytime and evening skating mid-Oct through Apr. Rentals available.

Lighting of the Christmas Tree, Rockefeller Center; (212) 698-2950.

Other Recommended Restaurants and Lodgings . . . .

NEW YORK

Carnegie Deli, 854 Seventh Ave. at Fifty-fifth Streets; (212) 757-2245; www.carnegiedeli.com. Famous for their pastrami, corned beef, and cheesecake. Open for breakfast, lunch, and dinner seven days a week from 6:30 a.m. until 4 a.m. $–$$.

Craftbar, 900 Broadway; (212) 461-4300; www.craftrestaurant .com. Food Network top chef co-host Tom Colicchio's casual dining spot serves sexy seasonal fare. Dinner $–$$.

Crepes on Columbus, 990 Columbus Ave. between Hundred-and-eighth and Hundred-and-ninth; (212) 222-0259; www.crepeson columbus.com. Breakfast and dinner all day. Sweet and savory crepes and other entrees. $–$$. Open daily 8 a.m. to 10 p.m.

Fitzpatrick Grand Central, 141 East Forty-fourth St. at Lexington Avenue; (212) 351-6800; www.fitzpatrickhotels.com. European-style Midtown boutique hotel. $$$.

Grand Central Oyster Bar, Grand Central Station Terminal, 89 E. Forty-second St. at Vanderbilt Avenue, between Vanderbilt and Lexington Avenues; (212) 490-6650; www.oysterbarny.com. More than forty types of oysters and a massive menu of other seafood. $ for sandwiches, $$ for entrees.

Hotel Wales, 1295 Madison Ave. at Ninety-second Street; (212) 876-6000; www.hotelwalesnyc.com. Beautifully restored late-19th-century boutique hotel located in the Carnegie Hall section of the Upper East Side. $$$.

Hotel Wolcott, 4 West Thirty-first St., between Fifth and Broadway; (212) 268-2900; www.wolcott.com. Ornate, gilded lobby, crystal chandeliers, and clean, comfy rooms in convenient Midtown location. $$–$$$.

Larchmont Hotel, 27 West Eleventh St.; (212) 989-9333; www .larchmonthotel.com. Lovely boutique hotel in Greenwich Village. Multi-lingual staff. $$–$$$.

Momofuku Noodle Bar, 171 First Ave. between Tenth & Eleventh Streets; (212) 777-7773; www.momofuku.com. Prix-fixe lunches and dinners, a la carte noodle bowls, steamed buns, other global dishes with Asian accents. $–$$. Open for lunch Mon to Fri noon to 4:30 p.m., Sat and Sun until 4 p.m.; for dinner Sun to Thurs 5:30 to 11 p.m., Fri and Sat until 2 a.m.

Union Square Cafe, 21 East Sixteenth St.; (212) 243-4020; www .unionsquarecafe.com. Seasonally inspired imaginative, unpretentious atmosphere. $$$. Lunch, too.

Washington Square Hotel, 103 Waverly Place; (212) 777-9515; www.washingtonsquarehotel.com. Cool Art Deco accommodation in Greenwich Village. $$$.

For More Information . . . .

NYC Information Center, 810 Seventh Ave., New York, NY 10019, between Fifty-second and Fifty-third Streets; (212) 484-1200; www.nycgo.com.

New York State Tourism; (800) CALL-NYS; www.iloveny.com.

INDEX